Hmong
and American

Hmong and American

Stories of Transition to a Strange Land

SUE MURPHY MOTE

McFarland & Company, Inc., Publishers
Jefferson, North Carolina, and London

Library of Congress Cataloguing-in-Publication Data

Mote, Sue Murphy, 1938–
    Hmong and American : stories of transition to a strange land /
Sue Murphy Mote
        p.   cm.
    Includes bibliographical references and index.

    ISBN 0-7864-1832-X (softcover : 50# alkaline paper)

    1. Hmong Americans—Cultural assimilation.   2. Hmong
Americans—Ethnic identity.   3. Hmong Americans—Biography.
4. Immigrants—United States—Biography.   5. Hmong (Asian
people)—History.   I. Title.
E184.H55M68   2004
305.895'942073 — dc22

                                              2004003505

British Library cataloguing data are available

On the cover: (inset) Jessica Moua at Hmong New Year in Santa Ana, California, November 1999; *(background)* Chestnut Mountain, Laos

Manufactured in the United States of America

McFarland & Company, Inc., Publishers
  Box 611, Jefferson, North Carolina 28640
    www.mcfarlandpub.com

To Mom,
who told me her story
hoping that I could understand

Contents

PART IV. MIDDLE WORLD: BEING HMONG IN AMERICA

Ni-yai … why do my mother and father lose my footprints,
    and go on the downhill side of the rock? …
Why do my young brothers and old brothers lose my footprints,
    and go on the downhill side of the fallen log?

—"Song About Being an Orphan:
    No Parents, No Cousins, No Homeland,"
    Vang and Lewis, *Grandmother's Path,*
    Grandfather's Way

Preface

I was not raised in some foreign embassy or mission outpost, speaking an exotic language and rubbing shoulders with unfamiliar people. I was instead the product of conventional, white, middle-class, America-dwelling parents. I saw with all–American eyes. I grew up on breakfasts of bacon and eggs and hot cocoa, fell off the monkey bars as a girl, craved more popularity than I got as a teenager, and, throughout, absorbed the precept that one stands on one's own two feet. In short, I was American. I took a secretarial job after graduation and acquired a husband and the regulation two children.

So what am I doing imprisoned in my own land by a four-foot-ten-inch granny from Southeast Asia who doesn't speak English, led by her through crowds of her people where she knows every third person and I stick out like a giraffe at a pony show? Granny grips my fingers protectively in her warm, rough hand. Although we are both in our fifties, I feel like a child. I am getting some kind of lesson from this day among strangers, something about who I am.

Around us proceeds the New Year's celebration of the Hmong people, held in a county park near Sacramento, California, on the American Thanksgiving weekend. I follow Granny — I have no choice, since she still has a grip on my left hand. She works her way around the Hmong chefs barbecuing chicken and fish on portable grills, Hmong salad makers mashing spices and sour condiments with vegetables in wooden mortars, Hmong women dishing out purple rice, Hmong young people selling Hmong audio and video tapes, and lines of teenage Hmong boys and girls tossing chartreuse tennis balls back and forth, the ritualized flirting that in their native Laos served as introductions to a possible spouse.

Granny pauses with a group she knows. I am not introduced. I try out my Hmong on the woman next to me, stumbling through my limited vocabulary. A sweet-faced girl hides behind the woman's arm as if it were a sturdy tree. Her daughter. How many children do you have? she asks. I have two children, I say, a son and a daughter. And a husband.

She looks around for a matching American. Didn't come, I answer. I've had this conversation before. I came by myself. My reply ends the conversation. We have lost connection.

I feel both amused and annoyed. If you have a husband, I can almost hear her chastising me, what are you doing here without him? But, I want to answer, I am free to do as I wish. I can stand on my own two feet.

Granny, my wrist now clamped to her ribs under a steel-muscled arm, moves on. My annoyance fades and again I revel in the feeling of warmth that always surfaces when I am with the Hmong — a feeling I can't put my finger on.

We pass a trio of giggling children spooning gaudy green and pink desserts out of plastic cups. I marvel at the distance between the bacon and eggs of my childhood, and the world of the Hmong, where breakfast is rice and vegetables and maybe meat in a soup with hot pepper sauce on the side, the same as lunch and dinner.

I didn't know a thing about the Hmong when they were helping the United States fight the Vietnam War in Laos in the 1960s and 1970s. Few Americans did. They broke upon my awareness later when they showed up in Sacramento as refugees. There they attracted news photographers with the neon-bright costumes they wear at the Hmong New Year gatherings. (Photographs don't convey the sounds of the girls' silver-coin-bedecked outfits nor the effect of brilliant apron ties swishing rhythmically behind them as they strut in twos and threes about the grounds.) The incongruity of it. Here were people, I read, who came out of a world lacking the "necessities of life"— electricity, roads, paying jobs, newspapers, dentists— and seemed to be merrily developing their own version of life in America.

My appetite for the unusual stirred. What are these people like? How do they act toward each other? What do they know? I believe I also needed to throw a bridge across a gulf.

Fortunately, I was in a position to pursue the matter. As a feature writer at the *Sacramento Union* with an editor willing to humor me and wise enough to insist on narrowing the story, I set out to find one Hmong person who had done something unusual. Through volunteers at a Third

World people's crafts boutique I immediately came up with the name of Chamy Thor, one of the first Hmong women to earn a college degree and a genius with embroidery thread. I found Chamy (pronounced "chay-mee") and did the story, which was published in January 1988.

But interviewing her and watching her at work and home only increased my curiosity. You can't absorb much about a culture in a couple of interviews. Besides, Chamy had an edge to her — she had spine. She was on the threshold of something exciting, it seemed to me, even dangerous— she was struggling to stand on her own two feet. I could relate to that.

Chamy introduced me to a shaman in Sacramento, an older woman who looked into my face and smiled a smile that invited me back for more.

The visit gave Chamy the chance to begin to explain Hmong beliefs about sickness and health. I could only scratch my head at the thought of multiple souls that wander. Maybe if I learned the language I could get inside Hmong heads. I found a refugee language program staffed by a man named Lue Vang and began learning the Hmong tonal language, which has no relation whatsoever to the Romance languages that teachers tried to impart to me.

I wrote a few more feature stories about the Hmong and their difficulties adapting to the United States. It seemed life wasn't so merry for them. Their hardships disturbed me. They were like fish trying to walk. I went back to school and wrote a master's thesis on the conflicts between the Hmong world of shamans and herbs and the American world of doctors, appointments, diagnostic testing, and surgery. Ancient wisdom, I learned, leads them to avoid endangering the body's wholeness with surgery or upsetting bodily harmony with too much medicine. Yet they also saw that the new kind of healing could yield astounding results.

I wanted to help. I could help! I could explain some things to them. I could tell the lady with the fallen uterus that her problem could be fixed and that it was not caused by doctor trickery but was the result of the number of children she had borne. I could help Chamy with some of the projects she was beginning to tell me about.

But help is tricky. A Japanese American friend tried to explain. "Maybe they don't want your help." Maybe they can solve their problems better themselves. Maybe I didn't know enough to help. Besides, "helping" could put me in a position of arrogance, a sure-fire contaminant of relationships.

I ran into other snags, too. A lot of the rules of American culture crash upon entry into Hmong culture. I needed to uncover the unwritten protocols about visiting, meals, gifts, and babies. I had to learn how to be a friend to people whose language doesn't include the word "friend." (They have borrowed the Chinese word, a carry-over of their centuries in China. When you ask a Hmong, most friends turn out to be relatives.)

Then there was the worry about intruding. Maybe they were content without an American friend. None of the Hmong I encountered appeared to be lacking friends. But then I would hear Chamy's voice on the phone, "Oh, hi, Sue!" Or I would go to a Hmong home and find myself sitting on the living room floor surrounded by non–English-speaking young mothers, fresh from the refugee camps in Thailand. They would sway their babies to sleep on their backs and laugh and chat to me in Hmong, whether I comprehended or not. Always, I would be effortlessly included, and a familial warmth would creep over me.

I am in awe of the Hmong for numerous reasons: their bamboo musical instrument that sings words, their capacity for work, their range of survival skills, and the intricacies of their crafts, from papermaking to houses to poetry. These I can admire but not duplicate. But they have also demonstrated something else, something that is changing the way I live: The Hmong are showing me the possibilities of standing on more than two feet.

Houseful after houseful of Hmong remind me that I overlook something important when I am too busy for relatives, neighbors, and friends. Ties to the people, to tribe, clan, and family — that's what has carried the Hmong intact through thousands of years of wandering and a sometimes precarious supply of food. It's those ties that brought Granny of the Iron Grip and the others to the New Year's festival that day, sending them strolling in search of relatives or news of relatives, eating Hmong food, hearing poem-chants that emphasized Hmong morals, and reassuring themselves, with the ritual tossing of the tennis ball, that new Hmong families would be formed and new Hmong children born. They are a people and they know it. They believe in it. They have made community an art.

But there are two sides to it. Ties can be a net that traps as well as a net that rescues. I noticed this as I began listening to young men and especially young women who were chafing against the heavy expectations laid upon them, for example, as sons or daughters-in-law. For myself, I do not plan to relinquish my independence or opinions in favor of my husband's (although he is smart and even wise).

Along with ties to the living — spouse, parents, aunts, uncles, grandparents, children, and endless cousins— Hmong are mindful of the relatives who have died. They dream about them. They receive advice and comfort from them. They also can be fussed at and chastised by them, as they are by living relatives.

Such attention to ancestors piqued my curiosity about my own. I already knew a few family stories, but I can't say I truly cared. But witnessing how real their ancestors are for the Hmong, I began to wonder if I did indeed have palpable ties to the Delmores and the Murphys, the Currans, McHughs, and Sloans. Is it possible that a spirit of adventure can be passed down over centuries? That Herbert de la Mer, Viking, a likely ancestor, passed down something more than a similarity of name to his descendant my grandfather, Capt. Hubert Delmore, U.S. Navy? That my hunger for the unknown has a history?

I've thought a lot about ancestors and the length of their shadows. I began trying, through those remembered bits of story told over the holiday table or sepia photos I've hung on the walls, to put myself in the presence of my family's pioneers. I've craved a time-traveler's chance to see their faces in motion, watch how they walk, hear their voices to know what they were like.

In place of that futile desire I've turned again to the Hmong. In many ways, the substitution works. I can imagine any of the Hmong I know as ancestors of mine — pioneering people. Granny of the Iron Grip is a good match for my Curran grandmother, who took her two young daughters alone on fifteen-hundred-mile automobile trips in the 1920s that featured driving on boards over desert sand. What flashes repeatedly on my mental screen, as I spend time with Hmong, is our sameness. Same emotions, same bodies. Only the thinking is different.

One other bonus. The journey in search of the Hmong, the Murphys, and the Delmores has enabled me to shuck the good-guys and bad-guys mode of thinking. ("My people are Irish and therefore all Irish are good guys.") In its place I've seen that there is great and not-so-great in everybody and in everybody's culture. That turns out to be a comforting thought.

Although I truly wanted and expected to write this book by myself, it has turned out to be a community effort. I have many people to thank for its completion. My gratitude is extended first to each person in this book who honored me with his or her personal story. Newcomers in America, particularly those from a culture as unfamiliar to Americans as that of the Hmong, take a risk in telling their stories. They open themselves to erroneous judgments that might isolate them. In the end it is their bravery that builds bridges. Chamy Thor is a star example of such an individual, and so I most warmly thank her and her husband, Nom Npis Lis, for taking me into their lives. Mistakes found in these pages must not be charged against any of them who tried to help me understand. Rather, errors are due to my own limitations.

Thank you to the congregation of Sacramento Hmong Alliance Church for befriending me. To Nom Pao Mouayaaj who knew a floundering individual when he saw one and offered his interpreting services; he was typical of the warmth with which I was aided by so many Hmong. Thanks to Niam Tais (grandmother) Kao and Chue Lee for language help. To the Cha family for so much information, yes, but even more for modeling Hmong hospitality. Thank you also to the family of Chue Kao Thao, who in telling how their father died in saving a little girl — not even a Hmong — showed me what Hmong mean by leadership.

Thank you to Nellie, Alice, Grace, John, Beverly, and Jayne for prying open the door to Asia for me in the first place. Thank you to Laura Leonelli of Sacramento Lao Family Community, Inc., for challenging me to learn more about the Hmong and to Judy Lewis and Lue Vang of the Southeast Asia Community Resource Center, who made visiting their trailer office not only an important aspect of my education but an occasion for laughter and friendship. Judy also read the manuscript and, as always, offered enthusiasm as well as valuable insights. I am also grateful to Jan Hunt, director of the Indochinese Assistance Center in Sacramento, and for all that the late Ninh Van Nguyen taught me about being Southeast Asian.

Thank you to Professor Bernadette Tarallo at the University of California at Davis, who opened my mind to the complexities of cultures in transition, and to Faith Boucher and Isao Fujimoto, also at UC Davis, who taught and encouraged me through a master's degree. Thank you also to Professor Martin Kenney, who gave me tools to see how economics and culture shape each other.

Thank you to all those who encouraged me: my father, Ray Murphy, who not only exemplified respect for Native Americans from the day I was born but was also, during the creation of this book, a one-man clipping service; his wife, Carolyn W. Murphy, one of many who expressed enthusiasm and asked valuable questions; Patricia Woy, probably the world's best and gentlest writing teacher, sadly now gone; and members of the Writers Club of Whittier, especially Marla Miller, who understood what I was after before I did.

Thank you to those others who read the manuscript: Linda Cruikshank, my former editor at the *Vacaville Reporter*; Linda Hickman, also a newspaper editor, generous with compliments and astute with criticism; and Gayle L. Morrison, a true and helpful scholar with extensive personal knowledge of the Hmong. Family members who bravely read the manuscript include my son, Phil Mote, a scientist, writer and editor; my daughter, Sarah Williams, wise as well as educated in the matter of cultures; and

Cynthia Bird, a discerning reader and seller of good books. All of these loved me enough to wield a pencil.

To Elaine Walton, who prayed me through to the end: Thanks, dear friend!

Because of the complexities encountered in studying an unfamiliar culture, I feel special gratitude toward those who over the years have written about the Hmong, especially Hmong writers! Some are named in the Bibliography. These and all those others who think deeply about culture offer special hope to the human family.

Finally, I owe more than I can say to my late mother, Eileen Murphy, herself a writer, whose love for the Samoans translated into a lifetime of respect for other cultures, and to my husband, Dave, with whom I share the certainty that one day peoples of all sorts will sit down together for one big, joyous meal.

A Note to Hmong Readers:

"... *Saum toj no mas kuv tias yam twg uas yog nej xav tias yuav zoo no los nej ho khaws, yam twg nej tias tsis zoo no los neg ho muab pov-tseg.*"

"If there is anything here that makes sense, people can keep it, and if there is anything that is not good, people can disregard it."

— Shue-long Vue[1]

Introduction

"Will They Eat Me?"

In a small room, the man sits ramrod-straight across a beige Formica desk from a welfare worker, a woman with black hair and pale beige skin. He listens closely as she speaks to him in their common tongue — Hmong. The man leans forward, frowns slightly. "Hanh?" The worker repeats. I have no idea what they are saying. Perched on a metal chair with my knees squeezed against the desk, reporter's spiral notepad on my lap, I try to fade into the wall.

Once or twice during the meeting, Chamy Thor, the welfare worker and pioneer college graduate, turns to me with a quick English explanation of what's going on. She appears calm enough — she has a serious face and speaks with an even voice — but her white sweater and pale pink slacks suggest — what? A beginner's vulnerability? Chamy has already explained to the man that I am writing a story about her for the newspaper. I detect no response to the information.

The man wears spotless white jogging shoes, gray slacks, and a gray T-shirt that says, "Northern California/The 116th/Chevrolet Dealers." His brown arms are folded, and his black hair stands at attention in a crew cut. They talk about his health.

He is Hmong, one of the mountain tribes from Laos that, recruited and supported by the United States' Central Intelligence Agency, battled communism in Laos in the 1960s and 1970s.[1]

He arrived in the United States three months before this Northern California welfare office visit in 1987, along with his wife and three sons. Before his country fell to the communist Pathet Lao in 1975, he had served for seven years in the Royal Lao Army, Hmong Division. After Laos fell, he fled with his family into the jungle — just as Chamy did with her family — and carried on a guerrilla battle for eight more years. Finally, in 1983, the family escaped to Thailand and, after four years in refugee camps, came to America.

Now, in an institutional room in Marysville, California, he is sorting out his future with Chamy's help. To qualify for benefits, she tells him, he must go to school, learn English, and attend a job club.

But he is claiming disability, hoping to be exempted from the work requirement. He can barely see with his right eye or hear with his right ear, he says, due to years of firing a rifle. Also, there's no transportation.

Over the manila file on the desk between them, the two discuss where he can find a doctor and when he will report back to her. Then Chamy slides a paper in front of him with short, strong fingers. He takes a pen and slowly prints his name.

On the surface, the scene looked straightforward. Bureaucratic business. I already know about that. It was not their encounters with American government but this people's culture that captivated me, their spectacular dress and unusual customs. But later, as I listened to Chamy while driving with her to meet a Hmong shaman, I began to see that the dynamics between her and her client were tumultuous, far more complex than the usual case worker/client interaction. Though Chamy was nominally in charge of the transaction, it was the man, not the woman, who was armed, by tradition, with power. I began to look more closely at Chamy.

Here in America, Chamy told me in the car, nothing is the way it was. "Everything change," she said, distress giving her voice a fleeting hardness as we drove south on Del Paso Boulevard. Never in their homeland, I understood, did a law say a man had to work or explain why he couldn't. Never was school required. Never from one end of life to the other did a Hmong need to hold a pencil or pen. And never would a normal adult male be subject to the decisions of a woman, especially concerning his livelihood.

I began to see that encounters such as this are awash in cultural chaos. The phone calls Chamy was receiving threatening her life attested to that. The ways of the people were being challenged by revolutionary ideas, and Chamy — with at least part of her heart — was leading one of the charges. Along with her pink-slacks vulnerability, Chamy had spine. That was evident from the way she tossed off the information about the threatening phone calls.

Before I knew it, Chamy had worked her way under my skin — Chamy first, for her courage, and then every other person portrayed in this book. This is a biased story: I have fallen in love with the Hmong, from the crumpled, warty old men with giant dignity to the perfectly named baby Sunshine. I love them for themselves and because they so innocently opened my mind.

The Hmong are among the latest of the immigrants who over the centuries have walked, sailed, ridden, driven, or flown to America. In 1998 they numbered about a quarter million in the United States. Estimates at the end of the '90s placed more than seventy thousand Hmong in California, more than sixty thousand in Minnesota, forty-five thousand in Wisconsin, ten thousand in North Carolina, six thousand in Michigan, five thousand in Colorado, two to four thousand in Georgia, Oregon, Pennsylvania, Rhode Island, and South Carolina, and a thousand down to as few as ten people (Arizona, New Jersey) in twenty-five other states. There are at least seven million Hmong worldwide, roughly equivalent to the population of Massachusetts or Virginia. Most of them are in China, but others have migrated to France, Australia, and Canada.

The Hmong have swamped communities such as Merced, California, and Green Bay, Wisconsin. Tensions in American communities can heat up, as shown by a report written for the United States Commission on Civil Rights with the no-nonsense title *The Hmong in Green Bay: A Clash of Cultures*. Businesses and public agencies try to adjust. Telephone companies, utilities, the courts, and the IRS have initiated interpreter programs in Hmong along with Spanish, Chinese, and Vietnamese.

Some observers say the Hmong have been one of the least prepared immigrants for what they found in America. No one has had to leap further to adapt to life here. Since 1975 they have confounded immigration and refugee workers with what even some Hmong call Stone Age ways. In their first days here, they were stumped by Western toilets and electric stoves, standing on the one and building cooking fires on the other. Snow looked like salt. One group of newly arrived Hmong were frightened by the hugs they received from a crowd of sponsors at the airport. They feared, as they were passed from one happy American to the next, that they were being scattered so that one of them could be stolen.

Parents and their children have been baffled by school, and teachers in turn have been baffled by the Hmong. Only a few Hmong experienced classrooms or written language in Laos. Some families resisted sending their daughters to school. And religious beliefs have been known to pop up in unexpected ways. The father of a kindergartener insists his son was spiritually harmed when a classmate poked his finger with blunt-ended scissors.

The Hmong still frustrate physicians and nurses. Though Hmong will use medicine that they can see brings results, centuries of belief tells them that sickness is caused by the flight of souls.

Chamy told me one day at her dining table, where we have so often talked, about her mother's visit to the United States in the early 1990s.

"We went to the airport, and we picked her up. All the people came out [of the airplane], and we see no one came out anymore. We thought, Oh, how come we don't see her? And finally there's an airplane attendant brought her out, and she's very, very tiny! I couldn't believe it, because she's very tiny.

"And then when she saw us she start to cry very, very loud. She was so scared, she cry very loud, and so all the people just look. We draw a pretty good crowd! And then we were crying and crying."

It wasn't the airplane, Chamy said, nor being up in the air that scared her mother. It was the airport elevators. Chamy seemed amused.

"Whenever they took her to the elevator, she didn't know that it is [an] elevator. She thought they going to weigh her, how many pounds she had, and they going to eat her up. Weigh her and find out how many pounds she have. Is it good to eat yet or not? She really think about that. So she was very scared."

Mom's world and the world of elevators are like two circles sketched on paper that neither overlap nor touch. The worlds are as foreign to each other as those of a shaman and a medical doctor, or those of a child who works the field at age eight and a child who works a computer. Sitting in a neat middle-class apartment listening to Pang Foua Yang Rhodes, a Hmong woman graduate student, I drew two circles on my notepad. This is the Hmong world, I told her, and over here, not touching, is the American world.

The sketch struck a chord with Pang Foua. "I like your diagram because I think most people would do this." She grabbed a pencil and drew two overlapping circles next to mine. She poked the air toward my separate circles. In school, she said, "it definitely felt like there were two different worlds that you interacted in. Like on the weekends it was the Hmong world. You … visited with Hmong families. But on weekdays you were in school. This was a totally different world."

She continued. "We've been transplanted from a culture that didn't really allow room to transcend the cultural boundary. There wasn't a need to, and there was no stimulation to." Their world, high in the mountains, was largely self-contained.

While Chamy's mom, following her sojourn in America, has returned to the secure Hmong world in the hill country in Laos, people like Pang

Foua and Chamy and Chamy's client at the welfare office have stepped —
or been thrust — into a middle space. There they attempt the construction
of a new mental universe. For them, every thought and every mode of
behavior comes into question. They have to think about everything. The
mind becomes exhausted and the emotions raw. I could see it in Pang
Foua's and others' storytelling, their worries, their anger, their on-the-
ground experiments, their dreams and defeats. The man in the welfare
office was attempting to patch together a reasonable, dignified future as
best he knew how.

There in the middle space that they occupy, the forest is full of tigers.
Not everyone finds their way. The terrain is unfamiliar. The old mental
maps and tools no longer work. Some get eaten.

My wish in writing this book is to follow a few Hmong—friends,
now—from their home world into the middle forest of the tigers. I have
divided the book into sections so as to reflect that journey. Following a
portrayal of the exodus experienced by the Hmong over thousands of years
and by individuals in the last decades, the book turns in Part Two to the
world left behind by the Hmong, where the people we see now were
molded. Part Three, "America the Difficult," glimpses just how costly that
shift has been, and the final section touches on the accommodations people are making in order to create emotional and material shelter for themselves and their families.

The stories of most of the people in the book belong to one or another
of these sections, but others span the entire book.

Being an American writing an American book, I have gravitated to
the stories of individuals, even while describing a people accustomed to
taking their cues not from an inner, individual voice but from family and
community. Of the hundreds of Hmong I've met, most do not think of
themselves first as individuals. Ask them to describe themselves and most
would simply shrug or say something about their parents, grandfather,
siblings, clan, or people. One scholar who spends time thinking about
such things referred to East Asia — the ancestral home of the Hmong — as
a place "where the concept of the person as a separate entity is debatable."[2]
Like grapes, the Hmong come in bunches. You can't encounter the Hmong
without seeing their community. Only rarely do I visit a solitary Hmong.
In every apartment and home, someone is always coming in the door. The
phone is always ringing. They are always sharing information, housing,
food, rides, babysitting, marriage problems, a pickup truck. Young people arrive home with their friends— relatives, of course — and old people
come to pick something in the garden.

That's the circle labeled "Hmong world." The other circle, Pang Foua insisted, does not touch it. Compared in a study with fifty-two other countries, the United States topped out as the most individualistic nation on earth, with individualism defined as seeing the self as the basic unit of survival rather than the group.[3] It is the lone cowboy or inventor that lights our fires.

Now these Hmong, wedded as they are to communal ways, seem to be undertaking their internal reconstruction projects as individuals. Shelter is scarce in the middle forest. Few parents, grandparents, or older siblings — people who would normally pass on their knowledge — know this terrain either. Rarely anyone to say, This is how to do it. Can they survive as a community as they individually adapt to life in America? It is uncertain.

In telling the story of Chamy, I've chosen others who, together, suggest her context. Of the older ones, she is an heir. For the younger, an outrider. They are for the most part people I met along the way in my search to understand what's inside the heads of the Hmong. Several of them were introduced to me by Chamy. Only the gang member needed to be searched out. A few are outstanding persons, while others are typical Hmong Americans. I ended up loving them all — cranky, loving, misguided, funny, officious, defeatist, bright, troubled, talented, but always loyal.

The book's main figures are these, in the order in which they first appear:

Chamy Thor ("chay-mee tore"), a workaholic in her late forties at the time this was written, lives in Sacramento with her sociable husband, Nom Npis Lis ("naw bee lee"). Their grown children live with them. They are Johnny, married to Patty; Ken, married to Virginia; and May, married to Ku. Chamy's mother, Kia Lis ("kee-a lee"), lives and farms in Laos.

Pang Foua Yang Rhodes ("pahng fooah yang roads"), in her twenties, lives in Southern California with her American husband. She is a graduate student at a theological seminary.

Tou Ger Xiong ("too grr shyong"), an irrepressible comic, lives in Minnesota. He is a frequent presenter at Hmong conferences.

Mai Xiong ("my shyong"), warm-hearted, candid, is in her sixties. She is a retired shaman living in Sacramento.

Cho Lee, an earnest mother in her thirties, lives in Santa Ana with her talkative husband, Long Yang. She and Long are factory workers. Their children, a girl and three boys who are already imprinted with the classic Hmong open-handedness, are Zong, twelve; Lao ("lah-o"), nine; Feng, eight; and Dou ("doo"), seven.

Mai Xia Cha ("my see-a"), bright, passionate, is in her mid-twenties. She lives in San Diego with her husband, Zhen Fang, and their four small children. Mai Xia is a pioneer, looking for her moment.

Ly Vong Lynaolu ("lee vong lee-nah-o-loo"), angry, full of visions, was an officer in the Hmong Secret Army in the Vietnam War and a leader in the Sacramento Hmong community. His widow is the beautiful Pao Chao Lo ("pow chow loh"). Among their nine children are these grown daughters: Nouzong Lynaolu ("noo-zhong lee-nah-o-loo"), an activist; and personable Katie, or Noumoua ("noo-moo-a").

The handsome, charismatic Sai Sue Lor ("sigh su lor"), in his twenties, lives in Sacramento with his wife and baby. He is a former gang member, rescued in a surprising way by his culture.

Dr. Lue Vang ("lew vang"), a jocular educator and Christian in his late forties, lives in Sacramento with his family. He remembers being adopted.

These people and others contribute to the picture of how the Hmong are melding "Hmong" and "American." But the story belongs to Chamy Thor — complex, tireless, disarmingly open in our girl talks yet more often chary of talk, tough or "sweet," as she called herself, according to the situation, and above all courageous in leaving the familiar to scout out a new life as human beings have done since the beginning.

Working out a life in a land of tigers takes a toll. One day, recalling that many elder Hmong suffer depression due to losing family members and homeland, I asked Chamy if she ever felt depressed.

"Yeah, oh, yeah, I have a depression, but not in terms of old life or what I lose back there. What depress me is [that it's] very hard to adjust to a new country, very hard to compete with the people here to make a better life. Yeah, I do have depression. It make me a short temper and can't sleep, have to take sleeping pill." Then she laughed the sweet, lilting laugh of a well-schooled Hmong woman. "Even that, it doesn't help."

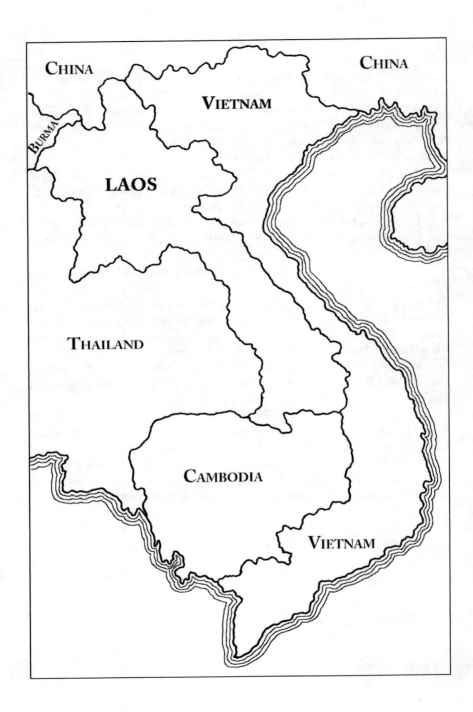

Southeast Asia

VIETNAM

Dien Bien Phu

LAOS

Sam Neua

Plain of Jars

Phonsavan

Luang Prabang

Lat Houang

Nong Het

Long Cheng

Xieng Khouang

Mouong Cha

Vang Vieng

Ban Son

Phou Bia

Mekong R.

13

Ban Vinai camp

VIENTIANE

Mekong R.

Nong Kai camp

THAILAND

Northern Laos — Hmong Country

Part I

JOURNEYS

Npaj sia ua: To risk
(Lit., to prepare the heart to do)[1]

1

Leaving: Chamy Thor

Whatever the old people tell you,
It just stay in your mind.
— Chamy Thor

Every human life is mysterious in its unfolding, the product of multiple influences and choices. In each life, some mysteries yield to thoughtful inquiring. Others never do.

Were it not for the intervention of one man, an uncle, in Laos, Chamy Thor's story might have read like this: Chamy Thor rises early on work days, dresses as befits a laborer in the family's fields, and sets out barefoot with the family crowd for the hours-long trek to the fields. At the end of the day, they might stay overnight in the fields, tired, hoping that the crop will feed them for the following year.

Instead, at the age of eight, she experienced an abrupt immersion in Western culture, before ever hearing of the United States. And so, her story runs like this: Chamy Thor rises early on work days, dresses as befits an accountant — she left her job at the welfare office — and climbs into her Toyota. At the end of the day, she leaves the concrete-and-glass California Department of Transportation building in Sacramento, tired but knowing, she once told me, that she's got the mortgage covered.

Chamy, the professional, is in her middle years, married, with kids. She is not a flashy person nor a chatterer like so many Hmong women. If you want to know something, you ask. She will tell it to you straight. But she will not offer information about herself, particularly if it is flattering.

21

Chamy Thor (right) and Nom Npis Lis. California, October 1994.

Chamy is loath to weep, except as required at a Hmong funeral. Even upon seeing sisters and brothers for the first time in decades, she did not weep. Perhaps, I thought, weeping opens too fearful a pathway. But in other ways she represents ideal Hmong womanhood: She is hard working, like a faithful water buffalo. She is impeccably hospitable. She smiles energetically, her short upper lip lifting off even white teeth to give an open and engaging countenance. And, more than most, she is courageous.

Chamy, her husband, three teenage kids, and — at this time in the story — a teenage daughter-in-law live on a skillet-flat acre of land north of Sacramento. The ranch-style gray house is fronted by roses that Chamy has planted, or ordered her sons to plant — "for color," she told me.

I have often gone to this house. Just inside the front door hangs a big needlework scene that Chamy stitched showing the Laotian mountain village life she once lived. It was only by chance that I learned of the prize she won for it.

Sometimes I spend the night on one of the daybeds in the family room, through which Chamy tries to control foot traffic. Mornings, I dress as quickly as possible in the bathroom shared by the four young people and then guess what's for breakfast — tea and fish-flavored crackers, a huge feast of rice and multiple meats, or nothing. With limited Hmong language at my disposal, I frequently don't know what's going on.

On a spring Saturday morning, after my bathroom sprint, Chamy buzzed through the family room, on a mission. She was dressed in slacks, shirt, and old shoes. She is not tall — five foot one, her husband Nom Npis measured for me — but her size-five feet are the widest I have ever seen.[1] "My foot hurt," she said, on the return trip past my bed. "I'm getting old," she wailed. I inquired how long she had been up. "I like to get up early and complain!" She laughed disarmingly.

Not long after, I heard the front door opening and shutting more than usual.

"We have dance practice today," Chamy told me. "Good!" I said, delighted for the bonus of music, dance, and children.

Quietly, a few children slipped through the front hallway into the converted garage, then some teenagers, then more and more until over thirty Hmong kids, mostly girls, had materialized. Chamy's husband, as always, joked with the little ones, who responded with shy smiles. The couple's daughter, May, acted as practice coach for Chamy's dance troupe. She poked a button to start the taped music. I crept in to watch. Ten of the girls in pants and T-shirts arranged themselves in a grid. Each carried a large woven bamboo tray used to winnow rice. These they swooped up and around as they danced in time to electronic music with a high nasal singer who, I learned, exhorted listeners to do right. The music issued from two huge speakers, one placed in a corner behind an exercise bike and a set of weights, the other next to a computer. On the walls Nom Npis had fastened four khengs, the big wooden pipes used by the Hmong in an unusual acrobatic-musical performance. Next, the dancers executed a dance, with curved-out fingers, in the Lao fashion.

Nom Npis, meanwhile, was having fun interacting with some of the younger ones waiting their turn in the family room. After chatting for a while he went outside to work on a building project — I didn't learn what.

The rehearsal went quietly — you begin to wonder *why* these children are so well-behaved — until a girl of about eight, who was waiting with others in the family room, broke into silent tears. She hid herself behind sofa cushions and continued to cry noiselessly. Chamy appeared and questioned the unhappy girl. The child, by then showing anger but still emitting no sound, could not answer. Chamy patted her sturdily on the shoulder, then, noticing my worried expression, laughed and said, "She's fine." A plate of pizza placed in the child's hands halted the crying.

I returned to the garage to watch a dance with Chinese paper umbrellas. "They haven't practiced this one before," Chamy said. One dancer with perfect light tan skin and sweet mouth looked like a child from an Asian travel video. Another, in glasses, looked like the American school-ground star she no doubt was. The dancing fell apart, and May showed them the choreography again. Later I would see a few of these same dancers' faces up close in the newspaper, dressed to the teeth in brilliant Hmong finery, performing the Hmong dances Chamy has taught for years and taken to events around California.

I learned to expect surprises on visits to Chamy's, snippets of the Hmong world that caught me off guard — the big dance class or the lengthy late night counseling session she and Nom Npis conducted for a young Hmong man whose Vietnamese wife had run off. One afternoon I found myself witness to a scene I had never experienced in my city life. The three of us returned to the house after an errand and found a farm truck backed into the side yard. I heard a loud pop. Then two cowboy-hatted and -booted Americans climbed back into their truck, studied me with quick but open curiosity, and drove away. Behind them remained a half dozen Hmong who set to work butchering the steer that had just been dispatched.

"I forgot they were coming today," Chamy said. "People from town come here to do this. You want to watch?"

Some months later, at a new house built for Chamy and Nom Npis a few miles from the old one, I was again caught by surprise when I began questioning Chamy about the Hmong funeral liturgy. On the previous day

I had gone with Chamy's family to part of a five-day-long ceremony in South Sacramento and was curious about the speeches I heard but did not understand. On this brisk February morning, I followed Chamy out of her new house, a few miles northeast of the old one. In her hand she carried a book in Hmong. We were heading no farther than to my car, parked in the gravel driveway. There, she explained, outside the house, she could translate aloud from the funeral text without bringing harm to her family. She was still Hmong.

After nearly an hour, my questions about the text had been answered. The little car was like a cocoon around us, and it occurred to me to probe a little deeper than I had before. Perhaps because of the miles we had traveled together or because I had just spent several days at her home, I asked a different order of question. "Take a look back at your life," I said. "What makes you sad or happy or regretful?"

"Oh, you want to know that?" Chamy frowned through the windshield. She began to blink rapidly, the sign of stress. For a decade, Chamy and I had spent hours together like this, me asking questions about Hmong culture, how she viewed different customs, details of her life, even family matters, in my effort to plumb her life. And every one of them she answered, sometimes at length, sometimes minimally. This was the first question of mine that brought her to a standstill. The question seemed simple, but questions about the sweep of one's life are the hardest. Maybe I had reached the boundary where Chamy closed down.

I sat quietly and waited. I wanted to understand her, this tough, inward person. I wanted to grasp the life she came from, to see how it illuminated what she is now, to know whether she had come through whole or damaged. I *wanted* her to have come through whole, for the sake of hope. A chill wind buffeted the little car and blew the wild green grasses in Chamy's yard into waves. "My goal is yard cleanup!" Chamy had told me earlier. Was she now slipping away from my question? Maybe the clues to her answer were already there in her story, which she had told me over so many visits. The clues might be there, but clues can mislead.

Leaving

The ordered world of Chamy's childhood, I had already learned, was overturned not by the enemy soldiers who marched into her village but by the quiet return of handsome twin uncles from the city. She was eight when this happened.

Right now, listening to her voice, I was sitting at her dining table in the old house where she often told me stories and fed me to bursting. Behind us in the kitchen, her daughter-in-law Patty was cooking a meal, quiet as a mouse. She was doing her duty as a Hmong daughter-in-law.

"I used to be a very shy girl," Chamy said. She was writing the words on a white lined pad—"very shy"—as if to emphasize that she had not gone looking for the event that changed everything for her.

"My two uncle, they went out to school in the city, and once they come back to the village, they try to teach us the Lao alphabet language." The twins had left the village as boys to go to a city school, something only a skimming of Hmong could do. They came from rich folks. Excited by the discovery of a broader world, they had returned, resolved to pick new scholars from among the nieces, nephews, brothers, and sisters who were old enough to leave home.

Chamy would have had black hair then, tan skin, and eyes shaped like the leaves of golden bamboo, as she does now. But she would have been small and thin as a rail. Carrying water, lugging a sibling, and working the rice pounder or the corn mill would guarantee that. Like all the mountain children, her nose would often have been plugged from infection.

"My uncles try to teach us to read," Chamy said. Four young students had been assembled. "The other three talk and laugh at each other. I was so shy that I never speak out." Then one uncle gave them a test—"You read, now you read, now you read," the uncle had said, pointing to each one. The noisy ones couldn't read but shy Chamy could, recalling the secrets of the curves and loops spread across the page.

And so she was picked to go to school in Vientiane, Laos's capital city. "But I didn't show any interest that I want to go. My mom didn't show any interest that she want to send me. Because my uncle picked, then we just go." Two boys—the ones usually chosen—and stepsister Mai were picked, too.

"And now we have to walk the whole day to wait for the airplane," Chamy said.

One of the uncles took them to the airstrip. No roads existed then between the village and the airstrip. Just paths. "We walk all day from very early in the dark."

The children knew nothing of planes. In two days, the small airplane came, and the uncle took them aboard.

"And when we in the airplane, small airplane, it go up, go down. Mai grab the right knee of my uncle and I grab the left knee, and we just hold very tight like that. Very scared." There still hangs on Chamy's wall a framed photo of the uncle, Nyiaj Thoj, who chose her and whose knee she clung to that day in fear. He stands, handsome, uniformed, beside the T-28 that he flew in the Secret War in Laos.

"And then they took us to the Catholic nun and leave us with them. That is 1964, August 1964. It's about four years that I didn't see my mom." My heart wept for the little girl.

Chamy might as well have been changing planets on her one-hour flight to Vientiane. With little warning she was plucked from an ancient tribal cocoon and dropped unprepared into French colonial culture. Chamy and an aunt of the same age who later came to school were the first females in their lineage to get an education.

By simply being a student, Chamy was a challenge to the rules. The Hmong long ago figured out a tightly structured way of life that served in tough times. It's similar to football or basketball. You play by the rules. You can't win without your teammates. It's the same with Hmong. There is a word *ntsuag*. Its meaning shades from "without parents, without wife or husband" to "destitute." Within your group you are safe—fed, clothed, sheltered. To be alone is to court death.

The flip side of social cohesion, however, is social pressure, and it can be severe. Team life works for people who can fit in, know their position, and follow rules. It was Hmong boys, not girls, who were to be educated. Education could ruin a future housewife. Without wishing it, Chamy had been transplanted to a spot where she would question the assumptions of the game.

As it turned out, that education would give Chamy a head start in grappling with life in America. The experience of questioning, triggered by her immersion in a culture so alien to her own, prepared her to function as an individual, to make choices not necessarily approved by family and clan.

From my place at Chamy's dining table, I saw that Patty, now joined by Chamy's daughter, May, was emptying contents of frying pans and pots into big flowered bowls—fried meat, fragrant herbs, and green onion. Steaming rice was heaped into another bowl. Chamy turned to me. "Dinnertime," she said. It was time to gather up my notes, the tape recorder, and the maps she had marked for me to help anchor her stories to earth. There would be other times to get her talking again.

The perfect opportunity came months later, on a three-week trip we took together to Laos. It was Chamy's first trip back to her homeland since she fled eighteen years before. Typically, she expressed no emotion about the prospect. I had initiated the trip, knowing I wanted to see the Hmong in their home setting to understand them better. I was delighted that

Chamy wanted to go. She wished to see relatives and attend the Hmong New Year celebrations. "Is it OK if Nom Npis come, too?" she had phoned to ask. "He can carry our luggage." She laughed.

Finally on a November day, right after Thanksgiving, my husband, daughter, and son-in-law saw the three of us off from the Los Angeles airport. Excitement bounced around inside my chest, but my two companions appeared cool. Gradually, above a wrinkled blue ocean, we settled in.

Chamy, I noticed, was fidgeting in her airplane seat. The overhead light shone on her newly permed hair. Unlike the sweats in which I intended to get some sleep, she was wearing trim slacks, a long-sleeved blouse with a pattern of leaves in soft browns, and neat gold earrings.

Almost immediately Nom Npis was snoring in the window seat. He made this trip a few years before, soon after the communist government of Laos cracked open its doors for outside visitors and, especially, for currency. He was taking a sensible approach to the flight; we had well more than a dozen hours before we would bump down in Bangkok.

"My body ache!" Chamy said, sealed off in her middle seat. She hates inaction. "Can I work on your apron?" Six years ago, Chamy had taught me some simple Hmong cross-stitches, and since then I had laboriously decorated chunks of cross-stitch cloth with brilliant pink, orange, blue, and green embroidery floss, colors the Hmong love. My efforts included the collar and cuffs for a traditional festival jacket, like the ones worn by Hmong women for New Year's festivities and for burial. Now I was worrying my needle down a fancy-dress apron. An interminable project.

Chamy took the apron and bent over it. Her short fingers raced. The silver needle never missed the tiny gap between threads in the cloth. X-shaped stitches zigzagged behind her needle, forming diamonds and triangles. Chamy worked like a machine. No garden to dig in, but a needle to ply. She seemed to feel better.

She began to tell more stories. Nom Npis loves to tell stories and will do so for any audience, at any time. Not Chamy. In her I see a mind hard at work, but folded quietly upon itself.

I asked her to pick up the story about going to Vientiane, to the French nuns, for school. Later, we would glimpse the empty building where her uncle deposited her after that first, frightening airplane trip. She calls it the "nuns' school"—actually a dormitory.

She remembered her misery.

"When I left my mom, I still pee at night in bed." Each student was given foam squares to sleep on, two if you were short, three if you were tall. The nuns expected these to be kept clean. "So every night when I pee,

I just turn that over. They don't know because I smart and turn it over so they can't catch it." That went on for a year.

Chamy and the other students walked two and a half miles down one of Vientiane's main streets to the parochial school, now police headquarters. Adjacent to the school was a Catholic church, which after 1975 and the banning of religion became home to multiple families.

"We were more skilled than people who go to Lao public school," Chamy offered. "If they have exam, people with nun school[ing] do better." Instruction was in French.

The school day started at five A.M. with a clanging bell. The students had fifteen minutes to wash up, "but we can't talk to each other." Another bell rang for prayers. When we later stood in front of the dorm, Chamy pointed out the room where they slept—"there." Then there was prayer (twenty minutes), study period (thirty minutes) to memorize geography or history, and thirty minutes to set tables or clean the yard before breakfast. Under the eye of the nuns, the girls washed their dishes and started out. In winter when it was cold, students heated stones in a fire and carried them to school "so hand not get stiff."

For Chamy, the walk was not pleasant. "The Lao bad people. Every day you go to school, at least ten people insult you. Even old people call you 'Meo, Meo, Meo.'" Meo is an old, mean-spirited term for Hmong. "Even Laotian men or little girl say, 'Meo, Meo, Meo, Meo!'"

It still hurts. She frowned. "You feel bad about yourself—humiliated—like you're nothing." Chamy continued to stitch on my apron. Flight attendants dressed in slim orchid-color Thai dresses and gold- and silver-threaded shoulder sashes came through the cabin delivering fragrant meals of rice and chicken. Nom Npis awoke, ready to eat.

After the school day there might be more chores or time for play, maybe jacks or another game in which the two sides threw a ball hard toward each other. "I could catch very strong throw and throw very strong," Chamy assured me.

A three-hour study period followed dinner. Three hours. "If you talk or don't study, they put a cross by your name. But I play smart." She threaded a new length of brilliant green through her needle. "You have to pretend to study even if you are done. If I want something from inside [my] desk, I use my hand to find it without looking. You get a cross if you look." The nuns gave orders "like a soldier."

Even as she was packing to fly to Laos, Chamy said, a familiar dream troubled her. The dormitory where she had lived was dilapidated. "I dream I went back to stay in that place. I even dream I take Npis there and live. Next day [after the dream], I feel sick."

Chamy lived with the nuns for nine years and then moved into a nice home rented by her uncle — the one who took her to the school and who had become a fighter pilot for the CIA. After eight grades, she advanced to the lycée. Continued success while others around her flunked gave Chamy a powerful view of her abilities. It gave birth to the mantra I've often heard, sometimes spoken jubilantly, sometimes as a flat-out challenge: "I can do that." "I can do that." Once I heard her laugh when she said it, as if amused at her audacity. Once, while she was still at the lycée, her self-confidence led her into trouble.

> We have about forty-eight girls [students] went on a regular playing schedule. Like a certain day we can go out [from school] and play whatever we want. So we went to the Mekong River, and we try to swim.
>
> I was probably thirteen. We wear regular suit like, you know the kind of dress that have a big pleat, French skirt, dark blue, and a regular shirt. [They swam in these clothes.]
>
> I think the river was high. Probably in September, just after the monsoon. Many, many girl in water.
>
> The Hmong believe that dragon lives in the water. So whoever drowns, that means the dragon took their spirit or took their body. Well, I believe in dragon, too! Whatever the old people tell you, it just stay in your mind!
>
> Only a few girls know [how to swim]. The majority don't. I try. I go further, further. I can't swim. I almost drown. A couple of friends pull me out.
>
> I never try again.

Chamy lived with her twin uncles for two years. These uncles were half-brothers of her father. The Hmong have wondrously complex family trees, in which an American can get completely lost. The customs of marrying back into your mother's clan, men marrying multiple wives, raising families with large numbers of children, and practicing what Old Testament scholars call the levirate — a widow marrying her dead husband's brother and continuing to have children — all produce multiple, overlapping kin designations.

The twin uncles had the same father as Chamy's father but were sons of a second wife. Their father, Chamy's grandfather, was a rich man whose large family occupied all of Phou Lac village in a war-zone province — Xieng Khouang. ("Phou Lac, Famous Mountain," said Nom Npis, laughing at his ad hoc translation.) Grandfather had many children — seventeen, from two wives. At that time the opium trade was legal, and a large family could prosper by growing it.

Phou Lac was a fine place for Chamy's forebears to grow opium. Traders would come to trade the boiled-down sap for silver bars. With the money, the grandfather sent three of his sons, including the twins, to Vientiane to the lycée Chamy later attended. They graduated and, while one worked in Vientiane, bringing his young relatives to school, the other spent four years as a military officer in Long Cheng. Long Cheng was the largest of the airbases built by Americans in Laos during the war in Vietnam.

Then both twins went to Thailand for fighter pilot training.

"One die in 1969, one in 1970. Both killed in airplane fighting." The family retrieved the remains of the first one and buried him behind their home in Long Cheng. The other died behind enemy lines. His body was never found.

Besides losing two uncles, men whom Chamy still reveres, Chamy and two young male students from her family lost their comfortable place to live. The uncle had paid rent out of his salary. For Chamy's last year and a half of school, the young students lived in two rooms at the end of a ramshackle wooden building, cooking outdoors in the back. "Maybe we go there to see how it looks now," Chamy said.

Before I could appreciate what a watershed it was for Chamy to leave home, I had to grasp the absolute centrality of kin to the Hmong. In place of an entire village of relatives, she spent her time almost exclusively among strangers. In place of a hubbub of aunts and uncles, grandmothers and grandfathers to keep her headed the right way, a French nun demanded silence. In place of a life regulated by roosters and the sun, days were divided mathematically. Mental effort replaced physical labor. She was an animist — a belief that everything in nature has a soul separate from its physical aspect — in a French Catholic school. She learned aloneness. If she was going to do anything, she would have to do it herself. The Hmong circle had been breached.

Chamy graduated from Lycée Vientiane and returned to the village. She taught in the school, a rare female Hmong teacher. But soon she would set all her education aside and revert to the ancient role of wife.

Partners

Refreshed by his dinner, Nom Npis decided it was time to get up and walk around the plane. A caught pants leg revealed a bulging, muscled calf. Having observed him around his house and yard, I knew this short, sturdy man was strong. On our plane were some fifty Hmong, mostly men, returning to Laos during the Hmong New Year to renew old ties and reminisce about warrior days. Maybe they could uncover recent news of guerrilla efforts to wrest the country back from the communists.

Now a few of them moved about in the crowded aisles, stopping in clusters to *sib tham* (pronounced "shee tah"), to chat. They came from California, Wisconsin, Minnesota, many states. Some of the men wore sport shirts and slacks; others, for the dignity they confer, wore business suits. An older Hmong woman was outfitted in lavender blouse, magenta slacks, red velvet jacket, and crisp navy blue tennis shoes. She hugged a big flowered bag. Beneath her soft ribbon-rimmed cap beamed a warm face, with an elfin, toothless smile. Though she was traveling alone from Green Bay, Wisconsin, to visit a daughter and son in Laos, she appeared wholly without fear.

Eventually, Nom Npis returned to his seat, in full story-telling mode. I asked Chamy and Nom Npis about their early married life. Their relationship intrigues me. I heard them call each other Grandfather and Grandmother long before they had grandchildren — *Yawg* and *Pog*, pronounced with a light, breathy grunt, yuh and pawh. Yet I catch a sense of independence between them, as if they were business partners rather than the kind of entwined pair fussing over, or at, each other that I see among some Americans.

Nom Npis spoke. "When we marry, I still dream about that house" where he first brought Chamy home as a bride. That was in a village near Phou Bia, the tallest mountain in Laos at over nine thousand feet. Chamy wasn't happy with what she saw. "I wanted to turn around and go home," she said. But why? "Because there were no trees! They had all been cut down for fields."

"Back up," I said. "Start at the beginning. How did you meet?"

"Like a cat met a rat!" Nom Npis blurted out.

It was a classic tale of a young man hungry for married life, and it illustrates Hmong kinship at work, as it continues to do in the U.S. Nom Npis, it seems, was teaching farming and animal husbandry in Hmong villages. He was employed by the Central Intelligence Agency and had been on the country's main highway when he encountered a cousin of Chamy's at the road off to Kilometer 22 — named for its distance from the primary town in the area, Ban Son. Chamy had been teaching school at Kilometer 22 since graduating from the lycée. The cousin invited Nom Npis home to Kilometer 22. "So we just went there, stop, and spend the night," Nom Npis said, "and I met with her uncle. Her uncle is related to my mom."

"And the man gave me the champagne, he tell me the story, he ask me lot of questions." Nom Npis laughed. "And he said, 'You have two or three aunties living here and they have girls. And if you want to marry, next time come back, stop.'" So he did, going to Chamy's house.

"My mom is his step-aunt," Chamy said, "and he's just come over to see his aunt. My mom cook and then my mom call him and we eat. And I don't think that he has any interest on me at all." She laughed. "He just keep talking with my mom.

"I finish the meal first, and I just went outside all by myself. Finally, he came after me. And he asked me things. I don't feel anything much. I just tell him whatever he ask."

A few weeks later he was back again, eating his step-auntie's food and chatting. "So he come back, come back, and whenever he come back my mom cook for him — very nice. So," she paused mischievously, "whenever he get hungry, then he come back." He was a bold man to pursue an educated woman such as Chamy.

But how, I asked, did a child from a village end up teaching agriculture for the CIA? And we were deep into *sib tham*, talking.

Nom Npis was born on the Plain of Jars— Plaine des Jarres, as he says it — around the time when the French were defeated at Dien Bien Phu, during the 1950s. His family lay in the path of the conflict spilling from Vietnam into Laos in the 1960s and 1970s.

Nom Npis was the third child but the first son. One day when he was seven, he wandered over to his uncle's home nearby. The uncle was at the front door making a bamboo basket. The uncle looked at his nephew and began to fasten a rope belt to a basket, like the ones used by hired Khmu laborers, swinging the heavy basket onto the back and placing the belt around the forehead. Then the uncle said, "Hey, son, how come you don't go to school? If you don't go to school, you going to be a slave, and they going to put a basket to your shoulder and this belt to your head."

Chamy explained: "To carry crop or firewood or whatever. Very heavy work. The old people say, 'If you don't go to school, you will be working hard like a slave.'" Social and economic status allowed some families to pursue education, giving them a head start over other Hmong in America.

Nom Npis continued. "I went back home and tell my mom when she came home late evening, 'Tomorrow I'm going to school.' And I did."

Npis's competitive nature bloomed. "When I went to school, I have to fight until win. I must do everything to be the head Number One." Nom Npis laughed. When he completed the three-year village school, he went to a school two days' walk away. There he and a friend "build tiny house" to live in. Nom Npis laughed off the indignity, but he didn't laugh about the ribbing he got from his home villagers.

"When I come back home, and the people who live in the village there — every year they have to cut and make the road get wider. And when they came home, they saw me and they didn't say nothing. They just use the hand" — he pressed his hands together in the Asian sign of respect — "'Oh, my lord's came home, my lord's came home.'

"They making fun! It's because Lis family is famous. I was *disappointed* to the people, because I don't like it that way!"

At home he talked with his grandmother. She gave him a good Hmong lesson. "That's OK, son. The people making fun, but one day they going to respect you."

After three years in the town school, Npis went to stay with a powerful uncle at the military base in Long Cheng for more school. This uncle served in the Lao senate, commuting between Long Cheng and Vientiane.

Npis traded his services for lodging. "When I stay with them, I respect them every day and never say no. I have to cook. I have to go get the firewood. I have to do *everything*, because I know the poor boy [has] to live with the rich, and how much difficult we are [to them]. Middle of the night, they say, 'You have to go with me,' for the minute I have to go. I cannot say, 'No, I'm tired.' I have to go and carry the book with me, and when walking, take a look the book, read the book and" — he laughed, holding two hands like an open book — "I walk in the street!"

In 1968, Npis joined the army. He was seventeen. Forty-five recruits were sent to Thailand for training. "We went to train how to shoot the big cannons, 55 millimeter," and Npis learned map reading. "They give me the directions and where [the target] is located. So I have to measure the map and see how far and we have to use [how much] powder."

Soldiers were given rifles, pistols, and ammunition at that time. "And a couple of bomb in the belt, grenade," Chamy added. "It's very common. You have grenade all around your waist, and you walk like you are a *big* man." Chamy laughed. Nom Npis appeared oblivious to the ribbing. Chamy's father and other men were given brief training and weapons to protect the village. "They called the Village Army, just to have a gun and to protect the village. [Father] doesn't have to really go to the field to shoot the communist."

After six months, Npis was based in the Plain of Jars. He was injured in an accident and spent two months in a U.S.-built hospital. A slot for the rank of second lieutenant opened up, and Npis pursued it: The man in charge was a relative. "I told him, 'Can you give the second lieutenant to me, because I am your nephew? I grow up with you. Every time we have to stay together, go together. You are my uncle.' But he said, 'No, you are still young.'" Angry, Npis stormed off to friends. One said, "Oh, we better quit the army, and everybody go back to school. Why, we crazy! The war's crazy! And the government keep all the money, and we die for nothing!"

So Npis turned in his gun and pistol on the ruse that he was going across the river "to play with the girl couple days and we come back."

"I never come back," Npis said.

So Npis completed agricultural school, near Vientiane, and then was hired by the CIA to carry his knowledge to people back in the mountains. He traveled between isolated villages in a helicopter and taught Hmong farmers how to grow better rice and how to keep their farm animals from dying of disease.

Eventually, he decided it was time to look for a wife. And on August 12, 1974, Chamy and Nom Npis were married.

Although marrying a Lis, Chamy retained her own clan name, in accordance with rules. Marriage isn't allowed between people with the same clan name, hence the importance of keeping your own as proof. (There are about eighteen clans, twelve main ones.[2]) However, you can marry your mother's niece or nephew.

But keeping your own name does not mean you are your own person. Chamy belonged to her in-laws' household once she married. A graduate of the lycée or not, she answered to her mother-in-law. A wife needed permission to visit her own family, and in case of a split, the father got the children. These rules remain strong in the U.S.

Only after their wedding did Chamy learn that Nom Npis had encountered resistance to the marriage. She was educated, the argument went, and she might be lazy. That kind of judgment, whispered about, is the rumor a Hmong wife most dreads. A Hmong proverb goes, "If the crops aren't good, you lose only one year; if your wife isn't good, you lose a whole lifetime."

The complainers could hardly be faulted for their worry. Chamy said: "When I was eight years old, I left the village and I live in the city and go to school, and I don't get used to do all the hard chore or hard working in the field like that. And they, they already expect that I will not be able to do that.

"But actually that's not true. I can do anything." She did not laugh.

Still, when she got married, she said, she got "so unlucky." Chamy became pregnant, with severe morning sickness. She couldn't drag herself out of bed. "I was throwing up, throwing up, throwing up" on the dirt floor of the bedroom. No one bothered to clean up the mess, she told me more than once, but only covered it with ashes—a symbol to Chamy of her low status.

Chamy was losing weight. Yet young wives are required to work. Once when Nom Npis was away, Chamy's sister-in-law came from the rice field with word that Chamy must help harvest. The field was half a day's walk away. Chamy got up, filled some cast-off I-V bottles with water and set out.

"It was a long walk and the road was very steep. I didn't have strength, so I had to lie down and rest after every couple of steps." She took all day getting there. The next day she began to cut rice. But the work brought her to the brink of collapse. The sight of her face, drained of all color, scared her mother-in-law. Chamy dragged grimly back down the trail toward home.

Word got to Chamy's mother. She and another daughter set out. Luckily, they ran across a relative who knew the way. With no maps, a traveler needs people in order to navigate the mountains. Chamy's mother arrived and nursed Chamy back to health.

When the CIA ended operations in Laos, Nom Npis lost his job. He decided on more education in Thailand and, depositing Chamy at her mother's home in Kilometer 22, headed south to Vientiane to apply. But enrollment was closed, and he returned to his pregnant wife. The two moved to the small field house in her mother's rice field where they helped Chamy's mother raise chickens and ducks away from the diseases that killed fowl in the village.

It was there that Chamy went into labor, two months early. Nom Npis and Chamy's mother helped her walk the long way back to the house. But "it's the Hmong culture that you can't give birth at your mom's house," Chamy explained, or bad luck will come to the family.

It was also true that Chamy knew nothing about labor or delivery. In her circle, no one talked about such things. Now Nom Npis reminded Chamy that they must go to the Lis family's new place, in Muong Cha. (Everybody was moving away from the war front.) Out on the road, they climbed into the covered back of a truck, sitting on side benches with other passengers. In Ban Son they transferred to a second truck. But suddenly Chamy felt pressure. "I thought I had to go to the bathroom." In fact, she was in the final stage of labor.

"We just get out of the truck and pay the truck and let the truck go on. And I gave birth to John there," beside the road. Chamy herself is astonished at this turn of events. Her mother broke off a piece of bamboo from a nearby clump to cut the umbilical cord. Then the little group — now with a premature infant — returned the way they had come, the young family passing up Mom's house to live apart in another small shelter.

Then world events snapped shut on Chamy and Nom Npis.

Flight

Vietnam fell to the communists in April 1975, and in May, Laos fell. The revered Hmong Gen. Vang Pao had been airlifted out of the military base in Long Cheng along with a few plane loads of key Hmong and their families. People like Nom Npis who had supported the Americans but were not evacuated saw the danger. Victorious Vietnamese were sweeping the country. The Hmong flight from death began.

By then, Chamy, Nom Npis, and little Johnny had reached Nom Npis's family home in Muong Cha, three days from Long Cheng. Half the families had already fled in terror. Nom Npis's father — also a soldier — decided they must go, too. He untied his beloved ox — his equivalent of a John Deere tractor — and let it go, weeping. Chamy wrote a college paper about what happened next.

"I was bent over beside my old bamboo dresser," she wrote, "packing clothes, when [Vietnamese soldiers] entered the house." They demanded food.

Chamy went to pull six hens from their nests. A soldier stopped her. "He waved his finger at me and pointed to our pig, which was in deep sleep in its usual muddy pond." Chamy dropped the hens, which fled to their nests. Nom Npis and his father killed the pig.

Once the soldiers ate and left, Nom Npis's father ordered the family to pack blankets, cooking pots, spoons, and knives into packs. Bags of rice would double as pillows. Mother, father, two daughters, three sons, and Chamy — everyone carried loads. Chamy also carried Johnny. The men carried M-6 rifles.

Half way down the mountain they hid between a curved rock wall and bamboo. They waited. Water dripped, dripped from above. Birds and insects sounded their notes.

That night they heard rustling in the trees. Blessedly, some forty Hmong guerrillas who worked for the CIA came out of the forest. The black-clothed "sky soldiers" — the CIA was called "Sky" — sat down around the fire, guns in hand, and talked until dawn. At first light, the whole group crept on, the soldiers looking for their wives and children.

The second night, a chill rain fell. After four days, they came to a huddle of banana-leaf huts and the soldiers' families. The children had distended bellies. Now the group numbered about one hundred fifty, a large number to hide even in dense jungle.

That night, a two-year-old girl died from a fever, the sixth child to die. Chamy worried about Johnny and the mosquito bites that puffed up everyone's faces. Malaria.

After twenty days the rice was gone. They abandoned the encampment in search of food, climbing ridge after ridge, eating banana tree hearts. Starving, Chamy would stagger down a hillside toward water, only to find it covered with leeches.

"Oooh, I'm scared, because leeches follow you," Chamy said. She had scraped the leeches away with a stick and lain down to drink.

They spotted a field of corn. The cobs were small and green, but everyone ate. Chamy's delight turned to alarm when, stimulated by the first food in days, she went into the forest to relieve herself. Her urine was red, and her bowel movement was black and full of live worms.

A woman carrying her little boy found some red berries. She ate and gave some to the child. Within moments she collapsed, vomiting. First the mother died and then the son.

They tried to hunt a band of monkeys in the trees overhead, but they were too weak. They ate tiny black snails, sucking the body out of the shell. A fig tree with rotten, wormy figs was another treasure. Chamy was vomiting blood and her lungs ached.

Nom Npis's mother was weakening. She had malaria. She lay on banana leaves all one night, breathing poorly. The next noon, in the rain, she died.

A proper funeral — a keystone of Hmong life — was out of the question. There could be no drumming, no hours-long chant to guide her spirits home to Heaven.

> We didn't know what to do. Beside her, we laid her old umbrella with her little skinny body hidden in her black rotten cloth. We covered her with a pile of decayed leaves.
>
> As we knelt there and cried, my brother-in-law Pao suddenly rasped, "Go on, go on. Leave me alone. I am going to die right here with her," he said. He pointed his rifle at his chest and shot himself dead.

Years later Nom Npis told me: "My mother, she was very polite, and she had the perfect skin. She gave good advice, the right advice, and people followed it. When she died, I cried and cried.

"After that, I never cry again."

Icy mist condensed on leaves and dripped onto them. They walked and walked, the men listening for the sound just out of hearing, watching for the movement just beyond sight.

At a cave they built shelters. During the day, men would search for food and for Vietnamese soldiers to kill. "I was so frightened one day, they came back with no food but two dead bodies of Communists that they killed. They asked us if anyone wanted to eat them." Chamy was horrified. No one ate.

That night, perhaps because of the soldiers killed, they were discovered. Enemy gunfire roared from surrounding trees, and the embattled Hmong fled crowding into the cave. The men backed in, firing out into the gun smoke. But too soon their ammunition ran out, and the deafening roar of the rifles in the cave ceased. A frightening silence. Then a rifle blasted, and an old woman in front of Chamy fell with a bullet in her forehead. "'That's the end of me,' I thought."

Enraged by the elusive, hostile Hmong, soldiers smashed two men on the head with their rifle butts and jammed gun muzzles against their throats. Chamy and other women were roped together and commanded to march.

They marched for miles. Nearly half the group had died.

They were taken to a prison west of the mountains. It was surrounded by a fifteen-foot fence topped with spikes. Chamy and the eighty others from their group were jammed into one forty-foot-long dark room. The crowd was imprisoned together for two months.

But in a stroke of lucky deprivation the prison ran out of food. The prisoners were trucked east to Sam Neua Province to settle, under guard, with five hundred other Hmong.

The band of fugitives had failed in their attempt to escape. Many were sick and near starvation. Nom Npis's father's remaining household turned to clearing new fields, and Chamy again shouldered the daughter-in-law's burdens.

Life in the community was minutely regulated by communist overseers. Nom Npis must get seven signatures to travel to the next province, one to kill a chicken.

The situation deteriorated. Government authorities were sending men north for re-education. Few came back. Then it was announced that all men would be sent away for three years, with no contact allowed.

Chamy and Nom Npis fled again, this time with only eight adults. Chamy steamed and dried rice and put it into sacks sewn from old clothes. Johnny was still a baby.

One night, the eight adults and two older children crawled one by one into the forest. For six days they walked. Chamy's bare feet were bloody. Fatigue made her dopey. One night, they came upon a partly collapsed hut and went in for cover. With the morning light, Chamy saw two corpses in the corner, the lower bodies gone, as were most of the faces. "They were covered by thousands of ants and maggots," Chamy said.

But they had reached the Mekong River — their last hurdle. The sound of cackling chickens and barking dogs signaled a Lao village nearby. They must keep silent. Johnny cried and cried. "We just cover his mouth," Chamy told me, placing her hand over her own mouth and nose. "And I was very scared, because he keep crying and ... That's why a lot of people they do it until they — there's no sign left."

It's a grim, Sophie's-choice episode in many refugee families — save the baby or save the group. What follows is the story Dr. Mymee Her, the first Hmong clinical psychologist, heard from her Aunt Ying. In the story, Mai Mee (the name is pronounced the same as Mymee's) is Aunt Ying's eighteen-month-old baby.

> Awaiting words from the men [as to crossing the Mekong], Aunt Ying held Mai Mee close. ... As the delicate child slept, Aunt Ying stroked her head and kissed her tiny cheek.... Night came and the group slowly moved to the river bank.... The crowd heard the soldiers' footsteps and truck in the near distance....
>
> Mai Mee started to cry. The people harassed Aunt Ying about keeping her child quiet.... Aunt Ying pulled her child to her breast in hopes that, if she was being fed, she wouldn't cry anymore. It didn't work. The soldiers got closer and closer; Mai Mee cried louder....
>
> Aunt Ying could no longer control her baby's crying. She knew then that she had to make a decision — one that she would never be able to forgive herself for. Aunt Ying took the infant to the water. With tears blinding her eyes, she dipped the head of her pride and joy, her hope, into the river. As the baby struggled for breath, Aunt Ying wanted so much to pull her out and hold her tight, but she knew what she had to do. It was either her daughter's life, or the people's.[3]

The Mekong River rushing before Chamy was deep and wide. Blessedly, Johnny had quieted. Nom Npis and the other men built a raft out of banana trees, using knives and tying it together with a red vine. Standing deep in swampy water, the men launched the raft into the current. Nom Npis guided it from the stern with a makeshift paddle, and the swimmers scissor-kicked as they swept downstream.

Chamy's heart pounded. The sight of the water lapping at the top of the raft sent fear climbing in her gut. She remembered this river. The non-swimmer had barely escaped it once before. And now, she had a baby on her back. "If it sink, that's it."

Under pressure like this, I could imagine, Chamy would snap out of the required female docility. I picture her eyes blinking rapidly as she directed terrified ones where to sit, what to do. They had survived this far. She would not yield now.

For forty-five minutes they fought the water. These minutes burned themselves into dreams that still haunt Chamy a quarter century later. In them, she is trying to cross the river. Fear. The communists chase and catch them. Then, the raft goes under, water closing over their heads. And Chamy wakes in terror.

In fact, the raft reached shore. Two armed men waited for them, bellowing and finally snapping the gold chain from around Chamy's neck. Then a Thai policeman arrived and started them on their way to a refugee camp.

Thailand

Some fifty of us, tired from the long airplane flight to Thailand but thrilled to be near Laos, waited in the ornate lobby of a Bangkok hotel. We were an unsophisticated, rumpled jumble, all but one of us Hmong, shifting uneasily on cushioned sofas in a fancy lobby. Chamy, however, sat at ease in a leather chair, hands in her lap with fingers laced. Nom Npis discovered that the man carrying the kheng, a large flute-like instrument that sings words, is a great-uncle from Syracuse, New York. They hadn't seen each other in twenty years.

Boarding the plane to Laos from the concrete runway the next day, everyone crowded and pressed to get up the stairs. I recalled the stories of desperate Hmong scrambling to get on a plane to get out of the country before the soldiers came to kill. Chamy told me later that she was embarrassed by the behavior of her fellow Hmong, afraid I might be crowded off the airplane altogether.

After the terrifying crossing of the Mekong River in 1977, Chamy, Nom Npis, and baby Johnny arrived at a red-dirt refugee camp in Thailand. Camps like this one are pictured in panoramic photos that now hang in some Hmong homes like posters of Yellowstone.

For four months, jammed beside thousands of other Hmong, they lived in what they call a "tent" that Nom Npis built. As we made the brief airplane flight across the Mekong to Laos, Nom Npis and Chamy painted the picture. Camp authorities gave small families nine sections of thatched grass and enough poles as big as your wrist to build a frame. "But nothing to make a wall," Chamy picked it up, "so the wind blow the rain in." "Like a carport," Nom Npis described it, the words punctuated by laughter that scrunched his eyes to dots. "You got little tiny, tiny room I can have only one bed in there, kind of like a cat," he said. Chamy said, "When windy, he had to take one or two pole. Each person." Nom Npis broke in.

"It's raining!" Then Chamy, "Each person will be on one side to hold on, keeping [it] from blowing over. [Otherwise] if the wind blow, then you will all get wet."

Nom Npis seemed to find this genuinely funny. With Chamy it was more like laughing off humiliation. But the funniest to both of them was the shelter built by Nom Npis's step-brother. It stood only three feet tall. Chamy said, "I never got to see how their house looks like, because I don't want to crawl. Every single time they crawl [into] their house, I keep laughing."

Chamy cooked out front over a wood fire between two stones. She used a fruit can from the dump. On it she set a cheap bamboo basket for steaming rice. Firewood was scarce. Nom Npis devised a Thai-style clay stove. Taking an old five-gallon can, also from the dump, he punched a hole in its side near the bottom and shoved in a fat pole. Packing mud into the bottom of the can, he stood another pole up at right angles to the first one and continued to push in more mud. Once the mud dried hard, Nom Npis pulled out the poles. The resulting tunnel let the fire breathe. Then he traded labor at a nearby Thai sawmill for sawdust. This he packed into the stove each morning for the day's cooking. "And that is the best way to save the money and learn how to cook in a can," Nom Npis said, tilting his head toward me in amusement.

They lived on handouts of "rice and fish sauce and, once a month, one chicken per five people, plus vegetables," Chamy told me. "Otherwise you had to buy food or eat just rice and fish sauce." Even then, you were never filled up. A few, pushed by the extremity, stole.

Hunger was hard on babies. "I didn't have enough milk to feed Johnny because there was not enough to eat," Chamy said. The young mother, hungry herself, chewed rice and fed it to him. Johnny had worms, and soon he had a bloated stomach.

"He cried a lot."

Twice in the refugee camp, they thought he would die. "One sickness, a baby cry and cry and have black spots like a snail all over its body and die. Very few people survive." Johnny got this disease, but an uncle's wife knew a cure. "She use a needle and poke the spots so it will come out." Once again, Johnny pulled through.

The camp was filthy. An open latrine meant you could "see everything down there," Chamy said. A well was dug downhill from the latrine.

Johnny got sick again. Chamy and Nom Npis called a shaman, a woman practiced at traveling to the spirit world to bargain for the patient's wayward spirit. The shaman came in a rain so hard that it drowned the cook fire out front. In a gesture that captured their plight, Chamy and

Nom Npis stood in the downpour and held a piece of plastic aloft over the shaman as she performed the ancient ritual.

"You just think that life was miserable," Chamy said. People's nerves frayed under the stress.

Nom Npis weeded and picked crops for Thai farmers nearby, earning enough money to buy bamboo poles and slats to build a better shelter. Still, the walls were no more than bamboo lattice through which people could see. Here Ken was born.

After Johnny, Ken seemed tough. Nonetheless, Chamy had only just enough milk to keep him alive. "I eat pepper [sauce] and salt fish," instead of the chicken required by Hmong custom for the new mother's recovery. Also, "the Hmong custom, when you give birth to a baby you have to drink hot water, warm water, for the whole month. [But] we don't have wood to cook the water, so that's why I used to put the water [in a can on top of] the house, so that the sun make the water warm and then you can drink it." Hmong women will tell you that drinking cold water or failing to eat properly after giving birth will lead to wrinkles, skin rash, or walking bent over. It's not superstition, Chamy explained. "It's just for your own protection when you get old."

With only one or two buckets of water a day for a family the size of theirs, bathing a baby was out of the question. "You wrap your kids in old Laotian skirt, and when the baby poo-poo, you just shake it off."

In the camp, embroidered pieces such as I watched Chamy making on the airplane evolved into a life-saving labor to buy food. "When we live in the tent, I made *paj ntaub* (pronounced "pandow") to have money to buy vegetable." For the first time, Hmong women, and even men, began to stitch *paj ntaub* for sale rather than personal use. *Paj ntaub* means flowery cloth. Story cloths, on the other hand, were invented in refugee camps for the market, some depicting the golden age of farming cut short by flight ahead of the rifles. Pieces were sold in camp. A few ambitious Hmong set up booths patronized by foreign workers and Thai locals, the beginnings of business experience for them.

Chamy did cross-stitch, story cloths, and reverse appliqué. The latter requires good eyes and a surgeon's hand. You cut a design into a top layer of cloth, carefully turn under tiny raw edges, and stitch them down with invisible stitches to a base cloth of a contrasting color. Designs are of symbolic mountains, spider webs, crossroads, or mice tracks. Now few young Hmong American women attempt to learn this craft, only rolling their eyes when asked. In camp Chamy made two coffee table runners, selling one there and sending a second to a nun in Canada to sell for her. She was also hired by a Hmong shopkeeper in camp to supply his booth.

"Right after Ken was born I did this," Chamy related. For child care she wove a basket of split bamboo and hung it from a rope Nom Npis fastened to their shelter's center pole. Into this, Chamy put four-week-old Ken, then called by his Hmong name Keu. Old-style Hmong don't use cradles. They tie babies onto their backs with a rectangle of embroidered cloth with five-foot-long ties. Westerners glamorize this closeness, but carrying a baby is exhausting. "You get your shoulder very hurt if you have a baby long time on your back," Chamy said. So they adopted the Thai baby basket. "We came to Thailand, and you have new idea — more advanced."

Sitting in her shelter, Chamy would stitch at high speed and swing Ken's basket, swing and stitch, trying to keep him quiet, to earn money for food. "I would swing him very, very hard to scare him so he wouldn't cry. Mostly he spent [his] growing time in basket, one month to one year and a half." One time, Chamy admitted, she swung the basket so hard that Ken almost fell out. It terrified him.

Fifteen months after Ken, May was born. In Hmong her name is Maiv Ntxawm, a pet name. She was the last of Chamy and Nom Npis's children.

Once, after May was born, Chamy went outside the camp to work, like Nom Npis, weeding pineapples. Her first trip, solo, "no problem," and she earned ten baht, then about forty cents. The next time, she took two unmarried aunts. At the end of the day, three Thai men told them, "Follow us; we show shortcut to camp."

"We believed them. We were half mile, suddenly jungle. Usually it's rice field. In the jungle we didn't see the three men. We thought they hide. We skirted the jungle, and we never saw them come out." So they went back to camp. "We outsmarted them.

"After that, we decided it was the last time."

When she said that, I was reminded of an episode after we landed at the Bangkok airport and were organizing for rides to the hotel. Chamy and Nom Npis had located a taxi for the trip, since they had bought their airline tickets independently and were not officially part of the group as I was. As we stood curbside I watched Chamy, at five-foot-one, verbally overpower a big, tall Thai tour guide — in Thai — and spirit me away from the group bus into their taxi.

Later I commented on her blunt performance. Chamy laughed her laugh and said, "You can't hit the target if you don't get to the point." Assessing my awe, Chamy continued, "You'll see how I am in Laos — sweet. In Thailand they're tough, very strict, so I have to be that way — strong woman.

"I learned that in the camps."

After listening to Chamy over time, I began to notice how she uses speech. Unlike Nom Npis, who speaks to stay close to people, Chamy — at least outside her family — values talk almost exclusively for its utility. She rarely speaks to fill silences or to make someone feel good, but only to give or get information. She will question a youngster about his father's health because she needs to know. Or she will instruct her daughters-in-law in the correct way to prepare a dish because they need to know. (But, she once told me pointedly, she tempers instruction with patience for the girls' status as learners. Her compassion grew out of painful experience.)

Chamy is disinclined to initiate speech, but any time I ask about a Hmong practice or an occurrence, she answers at once, grappling now and then for the vocabulary and blinking rapidly when the subject troubles her. She rarely gives more than the question calls for, so I must ask again for detail. This is unlike most adult Hmong, who take a question as a starting point and weave a big, rich tapestry of experience and opinion. Maybe it's the mark of a Western-educated woman, or a shy one.

The brevity of Chamy's answers does not mean she hasn't thought about things. She knows a great deal about Hmong culture. And from dreams she relates I know she ponders her own journey in life.

Chamy always answers my questions with candor. I treasure this. It's a brave act for immigrants to tell their stories, especially when they cross a cultural divide as deep as this. The opportunity for misunderstanding and ridicule is always present. And yet the desire to be understood by others is compelling. Chamy always seems to be trying to keep her balance between telling enough and telling too much. With some people, this tension is resolved by hiding the pieces that might prove embarrassing. Although Chamy sometimes falls silent, the most comfortable place for a shy person, when she speaks, her words carry the marks of bald truth. It is the text of a real, not a constructed, person.

America

One March day in 1978, Chamy, Nom Npis, and the three children flew to the United States. Chamy was about twenty-one years old. They had passed health tests at the camp, showed that they could learn English, and proved that they had a relative who would sponsor them. For Chamy and Nom Npis, the United States was the one place in the world outside Laos where they had family. Because the Hmong were refugees, federal and charitable funds were made available for traveling to the United

States— money they would have to repay — and for getting started in the new country.

Chamy and Nom Npis remember that while waiting to catch their plane in Thailand, a Thai immigration officer said, "Why do you want to go to America? You want to starve?" On the airplane, a movie was shown about an American family that went West and failed. The father committed suicide.

Arriving in Los Angeles, Chamy and Nom Npis flew directly to South Carolina to the home of the step-uncle who sponsored them. This man, having completed all the studies available in Laos, had been sent to Canada in 1969 to study electrical engineering. He returned to Laos but fled in 1976. He still lives in South Carolina.

Unlike Chamy and Nom Npis, most Hmong in the early years were sponsored by strangers— through religious groups and non-profit organizations— since few had relatives here then. Civic clubs, community social service agencies, schools, and individuals, funded by the federal government and by private refugee resettlement agencies, stepped up to provide help: health screening, housing, orientation, ESL classes, and job training and referral. But not all services were available in every place, as Chamy and Nom Npis learned, nor did they wish to receive any more help than they absolutely needed.

The young couple did their best to succeed. Two weeks after arriving, with no English, Nom Npis went to work for a clothing manufacturer, a job Chamy's step-uncle located for him. Nom Npis earned $3.35 an hour. One week he worked days, the next week, nights.

Nom Npis and Chamy stayed for six months. Then, Chamy said, they pictured their meager future. Nom Npis's erratic schedule precluded school, and English classes were expensive. They began to feel "left behind and in the dark," Chamy said. But another step-uncle, in Portland, Oregon, said that there they could work and go to school, too. Chamy and Nom Npis packed their bags, becoming part of a mass rearrangement of people.

Only the rare Hmong family lives where they first settled. Scattering the new immigrants across the country seemed a good idea to the government, to avoid swamping two or three communities with a load of baffled mountain people. But one official's common sense is another person's disaster. One lone family in Nebraska believed they would die, but a Hmong family in Denver saw them on television and drove up to reassure them. The dispirited family quickly moved to Denver.

Like most immigrant groups with few resources, the Hmong cluster. A group can supply social, emotional, and even economic insurance. For a Hmong family, being isolated is like being deprived of heat. During a brief period after her stint as a welfare worker, when Chamy took her first job as an accountant for the Department of Transportation — in Southern California, far distant from extended family — she and Nom Npis would drive into the mountains and stand gazing north, where their people were.

Chamy and Nom Npis's road trip across country was harrowing.

"We took the Greyhound. And we have three little kids. Npis got two, one in each side, and I got one. And it's very hard for us to get out to get something to eat. They have only fifteen minutes' break [at] each stop. We just eat a little bit in the [bus]." The bus wandered from city to city, all day and all night.

"And you can hardly sleep because you have your hand full of babies. And one of them have diarrhea, too, so I smell all kinds of things—pee or diarrhea or whatever."

The bus kept going. "So when we get to Salt Lake City, we thought, OK, we got to Portland. We got off the bus. We so happy, and we keep looking, Let's see, where's my uncle? But when we look at the map, Portland still *way* over here." She was laughing. "At that time I thought, 'Ohhhh!' It took another long night's ride to Portland, Oregon."

Years later I saw a photo of Chamy in a framed collage on their living room wall. It was snapped in Portland not long after the bus ride. She is standing in a grassy yard, gaunt, wearing a Lao-style sarong skirt. The picture shows long curly black hair and a bony, solemn face.

In Portland, Nom Npis worked and went to school nights. Chamy learned she needed a high school diploma to get into a nursing program. California had no such requirement. Like their forebears hunting up new fields, they headed to California. There she plowed through a two-year degree, but, she said, "When I got that, I try to find a job. I saw it was not enough to feed the family."

In 1986, riding on her mantra, "I can do that," she finished a bachelor's degree in accounting and took the job as a welfare worker.

It was then I met Chamy. She was known in the social services community in Sacramento for her meticulously executed, lush *paj ntaub* and for her college education. She was, I learned, one of the first Hmong women to earn a degree. An inspiring kind of woman. I would do a profile for the newspaper.

Looking still very much the untested college-student-turned-office-worker in pink and white, she opened to me a world adjacent to mine but wholly separate, and reliably instructive.

Notes from my first interview show Chamy walking the vertiginous trail between Southeast Asian culture and America. Changing cultures, it appeared, plays havoc with one's grip on things. One gets lost in the confusion. Every habit gets fractured, large or small. Such "profound uncertainties about life, culture and trust," the scholar E. Valentine Daniel writes perceptively, lead to "ever-anxious vigilance."[4] Even Nom Npis, the cando, macho Nom Npis, would comment a dozen years after coming here that the psychological cost of switching cultures is steep. It's the hardest part of the journey.

Stepping into a new culture is more than learning a new language or eating unfamiliar food. Even a part-time shift can be unnerving. Even now, I smart when I recall being raged at by a man selling peaches in a Greek market. I had watched a local woman choose peaches and did what she did. "When in Rome...." But the dictum is wrong. Only women known to the seller were permitted to squeeze the peaches. The man shouted at me, grabbed the peaches and flung them on the ground. Multiply that by infractions involving landlords, bus drivers, grocery store clerks, doctors, nurses, receptionists, telephone operators, used car salesmen, drivers' license clerks, school teachers, government assistance workers, neighbors next door, and complete strangers on the street. Repeat it daily, and you've got stress.

And exhaustion. A Vietnamese refugee parent in Scandinavia said, "In Vietnam, everything was normal. Things happened because they happened. Words were not necessary. We knew, and the children knew. Every little thing has to be explained [here]. Words become so important. Everything is a problem. We are tired."[5]

"Laos and here, very opposite," Chamy told me on our day of meeting in 1987. "In Laos, if you're fat, you're good. Here, if thin, you're good." Being fat in Laos has a survival message. It means you have enough to eat.

"We have a very conflict, totally conflict, the custom, thinking, attitude totally different."

She went on. "I think now [our] people are really scared. They don't know American law system, don't know their rights. Like when I came, the apartment window was broken. The landlord said, 'You have to fix it yourself.' I thought that was it. I believed him." Eventually she learned landlords' and tenants' responsibilities, but fear could stop her from making them stick. Her sink plugged up, and she called the landlord. He came with his wife. The two of them stood before Chamy and fought, a kind of behavior shunned by Hmong. "I was scared to call them again."

And if she couldn't pronounce the necessary English, "I just pronounce French."

Nor could Hmong escape cultural collision by retreating to their homes, because American ideas crept through the walls and created tension between parents and children, males and females. In Laos, women stayed home and raised "as many kids as they can, eight or nine," Chamy said. Ordinarily, a man would not allow his wife to go to school or hold a job. Now in the United States, you needed cash for food and rent. Without fields to farm, one must take a job. The government could insist on it.

That adjustment remains of earthquake proportions to the Hmong. Chamy has not escaped the trauma. As when the women's movement brought upheaval to many American homes in the 1970s, changes in Hmong gender roles cause trouble.

"In Thailand, we hear some bad rumor that people coming to this country can't control their wife anymore, so they don't want to come," Chamy told me in 1987. "If they come, they have to let them go to school."

Fortunately for Chamy, Nom Npis had been undaunted by an educated female. But others in the Hmong community took exception to Chamy's status. Her achievement was proven to be evil when it became clear that, as a welfare case worker, she was requiring Hmong to attend school and look for work or lose government support. As she had told me, she received death threats, a distasteful form of social control not uncommon in human history.

Nom Npis told Chamy not to give up. And she plunged ahead.

After a few years, Chamy and Nom Npis bought a home and began planting. They call their place the ranch and lavish labor on it. I take it to be reassurance.

The gray stucco with sky blue trim rests behind a white board fence north of Sacramento. This is the house where I slept in the family room and watched children dance. The loosely assembled community, made up of people who cherish solitude, is called Rio Linda, Beautiful River in inaccurate Spanish. In the middle of the front lawn grow Chamy's roses, pink, white, purple, and deep red. The brilliance of the blooms reminds me of the red poinsettias that grow house-high in Hmong villages in Laos.

The Lis family seems to be on good terms with their neighbors. Most are non–Hmong, the usual Central Valley mix of Americans of African, Asian, European, Hispanic, and Native descent. Chamy's step-uncle, the one from Portland, lives several streets away, and another Hmong family — of the Thao clan like Chamy — lives a mile or two farther on. The head of this household is a man whose picture as a boy in a Hmong village appears in a 1974 *National Geographic* article. His younger brother is now a physician — a nice jolt to the presumption that individuals stay forever on glossy pages.

Chamy's family gardens compulsively. Johnny, whose quiet manner and will to work prove him the child of his mother, spent one summer digging a fish pond behind the house. He had built a smaller one at the far end of the property, but it became a heron's cafeteria. The new pond is the size of a modest living room and is edged with marigolds, geraniums, and cyclamens. In it three dozen big carp meander. "He like fish," Chamy explained.

Chamy and Nom Npis grow what is useful, but the younger generation feels no such compulsion. Nom Npis kept chickens and ducks in wire pens for a while, but the younger generation wouldn't eat them — "too stringy." Ken in turn filled the empty pens with exotic birds. A talker like his father, Ken recently married and now lives in one of the bedrooms with his young Hmong wife, Virginia. Johnny and Patty live in another, following the old ways. Soon daughter May brought her young husband home, too, contrary to custom. They tried living with his family in Wisconsin, but college proved too expensive there. Here, Chamy could house the whole lot of them, she said. And keep them pointed toward graduate school.

Four yard dogs belong to Johnny and Ken. An earlier dog was sold when he started to bite. This dog would fawn on Chamy. Chamy in turn would swing at it with a stick, driving it off in the same gunfire voice she used on the Thai tour operator in Bangkok. Most Southeast Asian villagers treat the ubiquitous village dogs this way. Dogs are garbage disposers, not companions.

Beyond the pond and the pens, the place is Chamy's. She has plugged a plant or tree into every square foot. Nine kinds of fruit trees, including peach, cherries, and mandarin orange, share space with green beans, sugar cane, Japanese eggplant, cilantro, mint, Hmong squash, and green onions, with lemon grass along the edge.

Alongside these Chamy has planted herbs, one with an almond-shaped leaf for cramps and another with a toothed leaf for seasoning the chicken dishes required after childbirth — none of them plants I recognized. Much has given way before American influence but not the commitment to herbs. In a nostalgic gesture, Nom Npis once built a frame of two-by-fours so Chamy could grow the gourds used in Laos to dip water.

Above everything, Chamy's specialty is bamboo, the clumping kind that grows into tall fountains in Laos and is used for construction and musical instruments. Nom Npis acquired some thin-walled bamboo from an American friend, but the cold winters stunt its growth. Bamboo in the side yard successfully produces tender shoots that cook up quickly, Chamy told me. But bamboo for flute-making eludes her.

Still, she supplies nearby shamans with bamboo for the New Year ritual. Stalks attached to a shaman's ceiling represent the bridge connecting the shaman's altar to the spiritual homeland in China. The bridge is replaced every year.

Before Nom Npis got a rototiller, he and Chamy turned the soil with pick and shovel. An irrigation system that Nom Npis is laying was expected to shorten Chamy's hours with the hose, a blessing in spring when hay fever wreaks havoc with her night's sleep.

Viewing Chamy and Nom Npis's huge garden, I recognized something powerful. In both the choice of plantings and the ritual of hard work, the garden is history, personal story, some beauty, opportunity to ponder, and a promise that results still issue from enough hard work.

Chamy loves her garden. When we had been in Laos for ten days Chamy told me, "I miss my children. I miss my *garden*."

In the air for the brief flight from Bangkok to Vientiane, I strained to take in everything from the little window. There it was. Laos. Green-wrapped hills and cleared fields like green silk scarves tossed down on the land. I noticed dark dots in the center of the fields—shelters, Chamy said, where families stayed while working fields far from home.

We landed at Vientiane airport and walked across the runway under a warm November sky to the two-story, white and blue concrete building. In the middle was a sign in graceful Lao script, with the English words below in red. "Vientiane Airport." Poking into the sky, red flags flew. As we drew closer, we noticed that much of the second story was an open gallery, jammed with hundreds of people peering down, searching faces for loved ones.

Chamy had dressed in freshly ironed slacks—Nom Npis does her ironing—along with a jewel-colored paisley blouse and earrings set with green stones. She looked beautiful. She strode far ahead of me, purposeful, then returned and walked beside me into customs. In the arrival room we moved in silence between two walls of human bodies. Eyes searched faces in near silence.

Only one or two from her large family would be here to welcome us, Chamy had told me, her youngest sister from a town south of Vientiane and the sister's husband. No one else. The others, those who could make it, would be waiting in Luang Prabang or Mom's village far to the north. For now, a cousin of Nom Npis's who works at the airport would help transport us and our seven huge bags to a low-priced guest house.

We reached the end of the human tunnel with no signs of recognition. Nom Npis pointed out the baggage claim area through the crowds to our right. Suddenly Chamy disappeared from sight, surrounded by the arms and bodies of more than half a dozen bone-thin Hmong, men and women, children and babies, relatives. And the tears began to flow.

2

What Makes
the Hmong, Hmong

The mouth tastes food; the heart tastes words.
— Hmong proverb[1]

"What does it mean to be Hmong?" The performer slows the frenetic pace of his serio-comic routine to fling the question to the Hmong gathered in a Denver ballroom. "Somebody told me it's saying 'No, I'm not hungry' when their stomach is growling," Tou Ger Xiong answers himself. Laughter.

He pauses, shoving his eyeglasses back up and peering through spotlights to the well-dressed, mostly young and middle-aged Hmong conference goers— the essence of people in the throes of adapting. Three or four hundred have gathered here this evening. They're right with him. I try to take notes without taking my eyes off this funny man on stage.

"Or having parents who never say 'I love you.'

"Or not raising your hand to answer my question." More laughter. Tou Ger is poking his arms this way and that and doing a jester's dance, perpetual motion, trying to induce a little looseness in the reserved assembly.

He does some Simon-says testing to see if listeners' arms are indeed capable of rising above their heads. A good number manage the challenge. "Now, what does it mean to be Hmong?" Finally he gets some answers from the group.

"A refugee," a young woman calls out.

"A people," from someone else.

"A culture." Now the answers pop. "A language." "Clothing." "Food."

"Good! Good!" he encourages them. He's pleased with the responses. "Well, I've come up with my own list," Tou Ger offers generously. He will even rank them, he says, one to ten. A helper, marker in her hand, poises before newsprint clipped to an easel. People crane so they can see. I love this— people describing themselves.

Tou Ger's list grows item by item, and the helper writes them down, squeak, squeak, with Tou Ger offering brief examples of each one. Number ten is "psyche." He paints the Hmong psyche with quick verbal brush strokes.

"*Peb tsis muaj nyiaj* [we don't have money] and that's OK," Tou Ger says.

"We were four thousand years in China. A third of our people died in Laos in the Vietnam War." He pauses.

"There are seven to eight million Hmong still in China." Such is the content of the Hmong psyche.

Next on the newsprint is artwork, dance, and music: Tou Ger mimics his father crouched down in the dark outside a wooden Hmong house, courting Tou Ger's mother through her bedroom wall. He mimics whispering and playing "words" on a little jaw harp. "Or if you don't have that," Tou Ger advises, just play on a folded leaf.

Another distinguishing feature, Tou Ger says, is ritual: New Year rites, funerals, shaman's healings.

And weddings. Tou Ger says, "Do the bride and groom kiss after the ceremony?" To knowing laughter he dismisses the idea with a roll of his eyes. "No!" He demonstrates the forehead-to-floor kowtowing that grooms must perform in front of their new in-laws. No touching the bride!

"And the funeral. Ritualized crying. It's our way of saying we love this person."

Another item goes on the newsprint list: family and clan. Tou Ger jokingly teaches the audience the Hmong equivalents of "Umhmm" and "Really?" necessary to "converse" with grandfathers and grandmothers, the old ones with stories to whom one listens and listens and listens.

But the items he considers most defining of the Hmong are food, clothing, and language. Food is always in abundance at special occasions such as weddings, as I've learned. "I was invited to an American wedding," Tou Ger says, hands shoved in his pockets, "so I didn't eat any food that day." The few non–Hmong in the audience know what's coming. Tou Ger continues. "At the reception a server came around with a beautiful silver tray with teeny, tiny sandwiches." His audience is grinning, laughing. Tou Ger

doesn't need to describe the tubs of rice, the pans of barbecued beef and pork and chicken, the platters of spicy vegetables, the fifteen-gallon pots of soup. "Hmong — they eat." More mimicry. "And kids carry around an open can of Mountain Dew without drinking it." Laughter of recognition.

Tou Ger's number one characteristic in defining the Hmong is language. This ancient tongue, possibly a branch of the Chinese-Tibetan family, is unlike the language of any people among whom they have lived, with the exception of the Mien, a number of whom also fled from the encroaching communists in the 1970s. Although the Hmong language may have had a written form long ago, it has been exclusively oral for more than four thousand years. All the creativity that literate cultures pack onto pages the Hmong lavish upon the spoken word. The secret code-language of sweethearts, proverbs, the plain language of morality tales and ancestral stories, the flowery speech of the elders, the antique language of wedding and funeral rituals that may take days to recite, the non-linear way an idea is wrapped round and round in words. The Hmong are a talking people.

Tou Ger demonstrates with a verse of sung poetry, a nasal, chanting kind of song that most young Hmong are not learning. The song begins with a sustained syllable on a high note before it slides down to a stylization of the tones of daily speech. "A long time ago ..." A few young people laugh at the old-fashioned sound. The older ones do not. The laughter must hurt. These poem-songs live deep in the old ones' hearts.

The following sung poem exemplifies not only Hmong communication style but the centrality of *sib tham*, talking together, in the fabric of Hmong society. It is from Song About Being an Orphan: No Parents, No Cousins, No Homeland.[2]

> *Nij yai....ntuj-teb os ib zeej txiv leej tub,*
> *noob txheej-tshoj los thaum i ais ...*

> Ni-yai....oh heaven and earth, all people, men and boys.
> Once long ago,
> I am with my mother and father, living together;
> I have finished eating only a little, and
> I have worn only a few of the clothes.
> Ni-yai....why didn't the old know how to love and care for the young?
> Now I leave my mother and father,
> young brothers and old brothers,
> abandoned in Indochina, far behind;
> now all I can do is to think over what has happened.

Opposite: Jessica Moua, with her father, Vue Moua, at Hmong New Year is learning about old ways, Santa Ana, California, November 1999.

Ni-yai ... once long ago,
I live with young brothers and old brothers, all together;
I have finished eating only a little,
I have worn only a few of the clothes.
The young did not know how to love and respect the old;
now I abandon my young brothers and old brothers.
I come to this foreign country,
now all I know is worry and trouble....

Ni-yai ... why do my mother and father lose my footprints,
and go on the downhill side of the rock?
Now they leave this young son to come all alone to live his life,
lonely in this foreign land called Thailand.
Why do my young brothers and old brothers lose my footprints,
and go on the downhill side of the fallen log?
Now they abandon this young man to come all alone to make his way,
in this foreign land, on American soil, oh Hmong cousins....
Hmong cousins, the others have young brothers and old brothers.
They finish a meal and talk together about caring for each other.
This young man has no young brothers, no old brothers, to finish a meal,
has no place to come and talk for a day, oh Hmong cousins.

The others have young brothers and old brothers.
They finish a meal and talk together about remembering each other.
This young man has no mother, no father, and
the young brothers and the old brothers did not come to this country,
    to finish a meal,
and there's no place to bring a wife and children, with sweat-streaked faces,
to come and talk for a night, oh Hmong cousins....

3

Keeper of the Past: Mai Xiong

> One thousand years without weakness, forever
> without sickness, you will be our advisors, you
> will be our elders, you will live until your hair
> is completely white.
>
> — Vang & Lewis[1]

April, a pleasant afternoon, and I was in Sacramento.

But what I found on a corner of Martin Luther King Jr. Boulevard quickly metamorphosed, in my perception, from an ordinary American apartment building into a foreign village.

I parked on the street and, address in hand, walked through the open chain-link driveway gate into the courtyard of the two-story building. The modest stucco structure reached its short arms toward a phalanx of parking spaces where a few older cars, mostly Toyotas, stood ready to convey their owners between worlds.

In the concrete courtyard a loose knot of women looked toward me none too eagerly as if to ask, Government lady? Hmong children playing nearby paused, too. I moved closer and asked them in my best memorized Hmong, "*Mai Xyooj puas nyob tsev?*" Is Mai Xiong home? Faces relaxed — it was the Hmong language that did it — and Mai Xiong (pronounced "my shyong") emerged from the half dozen women. The grandmotherly Mai hugged me — we had met before, in other settings. The first time had been several years ago, in a different apartment a few miles north of here. Chamy Thor had taken me to her for my first lesson in Hmong religion. Apparently

Mai Xiong with friends and relatives, Sacramento, California, October 1994.

Chamy believed that Mai Xiong was key to understanding the Hmong, since Mai is a shaman.

Today, I saw that Mai also is an individual around whom people congregate. Even after the two of us climbed the outside stairs and walked along the balcony to her small apartment, a few of the other women drifted inside with us to *sib tham*, to chat. Children bunched outside the living room window, which looks out on the walkway, their eyes shielded by cupped hands pressed against the screen. Visitors are group entertainment. Soon four or five of the children, dressed in play-dirtied shirts and pants, wandered inside. Two hid behind Mai's comfortable shape, and the others stood boldly in the middle, as if hypnotized. I caught a boy's eye and he gave me a wide kid smile.

Mai Xiong smiled a heart-warming smile, too, all glittering teeth with a flash of gold. Her lips are full and wide, like her laugh. Most Hmong women I meet have warm smiles, but Mai's comes from some deeply confident place.

She speaks slowly and distinctly in an alto voice, with a regular rhythm, and for that I was grateful since I had come to practice Hmong. After months of classroom work, I needed real-world experience. Mai would force me to practice, because she speaks about twelve words of English. ("Come!" "Sit!" and "Meh-ka" for American). She hoped to learn more English during our visits.

Mai explained to one of the older women who followed us into her apartment where she got this stranger. I figured it out from their gestures and from hearing the name of a refugee organization. Then I heard the words "Reno" and "Tahoe" among the mostly unfamiliar sounds. I knew this referred to a possible bus excursion to gaming venues, something that appeals to a lot of Asian seniors seeking escape from their apartments.

Hampered by the lack of a common language, I tried to extract clues about her from objects I saw. Coming in I had passed a hoe, some beat-up aluminum pans, squashes, and muddy gardening shoes. I could imagine Mai returning from gardening chores and slipping out of the shoes before stepping indoors. Over the doorway I had seen cut paper, to ensure protection by a gatekeeper spirit, a book later told me.

Inside, in the living room, two of the older children sat on a thin double-bed mattress that had been folded in half and pushed against the wall opposite the window. The children poked each other, and then fell to wrestling. Mai halted them with brief words. "*Tsis txhob.*" Eventually I recognized the folded-up mattress as an American stand-in for the bamboo guest platform in the main room of traditional Hmong homes.

While Mai and one of the other women sat on foot-high bamboo stools and chatted, I discreetly considered the astonishing business on Mai's ceiling. Spread across the ceiling from the far wall to the door was a geometric string design into which had been worked two long stalks of bamboo. This is the bamboo Chamy grows, dried to white. The string pattern fanned out from a spot on the far wall at the top of an altar fastened there, a boxlike rectangle of wood. Mai had placed on the altar small bowls with rice, water, and sticks of incense. I told myself to look up the vocabulary for this, but I wondered how far two people without a common language could get discussing anything as complex as religion. Then I wondered who climbed up to tack the string and bamboo in place.

I looked at Mai again. Though only a bit above five feet tall, she conveyed largeness of spirit. Eventually, the visiting women left. The children had already melted out the door. I heard their shouts and laughter in the courtyard below.

Mai and I practiced talking. With nods, rolled eyes, multiple facial expressions, and a few recognizable phrases, we discussed how poorly we speak each other's language. She said I'd be speaking in one year, maybe two—"*ib xyoo ob xyoo.*" Then giving in to mirth she described what happens when a non–Hmong speaker comes to her door. The comedy routine featured her gold-flashing grin and, unlike the properly reserved Hmong female, gesticulating arms and waggling head. She mimed responding to a knock on the door, greeting the hapless visitor with another of her English words, "Hello," followed by the clear command "Go!" And then she shuts the door. I could almost see the would-be visitor standing outside not knowing whether he had just experienced sunshine or rain.

Vocabulary. I struggled for the Hmong word for telephone, and she said, "te-le-phong," in a manner that sounds altogether un–English. "Phong," she repeated, and we laughed. Then in Hmong we talked about the flowers I had brought — their colors, how many grow on a bush. We discussed our relative height, and I pointed to my big feet next to her small ones. She pointed out that I'm tall, while she is "small and big." She told me she wants to dress me up in Hmong clothes so we could be photographed together. As always, much of this conversation was a work of performance art.

On top of the TV in the corner I noticed a toy stuffed cat. "*Miv,*" I said. "*Tus miv,*" Mai repeated, adding the classifier for living things. She meowed for me and I meowed back. My mind briefly flew to Chamy, whom I would never catch meowing at anyone. Then Mai told me something about cats and her stomach, patting it and giving its name *plab*. I didn't get the story line.

Mai pointed me to a place on the sofa and sat down beside me. While we talked, people continued to come and go. One of Mai's friends, probably a relative, who let herself in and sat down on a folding chair, asked me in Hmong where I live. I gestured toward the west and rummaged in my brain for words of distance. I reported, to their dismay, that I have only two children. I showed them photographs of my husband, children, and children's spouses.

Mai turned to tell me something earnest but incomprehensible. Fortunately, a young neighbor who had dropped in, blessedly bilingual, interpreted. "She is not feeding you a meal because she didn't have time to prepare chicken and beef" between my phone call and my arrival. I had not anticipate that food would be part of the language-study arrangement.

I wondered if Mai felt as hampered by the lack of language in this relationship as I. Words connect people. Little of that here. I am watching a movie starring Mai Xiong with the sound turned off.

Determined not to fall back on an interpreter, over the visits that followed I watched closely, then read and mulled over what I saw. I watched Mai watering her vegetables in the community garden, cooking in her kitchen, seated by the window stitching elaborate decoration onto clothing. Though I never saw her perform, I also imagined Mai practicing the mysterious shaman's rituals. Only after months of visiting did I begin to appreciate what I was seeing. Maybe more powerfully than she could ever have done consciously and with words, Mai was revealing to me what it means to live as a Hmong.

Thursday was my day to make the trek to Mai's upstairs apartment for language practice. Responding to my knock on the door or sometimes spotting me coming into the courtyard, she would open the door, grin, and say in her best English, "Come ing!" Then "*Zaum!*" she would say with a nod toward the sofa, and after I sat we would *sib tham*.

One Thursday morning Mai brought out some *paj ntaub* she had recently finished. It was a wide belt of squares covered with triangles and zigzags in tiny, tiny stitches. The squares were edged in blinding pink and chartreuse and were sewn together onto black satin. A girl wearing such a belt in the home country would stand out against nature's sober browns and dark greens like a flashing neon advertisement. That's likely the point. With a companion who had let herself in Mai's door a few minutes after I arrived, Mai discussed how much money such an item would bring. My clue was the word "dollah."

On this day I had brought my cross-stitched collar to show Mai, along with the start of a cuff I was working on. She looked the cuff over carefully—without glasses—and added a few stitches. I explained that Chamy

Thor taught me at her children's embroidery class at a Sacramento school. Mai considered my tale — or wondered what the dickens I was babbling about — and peered at my work. She was keen to upgrade one of my stitches. She demonstrated. It entailed adding an extra stitch to each triangle, placed just right, to give a fuller look. I took the cuff and did as she did. We were both pleased. I went home and stitched away at odd moments with my new stitch.

On a later visit Mai inspected my work and pronounced swift judgment: "*Phem!*," pronounced "pay." Unfortunately, it was a word I knew. It means bad. Or rather evil, wicked. My work was not just unacceptable; it was pernicious. I watched as Mai took out her small scissors and began to rid my piece of the offending stitches. Tiny bits of bright colored thread that I had earnestly applied drifted down onto the lap of Mai's black slacks. Silence filled the room. No reflection on me, but the high standards of the art were not to be diluted.

In other homes I had discovered something else about the culture of stitching. Hmong women with sarong-type skirts and dark hair knotted just below the crown of the head would ask to see my handiwork. They would smile at it and proceed to pull the needle from the cloth and add stitches. No one ever asked if I minded. My piece of stitching was group property.

I have an old red-bordered piece of Hmong stitching that is five and a half inches square with a black backing and wobbly red edging, a little bigger than a coaster. Some Hmong girl spent hours bent over this small piece, bought in a Lao shop. Inside lapped edges of green, blue, and bright pink cloth is a three-inch-square magenta piece woven from rough-looking thread. I wondered if the cloth was handmade. I knew Hmong grew hemp and spun it into thread on homemade spinning wheels, making skeins on the six-foot Hmong frame and weaving it on a handmade loom.

Curious about its purpose, I took it to show a friend, Cho Lee. She said yes, it is probably a practice piece for the pillow cloth that is always given by young couples to their parents against the day of their death. The decorated cloth will be placed under the loved one's head, while other mourners take squares to the funeral and place them on top of the body.

That is the practice of the White Hmong, Cho told me. The custom of the Blue (Green) Hmong — the other major subdivision of the Hmong, named for the women's batiked skirts — is far more elaborate. It is a ritual that stitches families together, the cloth squares carrying meaning as a diamond ring does. Lue Vang describes it in his book *Grandmother's Path, Grandfather's Way*.[2] The word *noob* means seed in the old-fashioned English sense of descendants.

According to ways of our great-grandmothers and great-grandfathers, today we still perform the traditions related to the needlework squares. There are two kinds of *noob-ncoos*, pronounced nong-dyong. One is called *noob-ncoos-tsha* and the other is *noob-ncoos-la*.

The tradition is for the young couple to give the nong-dyong to the girl's parents or the boy's parents.

If both the mother-in-law and father-in-law are still alive, then they make two *noob-ncoos-tsha* and give one to each parent. If one of the parents-in-law has already died, they make an appliquéd *noob-ncoos-tsha* for the living parent and the undecorated *noob-ncoos-lab* for the deceased parent.

It is the true custom to give the *noob-ncoos* to the parents-in-law according to the traditions: One cannot just casually give the pieces to the parents. ...[T]he son-in-law has to prepare one bottle of corn liquor and a pair of boiled chickens. When they reach the home of the in-laws, the two chickens are chopped up and put on two plates on the table, and two glasses are filled with corn liquor and placed on the table. When all is ready, the parents-in-law are called to sit on one side of the table. The son-in-law stands on the other side of the table, and puts the two pieces of *noob-ncoos* on the table, and says, "*Ah...mother and father...we, your daughter and son-in-law, have not given you anything to bless you. But this year, your daughter and son-in-law bring these small pieces of cloth as a sign of blessing for you. May you two receive good health and wealth, have long lives, and remain strong forever. ONE THOUSAND YEARS WITHOUT WEAKNESS, FOREVER WITHOUT SICKNESS, YOU WILL BE OUR ADVISORS, YOU WILL BE OUR ELDERS, YOU WILL LIVE UNTIL YOUR HAIR IS COMPLETELY WHITE.*"

The text explains, "This blessing, along with the *noob-ncoos*, provides an extension to the 'visa' with which each person enters this life; each *noob-ncoos* therefore extends the person's life."

The day's ritual concludes with the son-in-law kneeling and bowing to his wife's parents, and then the corn liquor is drunk. The in-laws pay a price to the son-in-law and plan a reward feast for a later day, when a pig is slaughtered and the parents-in-law say thank you for "the pieces of cloth and the thread."

When extra cars are parked outside a Hmong home in Sacramento or St. Paul or San Diego all day long, and signs of a feast have spilled into the yard, a square of cloth may have been the trigger.

Learning appliqué is difficult, especially to the standards of the old women. But its difficulty may be its undoing. In Laos, girls practiced for hours outdoors, seated in a doorway, or beside the small indoor cooking fire. Now Hmong daughters learn to manipulate words and numbers, seated under fluorescent lights at school. Mothers and older sisters who would have taught them may be at work. A group of Hmong college girls told me that not one of them knows reverse appliqué. Nor are they likely to learn. That loss will alter the character of ties between generations.

At some point during visits to Mai Xiong's apartment, after we had stitched awhile, chatted, or watched "Gunsmoke," Mai would excuse herself and disappear into the kitchen. It was a two-person affair facing onto the street below. At one end stands a laminated-plastic table. Under this American table, used as a pantry, Mai has stashed a two-foot-wide, low bamboo table, the one she uses for eating.

I felt ambivalent when Mai headed for the kitchen. I understood that feeding guests was good manners, but I worried that she was feeding me out of spare provisions. Yet her meals were irresistible. I've eaten many Hmong meals, roast whole pig for a naming ceremony feast in San Diego; a welcoming feast in a village in Laos for which a cow was dispatched; and Hmong church potlucks, with the most delicious egg rolls I ever wish to eat. And yet those plain meals with Mai Xiong, sharing with her a bit of daily life, both seated on low stools at the small bamboo table and together dipping our spoons into common dishes, dripping savory juices on the newspaper tablecloth en route to the mouth — those meals remain my benchmark for blessed Hmong eating.

I could never in my kitchen duplicate what Mai Xiong did to the foot-long Chinese green beans. These appeared on her table in a quart-size flowered plastic dish such as are found in Chinese shops. You maneuver the beans into your mouth balanced on the plain aluminum tablespoon that the Hmong use, despite their having lived for millennia in the land of chopsticks. The beans, hot or cold, were always served in their broth, a treasure of vitamins that Westerners are inclined to empty down the drain. In a few Hmong homes, when the meal was nearing an end and it was time for a beverage, I have been tentatively offered this broth in a glass. Ordinarily I was not given a choice of drinks but simply handed something, usually a soft drink. My hosts weren't sure how I would take to the vegetable water. It was delicious.

One hot summer Thursday during my visit Mai went to her refrigerator and took out a fat green cucumber, another product of her garden. Taking a big knife in hand she peeled it three-quarters of the way down, to my horror drawing the blade swiftly toward her stomach. (The Hmong knife is a foot long, pointed sharply at the tip, widening to two inches midway along the blade, and narrowing again at the handle.) She handed the whole cucumber to me with the command, "*Noj!*" Munching away at it I decided it was a back-country ice cream cone.

Mai Xiong's meals for me always included a meat dish, perhaps small chunks of pork, beef, or chicken, depending on what she had found acceptable at the store. Farm-fresh is a tough standard to match in markets. I've watched Hmong study meats or vegetables as if they were fine china, turning them this way and that. Like greens, the meats Mai prepared also appeared with cooking broth, perfectly seasoned. Several times I joined her at her gas stove to watch as she dropped the chunks of meat into a pot of water and seasoned it with salt and a long leaf of lemon grass. As an accompaniment for this she would place on the low table a small bowl of a powerful mixture of fish sauce, green onion, lemon, cilantro, and the flaming hot peppers that make most Mexican chilis taste bland.

Every meal included rice. Mai, like most Hmong in America, now cooks hers in an electric cooker. But the soft, steaming rice she ladled into my bowl was always mild flavored and creamy with just enough firmness.

Now and then on my Thursday visits, someone would stop in not just to *sib tham* but to do some kind of business. Mai is, of course, a known healer. She handles ailments from simple to serious. Once when I came with my nose stuffed up, she disappeared into her back room and emerged with a small jar of mentholated ointment, imported from Thailand. She gently applied some of it to my nose. The fumes surged into my head and blasted a pathway. I recalled the Hmong word for nose, one of my favorites. It is *ntswg*, pronounced "ntchou"—rhyming with should, and it's said with a huff of air. When spoken, it sounds like a sneeze.

I looked at the little jar with its Thai script. I had seen visitors come to buy such preparations from Mai, including an ointment for insect bites. But I never saw evidence that she was selling any of the prescription drugs, such as antibiotics, that are sold over the counter in Southeast Asia and sometimes here, to the distress of U.S. authorities. Mai told me she herself has enjoyed excellent health, and I found no cause to dispute that. She apparently had never visited a doctor during her then eleven years in the United States, except for the checkup on arrival.

Like many older women, Mai raises herbs. One pot stands in her kitchen window, and a second pot at the apartment door holds a treatment for arthritis. These plants don't have English names. In the garden plot a mile away she has plugged in a few more plants beside her vegetables. Women pass seeds and cuttings from hand to hand.

Healing herbs overlap with flavoring herbs. I saw Mai drop unidentifiable green items into meat broths she fed me, perhaps to stimulate nose health.

In other Hmong homes I've encountered plants as much as three feet tall, tucked in a sunny window. Leaves from these may be added to a beverage or mashed and put directly on a wound. A succulent shown me is used for twisted ankle or bleeding, another for heart ailments and cancer. One man, a shaman like Mai, boils certain herbs and adds them to bath water in which he soaks for an hour, to alleviate the pain of a grenade wound on his knee. He uses it if his prescription medicine doesn't work. His daughter explained, "In two to three days the killing pain will go away."

Most homes have a resident specialist in herbs, and many include one who does massage of internal organs as well, a tricky business. Much rarer is the healer with the spiritual calling, consulted in serious cases and a key feature of traditional culture. Shamans are well-known and well-respected. Mai Xiong is one of the few female shamans.

Like all Hmong shamans, Mai did not seek the calling. "I didn't choose to do this; it just happened," she later told me through an interpreter. First the spirits called and "riled me up," and "I had to do it." She was almost curt in her explanation.

Mai Xiong is a familiar name to Sacramento Hmong. It was for this reason that Chamy Thor took me to meet her, back when I had known Chamy only a few days and was preparing to write about her for the newspaper. Chamy had wanted me to understand shamanism, part of her heritage. Perhaps she was also testing me. After our short visit with Mai that day, Chamy was curious about my reaction to her description of the healing ritual. "What do you think about the trance? You think that is real?" Years later Chamy confessed that she had actually been more concerned that I might notice the caged chicken on Mai's kitchen counter. Silently she had pleaded, "Don't move, chicken!" I had seen it and assumed it was for dinner. It was probably for a sacrifice.

Hmong shamans' rituals are strange to Westerners. Banged gongs and lengthy chants, pigs sacrificed and a shaman bouncing on a wooden bench — I was open to it but didn't know if a Westerner could make the mental leap.

Once when I arrived unannounced at Mai's, she was just lifting her hands gently from the tummy of a child lying on her shaman's bench, which I had earlier seen up-ended against a wall near her altar. The child's mother stood patiently near. The child had a cold, Mai made me understand. The healing was quickly concluded, and the mother and child left.

It is possible that Mai doesn't perform many major healings anymore. Shamans quite reasonably tend to wind down their practice as they get older, since the ritual is physically demanding. (Hmong commonly retire after age forty.) In any case, I have not seen her perform one.

But another occasion to observe came along. A relative of Chamy Thor's had been growing gaunt and listless. He was saying it was time to go back to heaven, Chamy's husband told me. "The family say it's not," Nom Npis Lis said. So they called for a shaman. Chamy, her adult children, and I drove together. What I saw was more than the healing of one person but the ritual renewal of family bonds.

The ritual was to take place in a family home off Mack Road in South Sacramento. The shaman, along with his eight-foot-long bench carved of oak, had already been driven by Nom Npis to the patient's house in a Chevy pickup. This shaman was later given an honorarium of fifty dollars and honored at a closing feast. "Sometimes they ask for an amount, but not this time,"

The patient lives with his brother, his youngest son, and the son's wife and nest of children. It's the classic old-country household, transplanted to a ranch-style house. Inside the front door, people were squeezed together on couches to watch TV. In the kitchen women chopped, mixed, and cooked heaps of meats and vegetables. A front bedroom held a computer, at which a knot of boys played games. Between this room and the kitchen an open area held a dining table. It, too, was alive with relatives. This became Chamy's favored spot.

Adjacent to the dining area was the family room. In the corner the cyclopic eye of a big-screen TV was hidden by sheaves of butcher paper. Two altars were fastened to the right-hand wall. They belonged to the patient and his brother, both of them also shamans. In this room the shaman would perform his ritual.

The shaman was tall, thin, and pale-skinned, with a thin, slightly hooked nose. He appeared to be about fifty years old. He was clothed in a black dress shirt unbuttoned at the top and traditional Hmong loose black pants. For the ritual he removed black socks and sandals and donned a black cloth covering for his face. This was fastened around his forehead with a band of black checked fabric. The covering reached to his shoulders in back and to his chin in front, a symbolic separation from the everyday world.

I was conducted to a sofa and inserted into a tight space next to the patient. It was the only piece of furniture in the room besides the shaman's small end table and a few metal folding chairs, ubiquitous in Hmong homes. In English I said to the patient, "They want you to get well, to stay with them." He shook his head and spoke at length in Hmong while he bumped his right palm against his thin arm, then his chest, showing them to me as proof of his hopeless condition. He used to smoke two packs of cigarettes a day, I had been told. Two or three times during the ceremony, he rose to go out the sliding glass patio doors to smoke. During the ritual he ran thin fingers through the gunmetal gray hair over his high forehead, daydreaming.

Soon after we arrived, cold rain began to sheet down, enough, I learned later, to cause flooding near downtown. More than once, lightning and thunder provided a rare sound-and-light backdrop to the drama indoors. Hail briefly pounded on a new patio cover outside the family room, a stout wooden structure admired at length by the men.

Later, when I sought Chamy out at her dining table post for interpretation, she explained that this healing was in fact the second part of a sequence. A month before, the shaman had made a diagnosis by journeying to the spirit world, the shaman's primary means of patient care. There he learned that the patient's soul was already "going back to look for reincarnation," Chamy said. "He's sick because his soul was sorry [offended], doesn't want to stay with his person." Another patient's diagnosis might have been angry spirits or needy ancestors. "If he get better in thirty days, they will do healing." Since the patient's health did improve, as can happen when one finally gets an explanation for feeling sick, it was apparent that intervention by that shaman could work. The souls of two pigs, bagged and waiting off-stage on the patio, would be sent during this healing in trade for those souls that had gone off.

I wanted to know where the patients' souls had gone off to. Chamy took my pad and wrote on it, *ntuj txiag teb tsaus* [sky-cold-land-dark]. She explained, "Place where [there is] no voice; dark, quiet place where nobody want to go." I thought about that. No voice. It was such a Hmong way of dividing the universe. Around us was the hum of forty or fifty people, talking. Adults trekked back and forth from kitchen to patio chattering. Children talked and played, a baby wailed briefly. Dark, quiet place would mean being *alone*.

The healing ceremony began with the shaman banging a hand-held gong and shaking small doughnut-shaped cymbals decked with red cloth and worn like rings on the fingers—all of it meaning something, I was sure. Chamy explained: "The shaman is not alone." (Of course. Why would anyone try to accomplish anything alone?) "He has helpers, several power, several people together." The string pattern on a shaman's ceiling is these spirits' pathway to the shaman. "So first time when shaman use drum [gong], he get everybody ready. 'Get ready,' he tell his fellowship.

'We're ready to go.'" She continued. "The ring represents helpers. Twelve [spirit] helpers," and the red cloth would be renewed once a year in gratitude. On this day, the shaman and his twelve spirit helpers would journey to find the patient's souls and bring them back to the house off Mack Road.

Two or three human helpers had also gathered around the shaman. They would beat the gong, spot for the shaman as he leaped on and off his bench, and apply a damp washcloth to his face, back, and stomach to cool him.

Now with the gong sounding in a steady rhythm, the shaman placed strips of paper symbolizing money on the bench and seated the patient on top of it. More "money" was draped on the patient's shoulder. Two men brought a sheet of plastic from the back patio and laid it on the beige carpet next to the sliding door. Then they brought one of the young pigs in a plastic grain sack and set it down on the plastic. The pig's snout stuck out a clipped bottom corner and its tail waggled from the tied end. It alternately rested and fought. Men took turns holding it down with a foot.

The shaman tied a length of thong around the pig's upper body and wrapped it twice around the patient. Then he took up a ritual sword with red and yellow tassels and held this before the pig. Later he described a circle in the air with it around a big iron ring on the floor. This ring was a principal tool of the shaman. It was a foot across and was fitted with half a dozen disks like those on a tambourine. It weighed a pound or two— easy to carry but a noticeable weight when shaken for four hours. The shaman took a small bowl of water from his altar, sipped the water, and sprayed it in a mist toward the patient.

Through everything, the shaman chanted in an unvarying rhythm. He interrupted the chant now and then with a Brrrrrr, made apparently with his lower lip. He held the iron ring in his hand (the little finger looked arthritic) and gave the lightest shake possible to set the disks a-jangle. After several hours, this steady sound, plus the banging on the gong, induced a hypnotic buzz in my head. The shaman had entered a trance.

Several men took turns banging the gong, another one tended the pig, and Nom Npis read the newspaper, seated a few feet from the sick relative on the bench. Three girls had taken the patient's place next to me on the couch. One leaned warmly against me, apparently oblivious that I was a stranger. I was grateful. My feet were freezing from the cold air drifting through the open sliding door, and the chill was creeping up my legs. I watched the pig squirm and wondered if it would be dispatched there in front of me. Luckily, the men carried it out to the patio and, laying it on a homemade bench, bled it into a stainless steel basin, its shrieking protests gradually diminishing. Then I got a lesson in pig butchering, which featured boiling water, a blow torch, and the back of a big knife to clean hair from the skin. The second, smaller pig likewise contributed its soul to the patient's health. The meat would be prepared for a feast later.

The shaman was chief actor in a drama, speaking to the pig, to the evil gate keeper, to the wayward souls. He also narrated in Hmong everything he was doing, referring to himself in the third person as Shee Yee Va. (Some boys are given the name Shee Yee.) "He is like Jesus," Chamy explained, "the savior. He refers to himself that way."

I turned to my guides for more explanations. Does the sound of the iron ring signify anything? Nom Npis: "Every time [California Governor] Pete Wilson go someplace very special, they have music. Every time shaman go, must have music." He continued. "He go to Heaven and to the guy who stands at the gate. He says, 'How come you let souls through? I'm coming to take them back. He has family, children, wife, granddaughter, and grandson. They crying and long for him in the earth.'" Chamy: "'His passport not expired yet.'" When the shaman had succeeded in talking his way past the gate, he addressed each soul. Chamy translated: "'Don't stay mad and stay away. Back on earth there are wife, children, granddaughter, and grandson. He has brothers, sisters. Don't be sorry.'"

The heart of the drama was the shaman's twelve journeys to recover the patient's souls. "Hmong have twelve souls," Chamy said. "He has to go get one soul from one place, another soul from another place." To claim a soul he found, the shaman jumped down off the bench and threw down the iron ring. Chamy: "He go, go, go, found soul asleep in a dying place. He drop ring and captures soul and comes back."

This recapture featured an astonishing leap backward by the shaman from floor to the two-foot-high bench. I had heard about it, didn't quite believe it, but now saw how the maneuver was accomplished. The shaman stood with his back to the bench. A helper schooled in the routine stood behind the bench and reached forward to grasp the shaman's waist. For his part, the shaman leaned forward, then flung his weight up and back while the helper guided him benchward. The shaman immediately resumed bouncing, the board sagging and squeaking with each step. Right foot, bounce, left foot, bounce, like a dance, his feet just clearing the board. Two men anchored the cross-braced ends for safety. Not all shamans stand to bounce. Some like Mai Xiong, from another part of Laos, use a shorter bench and sit to bounce. "Women [shamans] don't usually jump [bounce] that much." Chamy said.

I mentioned to Chamy that I had read that the bench is a symbolic horse. Chamy answered, "When shaman and his people go one place to another, so probably the horse." Nom Npis concurred: "Probably the horse."

At the end of more than four hours of chanting, bouncing, and shaking the iron ring, the shaman would not be tired. "If a shaman shakes, then they can do it without getting tired," Chamy said.

The atmosphere for this ceremony was decidedly unceremonious. Adults milled around. A three-year-old girl walked back and forth past the shaman, a baby bottle gripped in her teeth. The patient's brother tended his toenails on the patio. The patient snoozed on the sofa. The repetitive sounds filled the room —clanging, banging, jangling, chanting. I shut my eyes to listen. The shaman chanted in a jogging, sing-song rhythm with a long final beat: one, two, three, four, FIVE. One, two, three, four, five, six, SEVEN, repeated and repeated, with varied count. At the same time, I heard the iron ring's jangle, the bench's squeak, and the gong's tenor *clong!* Between chanting what seemed to be a refrain, the shaman talked, called out, shouted, or harangued, now rapidly, now slowly. Throughout the day, people asked me if this was my first shaman's ceremony and what I thought of it. They know it's strange to outsiders. And it was. To me, the music of man and instruments was unsettling. My brain doesn't resonate with these sounds. Opera, no problem. Latin mass, yes. Rap, sure. But I haven't had enough exposure to Asian timbre and tonality for this music to evoke any visceral meaning or emotion. I opened my eyes again. The patient's wife — his third, called Little Wife — sat in a dining table chair near Chamy holding a pink baby girl dressed in more pink. Little Wife swayed the baby forward and back and gazed into the room, looking at some far place.

Finally, the patient got up and left the house through the garage. Helpers put two small stair supports in the open patio door — a symbolic ladder — and placed the small pig carcass on top. The patient appeared outside the patio door. Chamy indicated the shaman. "He talk about the ladder. We have to put sections together so the soul have a way to come back. 'Come through this ladder. Come back. Stay forever.'" Then brothers, sons, sons-in-law, daughters-in-law, Chamy, and Nom Npis— all the sick man's relatives— stood inside the door and called the old man in. "Come back, come back. Stay forever."

The emotion of the ceremony touched me — the fuss, the gathering of the clan around one in need, the expression of the patient's worth, love made visible. Such a focus is wholly consistent with the meaning of "love," *hlub*, in Hmong thinking and the place of kin in Hmong society.

I could not, however, connect with the animist view of things— the belief that sees distinct spirits animating each bit of nature. But I looked for points of contact between Hmong views and mine. I was especially intrigued by the idea of escaped souls. The notion that you can lose something vital, something crucial, in times of stress has universality. We say figuratively someone fell apart or went to pieces. Someone tells you to pull yourself together. After sickness or a difficult task, you might say you feel drained. When a beloved person dies, you feel that something more than just the person has gone.

Many Hmong say a person has twelve souls. We talk of one. A few years ago I began gathering hand puppets against the day when I might have grandchildren. At least that was what I told myself. I was amused to realize that the different puppets—an eagle, a pig, a snail, an unruly bird—represent aspects of myself. My puppets now number eleven.

I sat across the low bamboo table from Mai Xiong, spooned long beans into my mouth, and thought about her. There *is* something about this woman. Thanks to whatever mix of personality and selection by the spirits, she is gifted. She mystically binds families together. They know it. Along with every Hmong shaman, she has been a force for endurance among the people. But this force may be on the wane.

4

Feast and Famine

Eat delicious [food], live well.
— Hmong greeting

"You want to eat?" Cho Lee turned to me. It was Cho who had explained the needlework square to me. We were sitting on concrete amphitheater benches on a college campus in Southern California, listening to one of the winners in the New Year sung-poem contest. It was a high-cloudy Saturday morning, a few days after Thanksgiving, and no students were on campus. On the other side of Cho sat two of her women relatives, people I had encountered now and then when in Cho's company.

When I had first arrived at the New Year festivities that morning — it was Day Three of the event — I had been scanning the crowd for Cho when her teenage daughter, Zong, touched me lightly on the arm. She pointed to Cho and quietly disappeared. Cho's youngest, a boy of eight, was also around, I learned, although Cho rarely saw him that morning. He and the hundred or so other children blended with the equal number of teens and adults without fuss.

"I'm ready!" I told Cho. I had already spotted the three food booths at the far end of the plaza. I love the food at these events, especially the barbecued meats and purple rice. Clambering up the back of the amphitheater to the grassy rim, the four of us women headed to a booth where, I guessed, Cho's friend would be in charge. She was. We went around to the back where another friend was barbecuing pork sausage on a big black grill. This was Hmong hospitality turned business.

73

"You like sausage?" Cho asked, glancing at me. "They make it themselves." The sausages looked beautiful—fat, even tubes with fine-grained meat and bits of green and red seasoning showing through the skin.

"I'll try it," I said, hoping this did not mean I was forgoing chicken. I should have known. Over my protests, Cho paid. "I invited *you*," she said. We left the stand, bearing Styrofoam boxes and tall containers of a sweet coconut-milk drink with pink and green gelatine shapes swimming in it, which Cho herself had stepped behind the counter to mix. We found a place nearby at a dry fountain where dozens of other eaters had spread their goodies.

More women and some small children joined us. I opened my box and released the fragrant warmth of sausage chunks, spicy shredded beef with cilantro, and a mountain of purple sticky rice, which you ball up with your fingers to eat. Immediately, chunks of chicken were plopped into my box, and I responded by dealing out sausage to the boxes of my neighbors. There were plastic forks, but we ate with our fingers. A sour papaya salad was eaten by picking it up in strips of iceberg lettuce, leaving fingers clean. But that dish is laced with fish sauce, which I don't like, so one taste for politeness was enough.

Cho's son Dou appeared, wiggling to be hand-fed clumps of meat and rice by his mother. "He still like me to feed him!" Cho said, scoffing but nonetheless responding to his silent pleading. "Feng, too. They still like that." The boys were eight and nine. Soon Dou took off.

Surrounded by these women and children, I was happy. My taste buds were happy. Evidently Cho was, too.

"We call it *noj peb caug*." Literally "eat thirty," referring to the last day of the year and the New Year feast. "So we eat!" Cho laughed. Her husband, who was at another location playing a men's war game with spinning tops, constantly tells Cho that she is overweight. But now he was not around to pester her, and she was relishing the food.

On this Thanksgiving weekend, the rest of America had just commemorated a time of hunger relieved by plenty. Now the Hmong, still an agricultural people in their hearts and bones, observed their own celebration of food. Personal knowledge of hunger lends piquant flavor to food. Being an all day eater, I don't like to think what a pitiful showing I'd make faced with real hunger, such as nearly all of my Hmong acquaintances have known. Likewise, I can only extrapolate from the few backyard vegetables

Opposite: When the Hmong arrived in Laos, the lowland fields were already taken. This field near Chestnut Mountain, Laos, belongs to Chamy Thor's mother, Kia Lee, December 1994.

I've presented at my dinner table to the intense relationship between grower and food where it's a life or death matter.

Every people has attachments to its foods. It has been observed that changing foods can be harder than changing religions. Tastes, textures, smells—from childhood they seem to work their way into our cells. I still find special solace in a mug of hot cocoa, while Hmong love their long beans, Asian cucumber, squash, and rice. Hmong I know will drive past innumerable mainstream supermarkets stocked with all kinds of rice to find a specific variety with the smell and taste of Laos. Some older people grow it in their backyards.

Subsistence farming has given the Hmong a certain way of seeing themselves. You catch it obliquely from the way they talk. A Hmong proverb begins slyly, "When the others work, you don't have to work with them. When the others eat, you can be the dog begging for scraps."[1] Knowledgeable, tough, and hardworking—those terms help define a true Hmong, and the traits are farm-based. If hard work brings arthritis, if bad weather, pests, or too few hands threaten the crops and tigers attack animals, so be it, they would say. You are what you conquer.

How to grow food is still a primary body of knowledge for older Hmong in America. In every backyard I've seen, tight rows are laid out for green onions, mustard greens, and healing herbs, with slender paths threading between. The resident grandmother knows everything about every plant. *Knowing how* gives dignity.

There was much to know. Chamy and her family, Tou Ger the comedian's family, the grandmother who clamped my hand under her arm and guided me around at the Sacramento Hmong New Year—all of these people who now lay into backyard soil with store-bought hoes once used tools made by one of their men. They hauled water from ponds and streams in lengths of thick bamboo slung over their backs, unless it was possible to dig a well or build a wooden aqueduct. Even Chamy, a Hmong outrider in a French school in Vientiane, was imprinted with this mode of life. She knew how her family spent their days, and it marked her as it did them — an inheritance. Now she no longer runs the danger of hunger, but somewhere in her bones, I believe, resides the message that one lives by laboring. Maybe that, as much as a craving for familiar tastes, is what sends her outdoors to do hard labor that leaves her sore, exhausted, and sneezing from Sacramento Valley's notorious pollens.

Hmong geography was tough. In America, mountains like those in Laos would be spangled with the most expensive mansions. Forested, quiet, and wreathed with morning cloud, they give off a Shangri La feel. But for the Hmong, the steep back country just meant hard farming. It was the only land available when the Hmong arrived in the nineteenth century. Now, neither equipment nor much expertise finds its way into the roadless mountains. Harvests can be meager, and the effort of farming burns a lot of calories.

Traditional Hmong farmers use the slash-and-burn method — some anthropologists call it swidden or shifting agriculture, language that to me glosses over the sweat and labor of cutting and burning trees using only human power. Slash-and-burn relies on no irrigation, fertilizer, or pesticides and is still much in use around the world. Hmong land was not "owned," only used.

You can see Hmong farming pictured cartoon-style on cloth. In the absence of writing and cameras, Hmong began to supplement oral storytelling a few decades ago with pictures embroidered on gray or iron-blue cloth. These depictions are favorites at craft fairs and can be quite detailed. On one of mine, small black-clad, barefooted figures — a family, I suppose — live the good, hard-working life on a farm. Tall corn stalks stitched in green thread bear thick, yellow-tasseled cobs, vines flaunt golden pumpkins, and a woman pokes mangos out of a tree with a stick. A man scatters corn to his chicken family with its handsome rooster dad. These are common embroidery themes, portrayed with Grandma Moses-style simplicity.

Bigger, more expensive story cloths than mine picture the details of farming, in sequence. These practices have survived centuries of trial-and-error testing. A book co-authored by Lue Vang, one of the Hmong pioneers in academic America, supplies commentary:

> The New Year is over, and it is time to look for new fields. We look in the thick jungles, looking especially for areas that are overgrown with vines, or we look on hillsides that have not been planted for six or seven years.... Finding lots of earthworm droppings in the surface of the soil is a good sign.[2]

Farmers mark their choice by notching a few trees with an ax and shoving a piece of wood horizontally into the cut, a symbolic split-rail fence. Then both genders set to work to clear fields — equality born of need. They use home-forged axes and brush knives. Later, a field shed will be built in the middle where they can spend the night if the walk home takes more than a few hours.

Even with such nice detail, it was hard for me to connect personally with the description on the page until I asked people I knew about it. Once I did, it began to come to life. Chamy's husband, Nom Npis Lis, bears a white scar on his chin acquired during clearing. One day at his house I asked about the scar. He was glad to oblige. His father had made a small-animal trap of split wood, it seemed, and set it out in a field one morning. At the end of the day, after felling a number of trees, he started across the rough hillside to see if anything had been trapped. Three-year-old Npis called out, "Oh! Let me go, too!" He ran to catch up, then tripped and fell on a fresh, jagged stump, tearing open his chin.

A decade later, he told me, he acquired a second scar. He quickly slipped out of a sock to show me. Two logs had been rigged together and propped against a large tree, high up where the trunk would be easier to cut. Twelve-year-old Npis, barefoot, clambered up this and began to chop with an ax. He swung and missed, grazing the skin near the toes on his left foot. "No broken bones," he said, grinning.

Once they have sweated their way through clearing trees, and the debris has dried in the hot sun, the men set their fields afire. "We all burn at the same time, for instance, at noon on a set day," Lue Vang writes. "The mountain tops and high valleys are all on fire, covered in red like being covered with a red cloth."

This kind of work does something to a person. In early America, once colonists moved beyond the fields previously cleared by Native Americans, they faced dense forest. Tobacco farmers in the South used Hmong-style slash-and-burn to clear land. In the Northeast, settlers girdled trees and let them die. As happens in Laos, the soil wore out in three years. Social historian David Freeman Hawke suggests that it was the labor of clearing forests, not religious precepts, that gave Americans their famous work ethic.[3] It has done the same for Hmong.

Along with melons, pumpkins, and cucumbers, Hmong plant tubers with engaging names such as bear-foot tuber, fragrant tuber, thorn tuber, egg tuber, nest tuber, and clay-pot tuber. They raise corn — early, late, purple or blood corn — for animals only. You have to be very hungry — or live above rice-growing elevations — to eat corn. Chamy grows lots of old-country vegetables at home, an edible essay on her heritage, but no corn.

A good percentage of a family's fields is devoted to vegetables, but rice is king. It's eaten at virtually every meal, every day. One story cloth shows two couples in traditional belted black pants and shirts, planting rice. The two women wear classic purple wrapped turbans, which I still see on the heads of purists at Hmong New Year's festivals, and the men wear a Chinese-style cap. The women in the picture are bent, dropping grains of rice into the holes their men have poked in the soil with a stick. The last one in line shoves dirt over the hole with her bare foot. These embroidered figures, though small, all have mouths, for *sib tham*, I like to think.

Assuming the war is won against weeds, insects, birds, and weather, the family hauls crops home to sheds built atop posts to discourage critters and to minimize rot. Neighbors might pool their muscle power in transporting the food. You carry Mr. A's crops one day, and he carries yours the next. Wealthy Hmong might own a horse to do the carrying, but failing that it's one foot in front of the other.

Bugs, heat, aching muscles get their share of a worker's attention. One of the many videotapes of Laos collected by Hmong in America shows a teenage girl with a basket full of corn on her back. She sits on a rock and saucily refuses to budge. There is laughter and bantering with fellow harvesters. Finally, refreshed by her complaints, she hoists herself and her basket, and the group files down the trail

About another significant crop, Hmong in America don't often talk, and I have learned not to ask — opium. Opium poppies were grown legally by the Hmong for centuries, but opium is illegal now both here and in Asia. Recent programs in Southeast Asia encourage substitution of other crops. In former times opium was their beer, their bourbon on the rocks, their double strength aspirin. Elders might smoke it or drink it as tea to dampen pain and speed healing. (A tincture of opium called laudanum was much used in North America and Europe in the 1700s. It was the best painkiller they had. Today another derivative, morphine, is a boon in hospice care.)

Having long used opium for medication, the Hmong were given added motivation to grow it in the nineteenth century. England, stressed by a trade imbalance and eager to open markets, forced China in battle (1839–1842) to accept imports of opium. The resulting addiction in China stimulated the populace to grow their own — not what the English had in mind. Hmong migrating south out of China carried their poppy seeds and knowledge with them. In Laos where they settled, as in the mountains of China, they found perfect growing conditions for opium — high altitude, cool weather, and poor soil. The French colonial government went into the opium trade, pressuring peoples such as the Hmong to grow it, then refining and selling it in government-operated dens.

Growing opium was both exhausting and exacting. You had to hoe, clear stones, weed, thin, weed again, then choose the exact time to score the heads with a curved knife — just so — and wait hours before circling back to scrape off the sap. Back home you boiled the sap down to a paste. But the effort paid off. The sap did not spoil and was easy to carry to market. It paid government head taxes, which were upped precisely to stimulate the growth of opium. In addition, a healthy return in silver bars or French piasters was available in the market. Cash could be exchanged for city goods that eased mountain life—cloth, cooking pots, salt, animals, metal. Sometimes, rice had to be bought to survive the year. Silver bars, a proud family possession, were essential when a groom's family was sealing a bridal contract. Occasionally, opium proceeds also paid to send a student away to school.

In subsistence farming, nobody takes a good harvest for granted. It requires staying in tune not only with the weather and the soil, but also with the spirits. If trouble threatens—nibbling animals, sparse rain—one may ask the spirits for help. Farmers worldwide understand prayer.

Chamy remembers helping with the farming enterprise as a child. She recalls when she was big enough to help around the house while her parents went to the farm. "At four or five or six you have to help watch the house and piggy your baby," she told me. Watching the house included hauling water from a creek. Little Chamy used a child-size bamboo tube to fill the two water barrels beside the clay cook stove inside the house. She shucked corn and learned to grind it in a stone mill, developing the exact pace required to keep the big wooden handle moving out and back, out and back. She might be alone at home, but someone, a grandmother or uncle, would be elsewhere in the cluster of houses, listening and watching.

If there were other children to tend the house, a child of even five or six would go along to the field to babysit. "You always have that baby on your back," Chamy said with a laugh, "almost all day, your little sister or little brother. Because they don't trust you if you just have it in your arm." The baby might weigh half as much as the child carrying it. When Chamy's charge cried hard, then Chamy would yell "*Niam!* Mom!" and her mother would come to nurse the baby.

Chamy said that sometimes a new mother who had no one around to help would strap a baby in its baby carrier to a tree trunk or a post indoors so she could get her work done. Chamy's mother did this with her first child. Leaving a baby loose asked for trouble, Chamy knew too well. Once when she was tending her youngest brother, he fell into the family's cooking fire, a ring always located near the center of the main room. "My mom have to take him to the bigger city," Chamy said. Chamy thought her brother would die. And it would be her fault. Mother and son were gone for two months. "I was very, very scared," Chamy said. But with access to medical care, he survived. I met him later in Vientiane, and his scars are still visible.

The accumulating stories of Chamy and other Hmong friends began to work a shift in my mind. Their words carried me beyond a museum view of Hmong life. Houses, stoves, clothing, and tools became animated by people I knew. I began to conjure noises and, in my head, watched Chamy produce the bump, bump, bump as she hulled rice in the foot-powered rice pounder. The people who made and used the knives and hoes and axes pictured in books began emerging as real to me, and soon I could imagine them laughing, crying, chatting, or falling into thoughtful silence.

Once I began questioning Hmong in the United States about their food, I turned up linguistic distinctions that far outrun Western vocabulary, most of all in the world of rice. Hmong differentiate between new rice, sweet rice, purple rice, and sticky rice. There is a word for rice still in the field, another for rice harvested and hulled, and another for cooked rice. For linguistic richness, rice parallels snow for native Alaskans, sand for Navajos, and construction nails for European Americans. Descriptions of rice can be vivid. When it ripens, filling out the heads in a perfect, scaly pattern, Hmong say it "makes a snake's stomach." Curiously, there is no word for just "rice."

I have cooked rice for years and find I must dress it up to make it appealing. Not so with the rice I've been fed in Hmong homes, where, unadorned, it is invariably delicious. Rice is so essential to Hmong that the invitation to eat, delivered with quick nods of the head and gestures toward the table, is *noj mov*— eat cooked rice! Later, at the table, your host repeats "*Noj!*" or "*Noj mov!*" like an Italian grandmother.

Preparing rice is clearly an art. I asked a Hmong woman, Grandmother Kao, to explain how it's done. A very bright Hmong student, male, whom I met at graduate school translated for us. No matter — Grandmother Kao's instructions were daunting. She described the old way to cook it over a fire. Although there is a short form that calls for boiling the grains in plenty of water and draining it to cook slowly, the five-star method begins the night before. You have, of course, already planted and raised the rice, harvested it, and carried it home. The day before, you — or a younger person over whom you have leverage — have poured raw rice into the wooden rice pounder's hollowed-out bowl and pushed the lever with your foot, rhythmically banging the hulls from the grains. After tossing the grains in a flat basket to clean them, you put the rice to soak. The next morning you drain and steam it over hot water in a bamboo basket.

"It will be cooked but still very hard after you steam it," our translator told me. (Cooked but still hard?) So it must be poured into a pot of boiling water, stirred well, and cooked until soft but not too soft so that "the rice is still whole rice." But you're not done yet. It needs another twenty minutes "because the rice is not fully cooked; you can still taste the rawness." The subtlety escaped me.

Of course much has changed since Hmong left their farms, and yet some things haven't. It may be easier to pick up a bag of rice at the store, but convenience isn't everything. A modern Hmong shopper doesn't know the farmer who grew the rice, for one thing. That is one reason they don't buy "American" rice, a young woman told me. Hmong ate American rice in the refugee camps "when they were so hungry," she explained, but it doesn't taste good. I'm not surprised: It's different. It doesn't carry sense memories.

After checking the rice on her gas stove, Grandmother Kao, who had warmed to the role of cooking instructor, set to work to show how to make stuffed chicken wings. I wrote down the recipe in my by-then grease-dotted notepad, a combination of her few words and a lot of observation. Here is what I learned:

Stuffed chicken wings
   Scrape chicken wings' skin with a knife until it's smooth. "Rinse neatly." Remove the last joint. Hold the wing upright on a firm surface. Using a small knife, scrape the meat away from the bone starting at the top. Turn the skin and meat inside out as you work. Avoid cutting through the skin. At the joint, remove the upper bone. Use the knife to break up the top of the second bone. Scrape and peel the meat back as before. Rinse it thoroughly.
   Stuff it with stuffing*, squeezing it into the cavity until the wing is full and hard, but not so full that you can't smooth the meat shut.
   Set the broiler rack at the second position from the top. Turn the oven to broil at 350 degrees. Put the wings on the broiler pan and cook them until done, turning often so the wings are evenly brown. Serve with cooked rice and hot sauce**.

*Stuffing
   Soak some vermicelli until it's soft. Chop the strips into two or three segments. Put them in a bowl. Add finely chopped cooked pork, about half as much as the vermicelli. Chop and add cilantro and green onion. Add salt, pepper if you want, and a little MSG. Stir and taste.
   (You may also use this to fill spring roll sheets to make egg rolls; fry them in oil.)

**Hot Sauce
   Chop some red and green hot peppers finely. Add a little salt, MSG, lime juice, water, and fish sauce (any kind). Add chopped cilantro and green onions if you like. It should taste salty and sweet.

In case I hadn't already grasped the care lavished on cooking, this production made it clear. Grandmother Kao is not unusual in her devotion. I have yet to meet a Hmong woman who can't cook delicious meals, even from modest ingredients, in the tradition of all good cooks. Some everyday dishes are simple, however, like sliced beef and ginger fried together in oil, baby pumpkin leaves lightly fried, or young squash leaves boiled with a little lemon grass. Of course, there were no cookbooks.

Hmong like to live near a Chinese or Vietnamese community because familiar items are available there. A Laotian store in South Sacramento, next door to a Hmong community center, offers a full array of fruits and vegetables, a freezer filled with fish, and dry goods such as Chinese aluminum cooking pots. Floor, shelves, and ceiling are dense with goods, including Asian clothing and fragrant soap in a green wrapper with a colorful parrot pictured on it. A Vietnamese market in Southern California popular with Hmong offers a vast array of fresh and live fish.

Hmong do love fish. Along with barbecued chicken and pork served at New Year's festivities, partygoers feast on sweet grilled fish. And at a restaurant dinner that Chamy, her brother, Nom Npis, and I enjoyed in Laos, Nom Npis ordered ten dishes for four of us. Every dish was fish or seafood, from sea turtle soup to grilled fish of unknown identity. Not a scrap of food remained for the waiter to carry away.

I got a fresh view of eating customs when my interpreter in Grandmother Kao's kitchen came with his family to eat at my home. At the dinner table, I overheard him and his wife teaching the children how to use table knives. Knives aren't used for eating at a Hmong table. In response to my questions about table customs, my student friend, normally a serious man, pointed out that the place of honor at an American table — the "head" — is considered the "end" to Hmong and pointed to his backside. We laughed. The Hmong place of honor is midway down the side, he said. From there you can reach all the food. And talk with all the people.

Afterwards in the kitchen, I also got a lesson in home remedies. The student's wife picked up a silver tablespoon, the size the Hmong use for eating. You can use a spoon like this to cure sinus pain, she said. Her high school-age sister nodded in agreement. My Western skepticism was on alert. Boil an egg and take out the yolk, I was told. Put the spoon — the bowl of it, I understood — inside the egg and wrap egg and spoon in black cotton cloth. It must be cotton. Rub the cloth-wrapped arrangement over your sinuses. "It will take away any sickness," the wife said.

By lucky accident that evening, and by my determination to overfeed these guests as they have overfed me, lots of food remained. So when the family immediately went for their coats to leave after dinner — standard Hmong timing, although I didn't know that and felt hurt — I pressed leftovers on them. Yes, they'd love to take some along. Someone was sure to get hungry. Later I learned that it is traditional etiquette to send guests away with food — a logical practice where a traveler would have a long walk back to the home village.

Tou Ger Xiong, the Hmong performer, named food as the third most important distinguishing characteristic of the Hmong, after language and dress. There are at least two levels of eating for the Hmong, as there are everywhere. The first is the daily, family eating that I experienced in a number of homes. The second is feasting.

One late-summer morning, under the misunderstanding that we were invited to a baby-naming ceremony for the first son of a young friend of mine, Mai Xia Cha, my husband, Dave, and I took a baby gift when we headed south two hours to San Diego. (Her name is pronounced "my see-ah chah.") We didn't need to take the gift. Mai Xia's explanation had been unclear only because I didn't know enough. This was in fact the day that Mai Xia's *husband*, Zhen Fang, would receive his adult name from *her* father. Should I have taken a gift for Zhen instead? No to that one, too.

At least we had correctly guessed that there would be food. But I couldn't drive out of my head the image of a modest baby shower luncheon. Entering the small living room of Mai Xia and Zhen's apartment, we beheld a whole roast pig, prepared by a local Chinese restaurant, reposing in majesty on a draped table in the center of the room. It was politely oriented face-front toward the door and featured a brilliant pink carnation between its roasted ears. On either side of the pig were a pair of plates holding two boiled chickens, with head and feet. This was prepared by the woman of the house. At the head of each chicken rested a cereal bowl filled with rice grains in which had been planted boiled eggs and a lighted candle — reminiscent of the shaman's ceremony. Another pair of plates held juice-size glasses filled to brimming with beer, Budweiser, to guess from the additional cans lined up around the table. A big bottle of Mountain Dew sat at the corner, which some of us drank in plastic cups. Near either end of the table stood platters mounded with peaches, bananas, green pears, and oranges. After a string-tying ceremony that symbolically bound the family together and after the ceremonial drinking of beer, women from the family heaped these fruits and eggs onto individual plates for the honored guests, including Dave and me.

While ten of us, plus babies, sat on folding chairs and ate away at our appetizers, a sister-in-law of Mai Xia's, protected by a black plastic garbage bag fastened sarong-style around her body, went after the pig's hindquarters with the big Hmong knife. I only nibbled at my fruit, reserving space for what I knew was piling up outside on tables in the side yard. There, another of Zhen's sisters, the one who organized the feast, was playing traffic cop for the crowd-sized foil pans arriving with egg rolls, seasoned meats, vegetable-and-meat mixtures, and other dishes I could not identify. There were also packaged salad greens and bottled dressing from the supermarket. And rice. And Mountain Dew. Eat! Eat!

Out front were fifty additional guests, mainly women and children sitting on blankets on the small lawn. This group apparently never went inside and paid no heed when Zhen ceremoniously received his additional name from his father-in-law—becoming Chun Zhen Fang. A majority of the guests were children, infants to teenagers. As I had come to expect, I heard little crying or complaining from them.

Dave and I ate to satiety. It is easy food to like, within the tastes of most Americans. Despite my hearty enjoyment of Hmong food, however, I have noticed that after every meal, I crave something chocolate. A retreat to the familiar.

Several years after this feast I had a curious experience. On the surface it did not relate to food or farming, but now I believe it did. Again, it was an event to which Cho Lee had invited me.

Cho called me one March afternoon. There would be an Easter picnic Saturday morning in a park next to her children's school. "Long [her husband] want me to call you to come," Cho said in her good, honest voice. "Can you come?" I could come. This time, I managed to be at the park just as the Hmong were arriving, about 9:30 in the morning. The sky was threatening. Soon Cho appeared in her car and I helped her set up the barbecue for chicken and hot dogs. Her boys swooped past, sweating, laughing, and red-faced, and I was given hugs by them, some perfunctory, some genuine. Cho's sweet daughter, Zong, her oldest child, smiled photogenically and giggled off with her cousin–best friend. Cho encouraged me to go visit the men gathered around the volleyball court where Hmong manhood was on display, and there I listened to an older man's tale of his astonishing recovery from kidney surgery.

Then it was time for the Easter egg hunt, to take place across the small parking lot from the picnicking and volleyball. Some forty or fifty children waited in developing rain for the signal to start the hunt. Two teenage girls in charge told the wiggling bunch that a few of the eggs had been marked for special prizes.

Parka hood pulled over my head against the rain, I held my breath. I had seen Easter egg hunts before, and I was not looking forward to the display of greed. Tweeeet went the whistle and off the kids ran, younger ones first. In a few minutes they were back, plastic sacks of eggs bouncing in their hands. Now, I thought, the whining, the quarreling will begin. It didn't happen. Still, I thought there might be some groaning when the winners of prizes were announced. A small dump truck went to a boy in a Donald Duck T-shirt, and Zong won a Barbie box of chocolates. I heard no groans, no tears of frustration, no parents complaining. The parents weren't even around. They had left the event in the hands of the two older girls and remained at distant picnic tables, chatting under umbrellas.

Then I witnessed something I have rarely seen. Kids who had somehow missed the bounty saw fistfuls of candy-filled eggs dumped into their bags by other kids. And all went off to show their treasures to parents and then went back to playing. Later, at Cho's house, I chatted with her four children about their take. Zong said she thought at first the Barbie box contained some doll accessory. Feng showed me his bag full, and I asked which was his favorite candy. "The kisses," he said. Then he fished through and picked most of them out. And gave them to me.

The whole thing made a mighty impression on me. Why can't we and our children have that spirit of sharing? I railed to myself. Since that day, I've turned the images over and over in my mind. Eventually I began to see that individual open-handedness is a natural accompaniment to an economy that lives or dies based on people's ability to share. Harmony is the sine qua non of survival in a world of subsistence, just as individual autonomy is what drives success in our society. The sharing of those Easter treats embodies for me the communitarian nature of Hmong society, but it also stands as a challenge to me to be less possessive of what I call mine.

New Year in the old country marks the end of one agricultural year and the start of the next. It's a treasured time. During that season, "the flowers are blooming all over, red, white, yellow, everywhere on the mountains," Vang wrote.

Hmong New Year captures the essence of a culture that survives on relationships. It is family reunion, county fair, cruising Main, and senior prom rolled into one. In Laos, people travel from one village to the next, young unmarried men to search for likely young women and older people to see scattered family and catch up on each others' news. In America, Hmong New Year's celebrations are assigned different dates in different cities so that people can get to more than one.

But Hmong New Year also has a spiritual dimension. On New Year's eve the head of the house calls the spirits of the family, animals, and crops back to the house. A chant goes:

> Toil so that silver fills the purse
> Farm so that crops fill the storehouse
> Raise children to fill the house
> Raise animals to fill the stable

Have new food, with others able to eat
Have new water, with others able to drink
Have food, have drink, have plenty of fine clothes to wear,
Don't be troubled, don't worry, don't envy others in the village
    or the country. [4]

5

Five Thousand Years, Ten Thousand Miles: The Hmong

Generally peaceable but with a wild, proud spirit
of independence ...
— Yang Dao, Ph.D.[1]

Origins

Here is a legend about the beginnings of the Hmong, the kind of story
told when families gather or when a father amuses his children before dinner. It has the rhythm of a story told aloud.[2]

The brother and sister Poj Cuas Ob Nus Muag are the ancestors of all
Hmong. [The name is pronounced "paw tyoo-ah aw noo moo-ah," one
name for the pair, as if it were Adam-and-Eve.]

One day God's flying horse told Poj Cuas Ob Nus Muag to open
God's stone gate so he could fly them to the earth. So they opened the
stone gate and the horse flew the brother and sister down to earth.
They were going to visit another couple.

The brother and sister landed at a place close to the desert where
hardly anything would grow. Now, says Hmong tradition, it is the
Middle East. God's flying horse left them there and said that he would
return to pick them up. But the horse did not return and they could
not find the couple they sought.

The brother and sister traveled to another place, where it snows all year and is very cold. They could not live there. So they traveled to a third place, where it is dark for six months and daylight for six months. They could not live there either, so finally they traveled to Muam Nkaug Lig Teb, which means Mongolia today.

Then one day they called to God. God came, and they told him how they came to be on earth — that God's horse had left them there. When God saw that the couple they wanted to visit had not had any babies as they were commanded, God asked the brother and sister to stay on earth and produce human beings. They protested, but finally agreed.

Then they asked God how they might eventually return to Home Heaven. God told them that he would grow bamboo on earth. When they did not want to live on earth anymore, they could use the bamboo to guide them back.

So today when Hmong die, a piece of bamboo will be the guide to take them back to where they were born. Then it will guide them back to Mongolia, then to the place where it is dark for six months, then to the place where it snows all year, and finally to the desert place, where God will send his horse to carry them home.

Look behind the mythic elements in this and you get a story that says something important to a much-traveled people. In the pre-historic period addressed by the legend, the founding couple travel to escape intolerable conditions— drought, cold, dark. After entering written history about five thousand years ago, the Hmong likewise were forced to move on, but this time, according to the record, in order to escape an engulfing people. The tale enshrines their wanderings.

Go far enough back and we're all descended from travelers— the humans who left Africa and over millennia covered the globe. To be sure many stayed put, as they do now. But as a people the Hmong, like Americans and unlike other nations, see migration as part of their identity. The urge is to give dignity to what was perhaps experienced as an undesired homelessness.

Who knows where the Hmong originated or, perhaps a better question, when they began to think of themselves as a people. Placing their origin in northern China because that is where they first appear in the records may cheat them of an accurate memory of ancient migration. Keith Quincy, a professor and author of *Hmong: History of a People*, writes that Hmong may well have originated on the Iranian plateau — which the Silk Road later crossed on its east-west journey — or in Southern Russia, from which many are known to have migrated into Siberia.[3]

If we understand that peoples do not begin as isolated, self-aware units moving intact through time and space, there is room to look seriously at the travels of Poj Cuas Ob Nus Muag.

Archaeology offers options. By maybe 20,000 years ago, modern human beings, with clothing and warm houses, made it from northern Africa, their presumed origin, to Siberia. Families and small bands of these people walking eastward may have supplanted archaic homo sapiens already there, simply because they were cleverer at devising ways to stay alive.

A look at a relief map suggests routes eastward. Travelers would reasonably avoid mountain ranges, making their way along the dry, grassy corridor that tied Africa to the Far East. Rather than setting out for a far-off destination, people wandered in a generally promising direction, a few miles per day or maybe per generation. Somebody — maybe with low tolerance for life in one place — might move on when the area got too crowded. Maybe the land or game was playing out, or the climate had taken an unfriendly turn. Maybe there was a last-straw fight.

Perhaps the proto–Hmong were among this initial drift. Or maybe they were part of the large migrations of predominantly Caucasian herders from Eastern Europe and the Iranian Plateau that took the same broad route toward Mongolia and Siberia much later, around 5000 B.C. By 4500 B.C., people are known to have settled in spots all the way from the present state of Romania eastward to the area north of the Gobi desert, farming and raising animals. Today, China is home to millions of people such as Tajiks, Uighurs, Kazakhs, Hui, Uzbeks and others— peoples whose countries form stepping stones eastward in an arc from Iran to China and could be classified physically as Caucasoid. Such tribes of Indo-European origin have been placed near the Upper Yellow River by around 2000–1700 B.C.

As to the Hmong's sojourn in Siberia, a good case is made based on the similarity between Hmong shamanism and that in Siberia, where the practice apparently originated. That link leads some scholars to place the Hmong there for more than a thousand years and lends credence to the reference to the cold and dark in the legend.

Siberia was not the end of the road for humans, however. People in the steppes continued their ancestors' migration, this time south toward China, through Mongolia. Hmong themselves believe that they lived in Mongolia before coming to China, mentioning the similarity of the word Hmong to the first syllable of Mongolia. A scholar writing about China's minorities, on the other hand, pinpoints a tribe called Meng-wu as the source of the name Mongolia.

It's worth noting that the Hmong language, a member of the Miao-

Yao family, is increasingly considered unrelated to any other language group. ("Yao" is the Chinese name for the Mien people, who share cultural traits, a history of migration and, now in America, neighborhoods with the Hmong.) This linguistic distinctiveness of the Hmong suggests a large and sufficiently successful people over a long enough period of time to resist being swallowed by others. Today, people who speak Miao-Yao, of which Hmong are the majority, constitute the fifth largest minority of fifty-five ethnic groups in China. Maybe thousands of years as a people with a unique language have contributed to the durable sense of identity they show in the United States today.

In China

Hmong legends say that it was to the region where the Yellow River flows silt-laden from the mountains that they drifted. This event may mark the beginning of their troubles. Other people were already settled there who had a crucial head start by virtue of having already stumbled upon agriculture.

These people had been foragers along the Yellow River when they turned their habit of choosing the best of the big grains into active cultivation, on soil as rich as that of the Fertile Crescent at roughly the same time, from 8000–3500 B.C. Similarly, they began to manage those animals adaptable to human company — pigs and dogs. They shaped clay pots, wove fabrics, and polished the stone tools they chipped out.

The people who made the shift to settled agriculture are called Yangshao, after an excavation site. They painted their pottery red and added markings that might be an early stage of Chinese characters. In the village of Banpo, inhabited from about 4500 B.C., the Yangshao people were growing millet.

At first, the Yangshao must have been clustered only in bands. Later, bands would have crystallized into different tribes with varying degrees of power and differing cultural attributes. People built villages and then, by 1800 or 1700 B.C., towns with fortifications. Within those walls, people slowly divided into social classes and distinct occupations. This could not have happened without well-developed agriculture, which provides enough food for a few people to turn their attention to non-essentials.

Into this scene the Hmong came, according to ancient records, maybe before 3000 B.C., but at least by 1200 B.C. The Hmong also built villages and fortified towns and at first continued the herding they had practiced on the Siberian steppe. But they were apparently open to new ideas, as they are now: From the Yangshao, they learned slash-and-burn farming, raising pigs, and building thatched houses with an indoor fireplace, the lifestyle Chamy's family pursues today. Archaeological sites suggest that the Yangshao and the Hmong were close neighbors. Site names suggestive of the Miao (Hmong)—such as Miaodigou and Miaoqiancun—are located within fifty to seventy-five miles of the Yangshao site.

Nicholas Tapp, writing in *Sovereignty and Rebellion*, suggests that it was here in China that the Hmong developed into a self-identifying people. Because they got on board the powerful agriculture train later than the Yangshao, they were probably dominated by them. Being squeezed by the Yangshao may have been enough to generate a sharpened self-awareness. Their late start with agriculture also proved to be a disadvantage they ultimately couldn't fully overcome, as has been true historically of peoples elsewhere. Without food surpluses, no writing could develop. Without writing, large groups of people couldn't be organized effectively, and useful knowledge gleaned from other times and places was not available to them. They could not record their own history—always a handicap. People who had these advantages ahead of others inevitably dominated.

Given that the Yangshao had the head start, the Hmong ultimately couldn't hold onto their land and had to bend or leave. A pattern was established: Leaving meant they lost the advantages and comforts they had acquired while settled. But for whatever reasons of history, beliefs, or character, they preferred independence to melting into another's culture. They dreamed of life on their terms, even at the price of a more abundant life. Portable nationhood, repeatedly challenged and modified, became part of who they were.

Eventually, the Hmong began to appear in Chinese writings. The references were not complimentary. Early documents use the term "Sanmiao" to describe a trouble-making people. "San" means three, and "miao," the term by which Hmong are still known in China today, means sons of the soil, savages, or barbarians. One of the Sanmiao's sins was pestering the gods with too much attention—the traditional Chinese view of animism. In the earliest record, the Sanmiao occupied northwestern China, perhaps west of the Yangshao people. Had they spread there naturally? Were they pushed? Other sources locate them also in Hunan, where Hmong still live today, well to the southeast of the Yellow River near another river, the Yangtze.

Some scholars believe the Sanmiao are not the same as the Miao (Hmong). I see no reason to exclude them from the group the Chinese called "barbarians," those whom they despised for lacking the common sense to become Chinese.

More Stories about the Hmong

Confucius seems to have had something to say about the Miao. According to the scholarly K.C. Wu, Confucius, who lived about 551–479 B.C., tried to regularize a history of China begun two thousand years earlier.[4] He must have researched texts produced by the dynasty called the Shang, which held power more than a thousand years before Confucius. These old texts mention the names of tribes and tribal confederations against whom the Chinese fought. It is doubtful just how much a time-traveler would find to verify the following episode recounted by Confucius. The story tells about the Yellow Emperor, called the Father of the Chinese Nation, who, tradition has it, reigned for one hundred years (2698–2599 B.C.). Obviously he couldn't have done that. Scholars mostly agree that the Yellow Emperor is mythical and that only later was there even a group who called themselves Chinese.

Here is Wu's story, which tells of the trouble some early Hmong caused. Ancient China was in a state of "frightful chaos," Wu writes. The leader of one strong family had claimed power over people north of the Yellow River but in fact were not in control. Some of these northern tribes, quarreling among themselves even though linked by marriage, began to increase in strength. Then a figure of obscure lineage from south of the Yangtze — "considered at that time to be the habitat of barbarians, with a culture inferior to that of the north," Wu writes — threatened to plunder and conquer with the help of metal weapons. In between the strong families wanting to dominate in the north and the barbarians to the south stood the man who would become the Yellow Emperor.

He chose first to face off against the northerners. The Yellow Emperor won. Then, with the defeated princes joining him, he turned to meet the oncoming "rapacious animist barbarians." The battle was fought on a plain, and the barbarian leader, called Ciyou, was captured and put to death. Thus, Wu recounts, the Yellow Emperor "unified China, or a very large part of it, by military force."

Quincy, in *Hmong: History of a People*, also uses legends to discuss the creation of China, but with pointed differences.[5] He identifies the barbarians clearly as Hmong and states that they were sufficiently powerful to win positions in government. One of those was a nobleman, Tche-you — a different rendering of Ciyou — who eventually grew angry at the emperor's mistreatment of the Hmong. Tche-you pulled together the Hmong tribes and routed the emperor's troops near modern Beijing. The successful Hmong tribal leaders began to talk about founding an independent state, but the Yellow Emperor defeated them with heavy losses on both sides and forced the Hmong into feudal peasantry. The particular pattern in which they were settled featured a grid of eight farms with a well in the center, a distinctive arrangement that places the events some time between 1600 and 800 B.C., not 2700–2600 B.C. as the legend would have it.

We may imagine that more than a few Hmong, especially those who had been close to the trouble-making Tche-you, chose to flee rather than submit to a feudal system. In so doing they must have suffered trauma and death not so different from the fleeing Hmong in our time. By around 1122 B.C., Hmong were to be found scattered in an arc beyond the original heartland, north and west toward the mountains and east along the Yellow River.[6]

Despite uncertainties clouding the picture of pre-history and early history, it is safe to say that, over some stretch of time, the ancestral Chinese grew stronger as they fought it out with "uncivilized" people such as the Hmong, who were increasingly pushed to the perimeters of the empire. Whatever the details of the antagonism, Hmong Americans savor the thought of having been so powerful a people as to hinder the formation of the Chinese empire. It was also their first big military defeat, spurring a continuation of the migrations already so much a part of their history.

The World Around the Hmong: Shang, Zhou and Han Dynasties

Out of the Yangshao's increasingly settled and powerful civilization grew the Shang dynasty, the first historically verifiable dynasty in China. The traditional dates of the Shang are 1766–1122 B.C. The Chinese landscape now included cities with thousands or tens of thousands of inhabitants, compared to the old farming settlements with populations in the hundreds.

The Sanmiao/Hmong, eventually spreading south and occupying a vast area along the Yangtze River, irritated the Shang leadership. Viewing it from the other side, one might say that the Shang became insupportably arrogant and grasping. According to Wu, the Shang co-emperor Shun couldn't get the tribes to agree to his flood control plans, so he forced them to move to the mountainous Gansu Province more than a thousand miles to the northwest. Historically reliable records show that many Hmong/Sanmiao did go. But after the floods, those who had stayed increased in number and again began to insist on being left alone. Wu reports that after military force had failed to bring them around, Shun stepped in and, by means of diplomacy, persuaded the Sanmiao to submit. Wu observes, however, that the threat of force probably strengthened the emperor's hand.

It's during this time, not that of the legendary Yellow Emperor, that the Hmong were forced to settle.

It was not peaceful settlement. Quincy says that Shang waged "more or less ... continuous war with their tribal neighbors, including the Hmong."[7] Later the area would become the state of Chu, covering a swath in the middle of China south of the Yangtze. The state, presumably still containing its Sanmiao, grew to be one of the most powerful of its time.

The Chou Dynasty

The idea of "China" seems to have developed around 1050 B.C. when the Shang dynasty was conquered by a semi-nomadic people from the west, the Chou — not to be confused with the Sanmiao-rich Chu state. The Chou spoke a different language from the Shang and were not Sinitic, that is, culturally Chinese. Although the Chinese trace their heritage through these two dynasties, it's not certain that the ancestors of either the Shang or the Chou spoke Chinese. Even more injurious to the Chinese desire for cultural purity, minority languages such as Hmong may well have influenced spoken Chinese.

The Chinese by this time were producing beautiful bronzes inlaid with silver, coins symbolizing spades and knives, and rich tombs for its kings and nobles. They also had iron farming tools, making it easier to grow food, and double-edged bronze swords, which made killing people easier.

Over the long span of time from 1122–221 B.C., the Chou dynasty's reach shrank from some 1,773 states to only thirteen. During the final stage, three were left. The largest of these was the state of Chu mentioned above, extending perhaps four hundred miles south from the Yellow River. Chu had cobbled together more than forty other states in the valley of the Yangtze River, which arises in the southern mountains before turning eastward to the sea in a channel nearly parallel to that of the Yellow. Tombs of the Chu wealthy have yielded musical instruments, elaborate wooden figurines, and silk paintings. Scholar Leo J. Moser reports that the population of Chu was "probably archaic Hmong (Miao), Yao, or Tai in background, perhaps some of all."[8] Although these people were regarded as inferior, the Sinitic peoples moving in didn't mind adopting from the Tai the growing of rice, which got its start in the south.

Some believe that Laozi, founder of Taoism, was from Chu. He may have been Hmong or Tai, these last the ancestors of present-day Thai and Lao. Laozi is generally considered to have been the teacher of Confucius. Once thought to have been a critique of Confucianism's rules for regulating human society, Taoism, with its focus on the way of nature, is now seen as complementary.[9] Nicholas Tapp notes a strong influence of Taoism on Hmong culture. The Hmong practice of shamanism finds its parallel in the trance still connected to folk Taoism today.

An amusing document called Lore of Chu paints a distinctly Chinese picture of the exotic state of Chu. Author Wu describes Chu as a kingdom that persisted for nine centuries (12th to 3rd century B.C.), but, because it was located near the "uncivilized" south, in modern Hubei, Hunan, and Jiangxi provinces, northern Chinese lumped it together with its neighbors and labeled the whole lot barbarians.[10] The Lore of Chu, which Wu translates, explains the development of relations since earliest, mythic times between gods and humans and the importance of not "bothering [the gods] with ceaseless entreaties." Since the Sanmiao recklessly mingled the spiritual with the mundane, the emperor sent in some good Chinese, along with troops, to "take charge again." Repeated subjugation and forced conversion to their more sensible religion was necessary, the Chinese discovered, since the tribes were disinclined to abandon their traditions.

A second of the three states, that of Yue, also had a number of people who spoke Miao-Yao, living in the mountains. This state was never conquered by the Han dynasty. Chu, however, was.

Moser describes the process by which Hmong and other tribespeople would be transformed into Chinese: Educate their elites using Chinese characters, immerse them in Chinese culture and rituals, and build alliances with them through marriage. Those people who went along were thereafter regarded as Chinese (Han), without respect to their racial or ethnic origins. Thus great numbers of ethnic minorities are now indistinguishable within the greater population.[11]

But always there was a significant remnant that escaped southward, losing goods and advantages but carrying the old identity with them. Although this remnant assimilated some foreign people and accepted some foreign ways, they held vigorously to the notion that they were *not Chinese*. In the third century A.D., these Tai, Miao, Yao, and others may have constituted a majority in the huge, warm southeastern third of China.

The Chou dynasty in the north gradually fell back before the onslaught of a non–Chinese, well-organized state called Qin. Later, the tomb of the first Qin emperor revealed the astonishing mustering of more than seven thousand life-size terra cotta soldiers. Before his death, this emperor sought to expand his realm southward by sending military expeditions into Guangxi and Guangdong provinces, followed by Chinese settlers. Always losing out in such projects were people such as the Hmong, who had to choose, as their ancestors had, between fighting, yielding, or looking for a better place.

Interestingly, two poor farmers—ethnic group not mentioned—from this muscular state of Chu gathered others angry about heavy taxation, which the emperor required for his luxuries, and rebelled. They had considerable success. Other rebellions followed, and the house of Qin collapsed after only fifteen years. One of the rebel leaders became the founder of the Han dynasty, the name by which today's Chinese still identify themselves.

During the Han period, flooding of the Yellow River, taxes, and the expanding grasp of landlords drove a significant portion of the northern Chinese population southward. These were accompanied by governmental policies designed to draw tribal leaders into the imperial structure, but no doubt severely squeezed the Hmong and others.

Ultimately the Han dynasty collapsed, at least in part due to the popularity of Taoist principles among hard-pressed peasants, which led to repeated and extremely bloody rebellions. These rebellions, according to Chinese historian Yih-Fu, included a Hmong outbreak in southern Hunan.[12] A contemptuous Chinese general sailed up the Yangtze ready to obliterate the Hmong, but instead of an easy conquest he and his entire force vanished. The replacement general and twenty thousand fresh troops were cornered by the Hmong in a gorge and, again, all died. The imperial response to this second embarrassment was three years of laying waste undefended Hmong villages and towns, killing the civilian inhabitants, and torching homes, another event paralleled in twentieth-century Laos. No doubt many fled.

Despite the Chinese certainty that they had devastated the rebellious tribe, the Hmong slipped back into control of much of Hunan, Guizhou, and Hubei provinces during the subsequent century, the second century A.D. They were joined by Hmong pushed out of Sichuan in the southwest by Tibetan nomads. Some drifted back into Henan, thus occupying or re-occupying much of central China around the Yangtze.

After the defeat of the Han, no single dynasty ruled the whole of China for more than three hundred years. Drought and disorder reigned. During this time, it is entirely possible that the Hmong experienced some kind of unified culture that they call a kingdom and others consider a reassuring fiction.

The Kingdom

Quincy describes a Hmong kingdom that covered a chunk of central and southern China from just below the Yellow River in Henan Province south through the middle of Hubei and Hunan provinces and into northern Guangxi, the province that abuts Vietnam. It occupied much the same territory as the old state of Chu.[13]

The term kingdom may be misleading to Westerners accustomed to European models. In the Hmong case, although the monarchy was supposedly hereditary, a king was not predetermined by order of birth but selected from among the deceased king's sons, who might be many. He was chosen by all "men capable of bearing arms." Further, most of the real power was exercised at the district and local levels, where leaders were chosen as Hmong villages choose them now: election based on a man's leadership abilities and only for as long as he remained the best. Given that the term "king" can be quite loose — the way we call Elvis Presley The King and as some Hmong now speak of their military hero Gen. Vang Pao as "like a king" — I suspect that the Hmong kingdom was not imaginary. The kingdom, which flourished roughly from A.D. 400 to 900 and then slowly disintegrated, may represent a time of relative prosperity when Hmong occupied territory that offered good travel and therefore a lively sense of themselves as a people. In this case, the king would have been a figurehead, symbolic of a flourishing sense of being Hmong.

Quincy makes the argument that the fiercely independent Hmong would never agree to hierarchical authority and therefore could not have had a king. It's known, however, that as populations increase, more complex organization and judicial structures become necessary to regulate interactions between strangers. Should a society fragment and revert to smaller entities, as happened to the Hmong, within which people again know each other, egalitarianism and localized control once more become the norm.

This isn't to say, however, that Hmong have not embellished the notion of a kingdom; it strengthens the spirit of a people with a long history of being overpowered. Yet discoveries to come may reveal that their stories are more factual than mythical.

During the period of the Hmong kingdom, Hmong used their military skills as leverage among Chinese rivals to secure their interests, even to attaining high positions in imperial courts.

Beginning with the Tang dynasty in the seventh century A.D., after several hundred years of the Hmong kingdom, Chinese administrators moved into Hmong territory. They sought to win over rebel leaders and, oh so gradually, to turn tribal people into good Chinese. Agriculture was thriving, making Southern China a prize possession, and in the tenth century the emperor sent in new military forces. In time, despite a legendary daughter of the Hmong king with magical powers, the king and his generals fell to the drive of the Sung dynasty. The Sung offered rebels the choice of surrendering and joining the imperial army or being wiped out.

A Sung document of the twelfth century, at a time when administrators were allowing some self-government for tribal peoples, describes the problem Hmong and other non–Chinese constituted. No hint is found that these peoples might have cause to be refractory. They are aggressive, says the document, and quick to anger. "Their customs are uncivilized and strange.... They use shoes made of leather and run up and down the mountains as if flying." Still, the writer registered grudging admiration for their strength, agility, and tenacity. A later policy document, of the Ming, on how to govern non–Chinese "barbarians" likens them to wild deer. Expecting Chinese magistrates to govern them "would be like herding deer into the main hall of a house and attempting to tame them." On the other hand, allowing the tribal chiefs to continue to govern as before would mean losing any semblance of proper control, "like releasing deer into the wilderness...." The solution was to divide the tribal holdings by administrative "fences," a policy the document likens to castrating a boar.[14]

Given the choice of yielding or being crushed, most Hmong left for Guizhou, Sichuan, and Yunnan provinces to the west, where they once again found empty land in the mountains and a measure of peace. Without the unifying force of a kingdom, the Hmong reverted to the clan-dominated tribal structure, such as now characterizes Hmong culture. Perhaps wishing to recapture past glory, and encouraged by the Chinese with their divide-and-conquer policy, clans developed a number of small kingdoms headed by "little kings" or kiatongs.

Toward the end of the Hmong kingdom, China contained more than one hundred million people, with the majority of them now located in the Yangtze River valley or south. Thus the pressure on Hmong and other non–Han peoples continually increased.

Around A.D.1275, Khubilai Khan was advancing southward, first destroying an independent state that had grown up in what is now Yunnan Province and then defeating the Sung dynasty, centered in the south. For the dynasty they thus founded, these Mongols gave themselves the Chinese-style name Yuan. During this decade Marco Polo made his trip to China, along with Christian missionaries, artisans, and merchants.

But Khublai Khan's descendants overextended themselves, and the dynasty collapsed, their soldiers defeated in 1368 by a peasant army led by a Buddhist monk-soldier. The successful warrior became the first emperor of the Ming dynasty, which was to last nearly three hundred years. The Ming sought tighter control of southwest China in order to push a trade route through Burma into Southeast Asia. The path took them through the heart of Hmong country, in Guizhou and Yunnan provinces. The Lolo ethnic group appointed to administer the area became tyranni- cal, especially toward the Hmong. In addition, during the sixteenth cen- tury, Chinese were encouraged to settle there and so came into conflict with Hmong and others living there. The Hmong retaliated frequently. Their fighters became bolder and more skilled with each confrontation. The Chinese sent in troops to crush them and established some two thousand garrisons. More than forty thousand Hmong were captured or killed.

Within fifty years, the Hmong were again fighting for their independ- ence, sometimes yearly. Guizhou Hmong also marauded into Hunan Province in search of better land. So serious were Hmong incursions that around 1500 the Ming built a ten-foot-high Hmong Wall, anchored by military outposts along its hundred-mile length. Like a modern chain- link border fence, it was constructed to stop Hmong migration. Today, descendants of those Hmong, and of the Han military who over time married Hmong, have been put to work restoring sections of the wall to attract tourism. To Hmong living there now, the wall is still a symbol of oppression.[15]

The Hmong were furious fighters. Since Shang times in the eighteenth to twelfth centuries B.C., their abilities had been sharpened by the need to defend what they desperately considered theirs. Guizhou Hmong, those against whom the Ming built the wall, dressed themselves in armor made of buffalo hide, copper, and iron mail. They carried a shield in one hand, a spear in the other, and a knife in the teeth. Crossbows and poisoned arrows rounded out the arsenal. In the late 1600s, a Chinese factional gen- eral multiplied the power of the Hmong juggernaut immeasurably when he left behind in a Hmong village some flintlock rifles, gunpowder, and cannons. Another Chinese general, whom the Hmong had sheltered, showed the Hmong how to manufacture their own flintlocks, or blunder- busses, an item used in colonial America around the same time. Hmong made them by the thousands. This same flintlock vastly improved their odds against Chinese military — though never quite enough — and was used by Hmong in Southeast Asia until recently.

At the same time, Hmong began breeding mountain ponies for war. These animals, able to race up and down mountainsides, were regarded by the Chinese as the best horses in the empire.

Refugees

The Manchu Dynasty, coming to power in 1643–44, expanded oppression of the Hmong. Stories of this period centuries in the past are still recounted by Hmong families in America, as I learned by listening to the widow of a Hmong military officer in Sacramento. That immediacy transforms one's experience of history. The horrendous stories, powerful enough on the page, are family history to those sitting before you, inheritors of millennia of frustrated nationhood.

Treatment by the Manchu was bound to engrave itself on the memory of the Hmong. By around 1700, many Hmong in Guizhou had settled in permanent villages, the wealthiest of them building elevated homes of sawed lumber, broad outside stairways, and decorative tile roofs. Soon, Manchu laws required the payment of heavy taxes in copper and lead, which had to be mined. Borrowing money was a dangerous alternative, since lenders pegged interest rates at five percent a month. Finally, Hmong farms were seized outright. Self-administration was withdrawn from the small Hmong kingdoms, and those Hmong who resisted were repeatedly and savagely crushed. Alfred W. McCoy writes: "When this policy [to abolish the Hmong kingdoms] met with resistance, the Manchus began to exterminate these troublesome tribes and to repopulate their lands with the more pliable ethnic Chinese. After a two hundred-year extermination campaign culminated in a series of bloody massacres in the mid nineteenth century, thousands of [Hmong] tribesmen fled southward toward Indochina."[16]

Tens of thousands of them were killed in battle, and thousands of women, children, and elders were executed. Many Hmong — termed "raw" or unsubdued — fled to the mountains. Others, perhaps because of the large size of their families, chose to hunker down and became tenants or servants of the Chinese. Still others fled south, including the man who was the forebear of my friend Ly Vong Lynaolu in Sacramento.

Several English-language documents provide glimpses of Hmong in China during this period. A Mr. Baber of the British Consular Service, writing some time before 1911, says of the Hmong that they are "a marvelous people, who have maintained a kind of empire of their own inside the Chinese Empire since the days of Yao and Shuen [emperors of the mythic Xia dynasty before 1750 B.C.], holding their own against the Chinese." In the 1880s T.L. Bullock said, "The Miao-tsz are wild, hardy mountaineers, who spend their time in hunting and wood-cutting, while their women cultivate the plots of land which supply them with grain. Their villages, which are strongly fortified, are perched on the most precipitous cliffs, surrounded by wood, and approached only by steep, and narrow paths."[17] They are also called peaceable and industrious, but they would not settle for being Chinese.

Out of China

The Hmong didn't want to leave China. Sorrow at the loss of their homeland remains with them today. They see themselves as a diaspora. Their sorrow is memorialized in a figure of speech meaning "very unhappy." It comes from a story of treachery. The Hmong phrase is *chim laj chim xeeb* (chee-la-chee-seng). *Chim* means unhappy, and *laj-xeeb*, divided into its two components for the rhythm of the phrase, is a small martial arts weapon. As the story goes, Chinese soldiers came to a Hmong village. They got to the Hmong guard, who was successfully bribed, tricked, or coerced — it doesn't matter which since all are humiliating — into killing the village chief. His weapon was a *laj-xeeb* hidden in his sleeve. The village was lost, and the people fled. The story appears in songs reminding Hmong of the lesson: A craven deed harms everyone.

The flight from Chinese oppression carried the Hmong into Southeast Asia, where once again they discovered the wisdom of living in the mountains. Hmong had first poured into the Tonkin delta of Vietnam, near Hanoi, looking for land to farm. But tropical diseases such as malaria, plus threats by the Vietnamese army with its terrifying elephant battalions, drove the Hmong back up into the Vietnamese mountains, where they remain today.

But about 1815–18, a group from the Lo clan traveled south from Vietnam into Laos, led by a Chinese trader who promised them land in the sparsely settled mountains that was good for farming and for growing the crop that interested him: opium. The trader's word proved good, and the Hmong settled down in the mountains around Nong Het, a town only six miles from Vietnam. More followed, and soon ten villages were established — the beginnings of the Hmong heartland in Laos. The virgin land was fertile, but tigers, reports have it, threatened children and old women. The men set out traps with string trip wires and dispatched the big cats with their flintlocks.

While still in China, the Hmong had been encouraged by the Chinese and indirectly by the British to expand their opium production beyond customary family needs. Chinese opium traders visited Hmong villages or lived in them. In Laos, the French and Americans would seek them out as suppliers of opium, too.

Long and Cho Lee Yang above Phonsavan, Xieng Khouang Province, the old Hmong heartland, March 2002. (Photograph courtesy of Cho Lee Yang.)

The French

French Catholic missionaries had been active in Vietnam, so near to the Hmong in Laos across the mountains, since the early 1600s. In 1664, the French East India Company set up shop in the region to generate trade.

More than two hundred years later, about 1885, the French needed help in finding and capturing a rebel Vietnamese emperor who was threatening the new French colony. Hmong gave them the needed help, the emperor was captured, and the French acquired respect for Hmong military ability in mountain warfare. Hmong could navigate steep mountain trails that would exhaust lowlanders, and they displayed a discipline, bravery, and determination that contrasted markedly with the easy-going lowland Lao.

And so began a relationship between the French, bearers of Western culture, and the Hmong, an Asian mountain people, a liaison weighted in favor of the French.

A decade later, in 1893, France established a protectorate in Laos—a guardianship—with the consent of Laotian rulers who were looking for help against the ever-encroaching Siamese to the west. The French soon demanded more opium from the Hmong to sell abroad, regardless of its consequences for the well-being of their sometime ally. The Hmong, incensed that this demand did not come through established Hmong channels, attacked the French provincial offices in Xieng Khouang City, capital of the province of the same name. Though the French succeeded in fending them off—with rifles that outclassed the Hmong flintlocks—they prudently opened talks with the Hmong and, locally at least, agreed to consult with the Hmong before making such decisions again. It was a matter of respect. Thereafter, Hmong leaders and French officials in Xieng Khouang cooperated.

Because the French found few resources besides opium in Laos, they spent a minimum of time and money running the country. Their direct influence in towns like Xieng Khouang City was slim. Whereas some forty thousand French people were deployed to administer Vietnam, at first fewer than a hundred went to Laos. Instead, they sent in French-educated Vietnamese to help run the colonial bureaucracy and militia. They also encouraged the Chinese to continue their centuries-long trade there. They left tax collecting and other matters of the law to the lowland Lao.

Still, French-Hmong associations could be close. Some Hmong villages contained French garrisons, and Hmong served French officers as guides and soldiers. Many American Hmong have fathers, grandfathers, and uncles who served in the French military, in regular positions or as guerrillas.

As in all things, Hmong were ingenious about weaponry. Along with swords, axes, and flintlocks, they used rock slides let loose from above and poisoned arrows shot from crossbows. They constructed barriers out of anything at hand and rolled them toward the enemy on logs, springing from behind at the last moment to do their damage. Verging on the comic, a story is told of a Hmong blacksmith who carved a cannon out of wood, banded it with iron, and stuffed it with knives, axes, chains, and junk from his blacksmith shop. When he fired it, the contraption not only killed a number of marauding Chinese looking to steal opium but terrified the rest, driving them into a French ambush.

Successful joint campaigns drew the Hmong and French together. The French leaned increasingly on the Hmong and, around 1915, supplied them with sixty modern rifles to defeat Chinese bandits. The pattern had begun.

Despite the developing military relationship, Hmong found themselves treated poorly by the French. First, their men were forced to build roads, an unpaid tour of duty that could wreck farm production. Hefty taxes were imposed, and ethnic Lao officials, who held the mountain peoples in contempt, collected taxes but pocketed most it. Should a Hmong want an interview with a Lao official, he must crawl head down into the man's presence and wait silently to be recognized. Humiliating! Eventually the Hmong were required to pay their taxes in grossly undervalued opium. Those who couldn't pay were tossed into prison. One can picture the angry late-night talks among village men clustered around someone's fire, a few of the wives nearby adding their pointed observations. How dare the French treat us like that! We are their allies!

Twenty years later, in 1916, the smoldering anger was ignited by a Vietnamese Hmong with magical powers, still honored in Hmong stories, who had escaped from Vietnam after initially successful rebellions against the French. Many Hmong men responded to his message of liberation by attacking French garrisons. Most of them were better equipped with ingenuity than weapons.

French infantry, with Laotian and Vietnamese militias, retaliated by burning crops and forcing entire villages of people out of the mountains to sites that could be more easily monitored. A few years later, in 1922, the man with the magical powers was assassinated, and the rebellion died for lack of food, ammunition, and spirit. At that point the French thought more carefully about their "enemy" and sensibly gave the Nong Het Hmong an autonomous district, headed by a Hmong *tasseng*, or area leader, appointed by the French.

There was more to life than war, and much of it proceeded as it had for centuries. Nearly all Hmong lived in villages or hamlets. Most of these were semi-permanent clusters of ten to fifteen wood-and-thatch houses, usually in isolated terrain. Because of the desire to govern themselves, a few Hmong went into the towns to join the civil service on behalf of the villages, becoming liaisons for and supervisors of the Hmong. In addition, forward-looking village leaders saw the importance of entering the market economy and encouraged villagers to carry their products into town on market days.

Not only the Hmong's military prowess but also their ambition and eagerness to improve their condition attracted the attention of the colonials. According to Hmong writer Yang See Koumarn,

> Our economic strength and our sense of cultural identity caused the colonial government to view us with more care than they did the other minorities in Laos, according to most writers; in any event, Hmong clan leaders came to be called upon by the Laotian district or provincial authorities to report on the status and living conditions of their people and to be given positions in local governments.[18]

Meanwhile, the Vietnamese were a recurrent, unwelcome factor in Laos. Vietnam had invaded Laos in the late 1400s via Xieng Khouang, traveling as far as the royal capital in Luang Prabang to the northwest. Xieng Khouang Province lay on one of only six routes through the Annamite mountain range, which divides the two countries. Until war made life there impossible, Xieng Khouang Province, and particularly the town of Nong Het, was the Hmong heartland in Laos. A look at a map shows an open-mouthed, thirty-mile-wide chunk of Vietnam pushing well into Laos at this point. Through that mouth, anyone with designs on Laos gained ready access.

Again in the 1830s, the Vietnamese had seized control of Xieng Khouang. The public execution of Xieng Khouang's native ruler and harsh methods of governing earned the Vietnamese the lasting hatred of the population. Because of events like this and bad experiences of Hmong who lived in Vietnam, the Hmong have a "deep traditional loathing of the Vietnamese," according to American writer Christopher Robbins.[19]

In Vietnam, meanwhile, the stage was being set for rebellion against the Western interlopers. French taxes reduced many Vietnamese farmers to the status of sharecroppers. This gained the French generous revenue in the short term but finally stimulated the Vietnamese to revolt. Early, unsuccessful action was followed in the 1940s by the ultimately successful communist Vietminh movement.

The Vietnamese were invited into Laos by an independence movement that had taken root there. The Vietnamese responded gladly. They were eager not only to remove the French but also to claim Xieng Khouang Province, which they believed belonged to them. They were supported in this claim by Vietnamese locals who already lived in a number of the towns near Hmong villages. As pressure built, the French looked about for allies against the Vietnamese. A French colonel, who had commanded a mountain post for six years and knew the Hmong, easily recruited Hmong and other highlanders of Laos and Vietnam — called montagnards at the time. It was not that the mountain peoples loved the French but that they hated the Vietnamese Vietminh, who for their part were also attempting to recruit them. From an initial force of two thousand guerrillas, the Frenchman in eighteen months assembled a force of twenty thousand. The American CIA supported this effort with weapons and an officer, while the French funded the guerrillas out of opium profits.

Step by step the Hmong were being drawn out of their cherished isolation. A Hmong military and political leader named Touby Lyfoung responded in a typically Hmong way. One of the first three Hmong to receive a high school diploma, in the 1920s, Touby eventually decided that politics, not military ability, would produce what the Hmong most wanted: freedom. So he went into politics, becoming Laos's minister of health and later minister of Post and Telecommunications. That made him a hero, and even now his photograph hangs in many Hmong homes.

Touby decided on a strategy of making the Hmong not just useful to the French but indispensable. The opportunity arose during World War II when the Japanese entered Laos in search of rice and minerals needed in their weapons factories. France had been subdued by Germany, leaving their possessions abroad unguarded. But once freed from German domination, France sent commandos parachuting into the Plain of Jars to establish guerrilla bases and regain their hold on Laos. (Japan, not interested in sharing Laos with France, had aligned itself with the anti–French people.) Under Touby's leadership Hmong guerrillas aided their old allies, the French. For his troubles, Touby was captured by the Japanese and probably would have been executed had his captors not been persuaded that a major Hmong uprising would surely result. Faydang Lo, a Hmong who had lost out to Touby in a bid for power, in anger sided with the Japanese and later became the leading Hmong in the communist Pathet Lao.

The list of participants is enough to make your head spin, but the array of interested parties, and their oblique reasons for choosing up sides, is characteristic of Southeast Asian history.

During this period a man appeared on stage who is now revered by many American Hmong as their leader, Vang Pao, the only Hmong to become a general in the Royal Lao Army. Vang Pao had started his military career while young. At fourteen he interpreted for Frenchmen recruiting in the Plain of Jars in the defense against the Japanese. After the Japanese surrendered in August 1945, he advanced to fighting Vietnamese and Chinese — oh, yes, they were involved, too — trying to seize regions of northern Laos. Now he was presented to the French colonel by Touby. The young guerrilla showed great promise, Touby told the Frenchman.

Vang Pao turned out to be highly skilled militarily, drawing admiration from Hmong and non–Hmong alike. It is as if he picked up the mantle that the legendary Hmong general Tche-you, opponent of the Yellow Emperor, laid down several thousand years before. From the start, Vang Pao's strength was guerrilla warfare. With his Hmong forces he would fight the growing war against communism in northern Laos virtually unaided. He was a tough commander, called by one writer "energetic, volatile, direct, and fearless."[20] He could also be brutal. Prisoners were often executed, and, as the war dragged on and victory eluded him, he was known to direct bombing and strafing missions against Hmong villages that were turning to the enemy. One of his own officers was found shot between the eyes; the man had been caught selling rice to the Pathet Lao.

Vang Pao's military and leadership skills were welcomed not only by the French but surprisingly by the Laotian government and later by the Americans. He quickly rose to the rank of major, a fact which, along with his ability to get foreign military support and food and medical aid for his people, carried Vang Pao to heights of leadership reminiscent of the Hmong kings of old.

But in 1954, France lost its colonial foothold in Southeast Asia to communist Vietnamese forces at Dien Bien Phu. The French packed up and went home.

The Americans

After 1960, the United States began inserting itself into Laos to stabilize what Dwight D. Eisenhower warned was the first domino, about to be toppled by communists. In response to shipments by the U.S.S.R. of military supplies to northeastern Laos, the U.S. sent military personnel and five hundred guns to Laos, an officially neutral country.

At that time the CIA, which was already instructing an elite police unit in Thailand, formed a partnership with the Hmong in Laos. For their part, the Hmong, who now numbered about three hundred thousand in Laos, about one tenth of the population, were eager to protect their lives and homeland, which lay directly in the path of the North Vietnamese swarming into the country. Americans would provide supplies to a Hmong guerrilla force, and the Thais would train them. This was the beginning of the Secret Army, or the SGU, Special Guerrilla Unit. For the Hmong, it was a relatively easy transition from a military relationship with the French to one with Americans. Hmong officers picked up English as they had acquired French.

As the war intensified, the CIA in 1962 began construction of an airbase at Long Cheng, in an isolated mountain valley between Vientiane and the Plain of Jars. It stood at an altitude of just over three thousand feet. Its landing strip, still visible from the air, ran up audaciously to the base of a jagged karst, "a *very* difficult mountain," as Hmong communications operator Nhia Vang put it.[21]

Here Hmong driven by war from their villages congregated. At its largest — nearly fifty thousand people — Long Cheng was the second biggest city in Laos. Crowded into its mountain bowl with limited cultivable space, residents couldn't hope to raise all their food. They had to rely at least in part on outsiders for food and other goods. To an American aid worker, the town markedly lacked such basics as water, sewage, waste management, and schools. (A Lao school north of the runway offered grades one to six.) There were, however, advantages beyond those available in the villages: a radio station, a hospital, outdoor markets for those who had goods or produce to sell, an agricultural development program and farm service center, and a movie theater, though one assumes few Hmong, many poorly nourished, had money for such a luxury.[22]

Long Cheng featured a mix of old-style Hmong houses and the concrete, technology-equipped American structures built for CIA officers and the Air America pilots who flew for them. Gen. Vang Pao's concrete home stood out, with anti-aircraft guns placed in front and on the roof. He held nightly dinners there with the Americans and Hmong officers, who also had substantial homes, to plan the next day's sorties.

Long Cheng's streets, all but one of them dirt, were filled with jeeps, trucks, and taxi trucks, plus crowds of mountain people on foot. More and more Hmong were wearing Lao or Western-style clothing, sarongs for the women and army-issue gear or civilian shirts and slacks for the men, in place of traditional black garb. Everything, of course, was dominated by the runway, airplanes, and soldiers.

By 1963 the Secret Army in Laos included about twenty thousand Hmong defending their own villages plus about ten thousand regular soldiers, most of them supplied with weapons delivered by Air America. Villages were assigned — ordered — to supply so many men, who, by the end of the war, came too often from the ranks of children and the middle aged. Hmong soldiers fought offensively in conventional battle, sprang guerrilla attacks, and defended the landing strips that had sprouted on the mountaintops. One unusual assignment, reported by Robbins, occurred when an American pilot made a forced landing on a runway built exclusively for short take-off and landing aircraft. After the plane was repaired, the pilot climbed in and directed Hmong soldiers on the ground to hold onto the plane's struts and tail until he revved it up to take-off speed. Then he "signaled to the [Hmong] to let go, roared down the strip until he had run out of runway, lowered the flaps, and staggered off across the trees under enemy small-arms fire."[23]

It was from this period that Hmong, along with other tribal peoples such as the Mien, recall "the promise," a verbal vow made by an American advisor or intelligence agent and passed around by the Hmong in several variations. The promise assured that if the war against communism were lost, Americans would "find a new place" for the Hmong and would help them.[24] This promise would color the attitude of Hmong toward the U.S. during flight, resettlement, and beyond.

As the easy-going lowland Lao's distaste for fighting became apparent, the Americans depended more and more on the Hmong and other tribal people, whom they provided with small salaries, food, materiel, and advisors. The goal in southern Laos was to prevent the flow of North Vietnamese goods along the Ho Chi Minh Trail to South Vietnam and, in the north, to stop a North Vietnam-backed Pathet Lao takeover. Hmong manned mortars and howitzers, which were helicoptered between battle sites, told American bombers where to find enemy targets, and, like Chamy Thor's twin uncles, flew fighter planes as Royal Lao Air Force pilots. The Hmong had indeed become indispensable.

Their faithfulness in rescuing downed American pilots and diverting attacks from American troops in South Vietnam earned them undying respect from Americans who knew of them. One of these, the late B.T. Collins, a Sacramento City councilman who had lost an arm in Vietnam, ignored his Sacramento doctor's orders and, sick with the flu, attended a Hmong gathering to which he had been invited. It was, he said, the least he could do.

In 1973 the Americans signed an international cease-fire agreement in Paris to get out of Laos. By then, they had dropped some 1.6 million tons of bombs on Laos, a quarter of all ordnance dropped during the Vietnam War. To compare, just one million tons were dropped by the U.S. during the Korean War. The Americans' departure left the Hmong and several other ethnic groups under Gen. Vang Pao to carry on the war in northeastern Laos. Both the Soviet Union and North Vietnam disregarded the cease-fire and continued a military presence.

The loss of Hmong life was staggering. More than one-tenth of those Hmong fighting in the war died — between 30,000 and 40,000. One third of the population of three hundred thousand was displaced, most of the villages were burned, and a large number of civilians died under fire or from physical privation. Another estimate figures the dead at seventeen thousand troops and fifty thousand civilians.[25]

In April 1975, first Cambodia and then South Vietnam fell. Despite ferocious fighting by the Hmong, North Vietnamese and Pathet Lao soldiers were prevailing in Laos as well. It rapidly became clear that, in the event of defeat, the Hmong would be in mortal danger. Yang Dao, the first Hmong to earn a Ph.D., in Paris in 1972, and vice chairman of economics for the government of Laos, reports that during a political trip to the German Democratic Republic in late April 1975, as communists were proclaiming victory in Cambodia and South Vietnam, he was berated by a member of the Presidium of the G.D.R. People's Chamber. Echoing statements that must have been made centuries before in China, the gentleman rose at a banquet, pointed at Yang Dao, and proclaimed that the "damn Meo" (another spelling for Miao) were responsible for the lengthy delay in bringing communism to Laos. In the U.S.S.R. on the same trip, Yang Dao watched as the chairman of the Presidium of the Supreme Soviet similarly threatened the Hmong and their allies, using a gesture to suggest decapitation. Back in Laos, on May 9, the Pathet Lao newspaper said, "We must eradicate the Meo minority completely."[26]

A few days later, isolated at his base in Long Cheng by a three-pronged formation of the enemy, Gen. Vang Pao was dissuaded from what would have been a suicidal offensive. He prepared to leave. About twenty-five hundred Hmong began a week-long, chaotic air evacuation to Thailand.

Laotian and Vietnamese communist forces started to kill the Hmong who remained and set fire to their villages. Hmong families fled into the jungle as Chamy's and others' families had, babies on backs and little children in hand. Already malnourished, many starved, died of disease, or were killed by soldiers. Some escaped across the Mekong River, while others drowned or were murdered by pirates. Many remained behind to continue the war from the jungle — they remain there today — or to try to adapt to the new regime. Of these, many died during forced labor and "re-education" from which few escaped.

Such is the history of the Hmong. It is a blend of ancient stories that reveal to the Hmong who they are and stories as modern and personal and silent as the vacant spaces at a family table.

Part II

HMONG WORLD: THAT WAS THEN

Cog ib tau kaum.
Plant one, reap ten.
— Hmong proverb

6

Old Royalty:
Ly Vong Lynaolu

> Tangled hair, use a comb to unsnarl it;
> Complicated dispute, use an elder to solve it.
> — Hmong proverb[1]

Ly Vong Lynaolu was a soldier and leader, a man of fiery temperament, but I didn't get his full story until after he had died.

I had met him several times, once at Chamy Thor's house. It was a small meeting of leaders of the Hmong arts organization that Chamy and her husband had founded. Ly Vong was its president, and he gave me a gracious ceremonial speech in which I could tell he was *zoo siab*, happy, and that his happiness related to me. His daughter, the group's treasurer, translated. They were honored to have me there, she explained. Then Ly Vong finished in English: "I think God send you to us." I thought so, too.

Ly Vong's involvement in the arts organization was critical to its survival, Nom Npis Lis later explained to me. Nom Npis was a kinsman of Ly Vong's. Without an elder of Ly Vong's stature, argument could swamp the group. Ly Vong was well respected in the Hmong community, had held an important role in the military in Laos, and now helped Hmong find their way in the new land. He supplied information and connections to help fellow refugees find housing and jobs, took them to the doctor and translated for them, gave them money and clothing. He gave advice to parents and children and counseled couples. He explained the lay of the land as best he could to terrified newcomers. Like all such community leaders, he was a one-man social service agency. In fact, he had helped found a mutual assistance association with Gen. Vang Pao, to whom he was related by marriage. Therefore, in the arts organization his word would be heeded.

But presiding over an arts organization and helping Hmong with their troubles were in turn important to Ly Vong: They were an emotional life raft for him. He was no longer the respected captain in the Hmong Secret Army who taught soldiers how to fight. These peacetime duties of leadership were important substitutes for former status. Other men his age without such roles to call upon often spent their first years in the United States shut in small apartments, ill-suited to meaningful work, afraid to go outside or even answer the door lest someone speak to them in English.

Physically, Ly Vong exuded dignity. I've never seen another Hmong carry himself the way this man did. At five feet seven inches he was far taller than the average five-foot-one Hmong. That alone brought him status. He had a light, smooth face, slightly protruding lower jaw, and a smile that turned down at the corners. I knew he had a temper. He told me so himself, and I would hear about it later from family members who had smarted under its lash. But to the Hmong he was a guide and godsend in the new land, a haven against the tigers.

My favorite image of Ly Vong comes from an exhibition of Hmong music and dance one November evening in 1992 at a Sacramento high school auditorium. This was what Chamy, Ly Vong, and the others were planning the night of the meeting. Thousands of Hmong had come from all over California to attend the Sacramento New Year, and this evening was one of the special attractions. The program opened with Ly Vong, in his smooth baritone, offering a stately welcome — a Hmong tradition. Then the Sacramento City councilman who had fought in Vietnam and knew how much the Hmong had done described his deep respect for those who fought. Teens and young adults in elegant Western formal dress milled restlessly around the edges of the audience waiting for the traditional performances to be over and the rock band to appear.

But first, to open the program of old-country music and dance, Ly Vong took to the polished hardwood floor to lead an impromptu procession that quickly grew into a community dance. Breaking with the Hmong father's traditional reticence toward daughters, he called his youngest, Katie, out of the crowd to accompany him as he led a growing line of people around the dance floor. With a recording of Lao music filling the auditorium, Ly Vong stepped in a stately one-two, one-two rhythm, moving his hands before him in a graceful, swirling motion. The universe, one could believe, belonged to this man.

Yet despite his finesse, he understood how much his kingdom had shrunk. And it was hard to swallow. He had made good choices all his life, it seemed, worked hard, and attained the double honor of community and military leadership. But outside forces had tipped the Hmong world on end and shaken him out. His abilities were now only occasionally relevant, his experiences no longer useful. He struggled to keep from lashing out in frustration and anger, he had told me. It was hard to steer others away from tigers when one was being eaten oneself.

That night, Ly Vong had only two and a half years to live.

Some months after he died, I visited his widow to ask about his early history. I wanted to know more about this big man whose world of glory had evaporated.

Directed by Chamy and Nom Npis, I went to visit Ly Vong's family on a perfect April morning five months after Ly Vong died. The family home was a plain stucco house in North Sacramento, enclosed by a chain-link fence. Katie, the youngest daughter, greeted me at the door. Inside, Ly Vong's widow, Pao Chao Lo, invited me to a seat near hers. She was as good-looking as the last time I saw her, if subdued.

Pao Chao had pre-empted the adjacent dining area for her cottage industry. ("My wife very smart lady—know how to sell for profit," Ly Vong had once said.) Stacks of blue, purple, and gray belt packs and other items she had decorated with Hmong designs were piled several feet high next to a sewing machine. Pao Chao has a booth at a flea market in the next town, but on the day of my visit she was disheartened. Mice had gotten into her storage shed near the booth and chewed up her inventory.

As we chatted, people slipped constantly in and out of the house. Most of these were sons or daughters of Pao Chao and Ly Vong. They would sit for a few minutes to add to their father's story and then leave. It was an easy atmosphere.

"Tell me about your husband and father. I want to know how he came to be a prominent leader."

Unsurprisingly, Pao Chao began with Ly Vong's great-grandfather, the last of a royal Hmong blood line in China, Katie translated for her mother. This was one of the small kingdoms that formed after the scattering of the great Hmong kingdom. Along with many sons, this ancestor had much money, animals, and power—everything. "They were the most suave, the most dynamic men around." Like Ly Vong, I thought. Seated near me, Katie, eighteen years old, spoke rapidly. She is bright and outgoing. As she translated, her face suggested that she was hearing some details for the first time. Pao Chao was now the keeper of family story.

The stories flowed from Pao Chao not in history-book fashion, fixed in linear time and a spot on a map, but in the Hmong way of reckoning, according to the stories' meanings. This suave ancestor lived in Yunnan Province in southern China, I had been told. Others say it was Szechwan. But the two provinces are adjacent, and borders can be vague on the ground. As we've seen, the kingdoms functioned independently within Imperial China and were ruled by princes or "little kings," called kiatong. Ly Vong's great-grandfather was one of these and is known to his descendants simply as Kiatong Ly. The nobles who surrounded him were probably also from the Ly/Lee clan.

By the time Kiatong Ly came to power in his kingdom, trouble had been deepening for several centuries, since the mid–1600s. It was then that Manchurians overthrew the ancient Ming dynasty and decided to abolish the Hmong kingdoms. Those territories were to be drawn into the imperial bureaucracy. Two centuries of resistance, extermination campaigns, and finally massacre had led many Hmong to flee toward Vietnam and Laos.

Pao Chao neatly condensed the same events this way: "There was a lot of war and a lot of fighting amongst everybody. And so, we didn't have much of an edge over them, so [the Hmong] migrated to other countries."

Alfred W. McCoy continues the story of Ly Vong's suave shaman-king ancestor, which he based on interviews with Lynhiavu clan leaders in Vientiane before 1972. These interviews personalize the broad story of migration out of China. "[The Ly] kaitong had been the leader of the [Hmong] resistance in Szechwan, and when the Chinese massacres began in 1856 he ordered his four sons to lead the survivors south while he remained to hold back the Chinese armies. His third son, Ly Nhiavu, was invested with the title of kaitong, and he led the survivors on a year-long march...."[2]

I realized that Ly Vong, whose photo looked down on us from the far wall as we talked, must have lived surrounded daily by his stately ancestors. Stories of such figures might have reassured him that the Hmong are a noble people, not pitiable refugees. But he might also have wondered, on occasion, if he measured up.

After a brief stop in Vietnam, first the kiatong of the Lo clan and then the newly invested Ly kiatong continued south with their followers into northeastern Laos. The Ly kiatong was Ly Vong's grandfather. "Grandfather," I reminded myself, can include great uncles.

Although the Lo clan got to Nong Het first, the Ly kiatong decided to go there, too. There was wisdom in settling near other clans, since marrying within one's own clan is taboo. In time, the fourth son of the Ly kiatong, Ly Yong Xeng Naolu, Ly Vong's father, was named kiatong.

Because of their proximity to Vietnam through a mountain pass — now a fairly brief walk along the French colonial road built from 1916 to 1924 — the people of Nong Het and the entire district were destined to be in the thick of things. It was there that Ly Vong's people had their first encounter with the French soldiers. Then followed the Lao, Japanese, Vietnamese. This was the tumultuous world into which Ly Vong was born.

Perhaps not surprisingly, given its position in the center of a war, Nong Het produced many of the major Hmong leaders in the Vietnam War. These included Touby Lyfoung, the chief Hmong political figure, and Gen. Vang Pao, the Hmong general who led his soldiers to astonishing victories. In addition, the brothers Nhiavu Lo Bliayao and Faydang Lo, key leaders with the communist Pathet Lao, also came from Nong Het. The seasoning of these leaders was surely aided by the political autonomy granted to the Nong Het region by the French, along with the constant military challenges that provided a hothouse for learning.

It is rare for a Hmong of Ly Vong's age to know the specific birthplace as he did — Green Pond Village. Usually they speak only of a province or area, since their settlements are temporary and the place of birth soon reverts to jungle. Moreover, in such a kin-oriented society, it only matters *to whom* you were born. Nor did he know *when* he was born. Hmong from mountain villages had no means or reason to record such information. Society revolves around the group, emphatically not around the individual.

When Vietnamese communists began to arrive in Green Pond Village, Ly Vong was a slender boy probably in his early teens. He was old enough to carry a little brother or sister on his back, his widow Pao Chao recalled. Like other males and a few females, Ly Vong already knew how to use a gun to defend his home.

One dreadful day in 1953 while battles raged between the Vietnamese and the French, some Vietnamese captured Ly Vong's father. Ly Vong was about fourteen years old. That night, the thirty remaining members of the family prepared to flee westward to Xieng Khouang City, the provincial capital more than forty miles away. For Ly Vong, that was the beginning of a decades-long flight.

It rained that night, Ly Vong had told author Gayle L. Morrison. The water sometimes reached halfway up his thighs, "and still we go." In the dark, everyone held hands to stay together.[3]

Already Ly Vong had finished elementary school. When the family fled to the small city of Xieng Khouang, Ly Vong went back to school, finishing secondary education and two years of college. By the time he was done, Ly Vong knew Lao, French, and some English.

I asked Pao Chao how a boy from a village with only the most tenuous awareness of formal learning was motivated to get an education. Though school was not much valued by Hmong in those days, it was different for the son of a royal house.

"It was a want from the ancestors," Pao Chao explained through Katie. "It had always been a desire, but they didn't have the means." Katie added her own explanation: "It's always been something expected, because the blood line was a royal blood line. That was something my father instilled in us, too."

Education. Living as the Hmong had within the reach of Chinese values, they could not help but understand that education brought status, and status was something they craved, if only for the power it would give to protect themselves.

War again intervened in his schooling, and "In 1958," Ly Vong had said, "I dropped the books and went into the army."

Along with education and service in the military — influences that opened disorienting worlds to Ly Vong — a third influence tugged him back toward tradition. He was learning how to be a Hmong man. And not just a man, but a leader worthy of the Ly name.

Training a boy up was the task of fathers, uncles, and older brothers. "When you start something, always finish it," boys were lectured at home or in the field. "Work hard to bring success to the family." Such traditional learning is a powerful thread that colors most of Hmong life. It has little relation to formal education.

Training in Hmong manhood hinges on the centrality of family. It produces the classic head of household and also village and clan leaders. These civilian leaders were pivotal to life in Laos and are still a keystone for Hmong in America. Here, however, they have had to take on unfamiliar tasks involving scientific medicine and independent-thinking children.

The subject of traditional male leadership in the Hmong community is a touchy one. On the one hand Hmong say, Why give up what has worked for millennia? On the other hand, the old-style exercise of male prerogative is unpopular — some of it illegal — in America. Public criticism can be experienced as humiliation by Hmong, an unforgivable social offense in a culture that accords high value to dignity. Why don't they just change? Americans ask. Many older Hmong feel they have been drowning in change. But just as America began to wrestle with the issue of gender equality on a grand scale a few decades ago, Hmong households, like it or not, are wrestling with it now. Many young women are seeing to it.

Within the traditional Hmong family, the father indeed looms. He is charged with protecting and strengthening his people. In the ideal model, he decides, broadly, who goes where and when. The wife may or may not hold her tongue when a decision is before her husband, but there is no shame to a man who does not consult with his spouse. This may seem harsh. But not to have a father, one Hmong man said, is "a little bit like living in a house that's not finished. You live in it with the wind blowing through and the rain coming in, and you haven't any shelter against the heat of the sun."[4] Many families experienced this feeling of vulnerability during the war years, and on many occasions, when no male relative was available to help, a woman became head of house. She might then turn around and require her boys to perform such female tasks as sweeping, cooking, and carrying water. When families fled for their lives after the communist takeover, a husband who had served in the army or had worked for a Western organization might separate from his wife and children in the jungle to protect them. In case of capture, he might well be killed, and so might they. One man who had been a medic did this, leaving his wife the job of getting herself and the children to Thailand.

I never asked Ly Vong about this aspect of his life, his role as head of household and later of the community, but other Hmong have filled me in on what the job looks like.

Txawv Vue (T.V.) Vang, a boyishly handsome, middle-aged man, was one of those trained in traditional leadership but practices it in the new American setting, a delicate proposition. T.V. explained.

"In a family, to me, I have to direct the family to the right direction, make sure that the family don't run around to do the wrong thing. So that if you are the leader within your family, that way the family can do better. He always have a good goal for the family to follow." During peacetime this meant he made family and farming decisions. During war, it might mean facing down enemy soldiers in one's front yard.

Peace or war, if the father does well and the family thrives, others begin to take their questions and problems to him. Continued success may bring him the job of village headman, especially if he is the son of a headman. Dr. Yang Dao writes, "They are nominated from among the clan's most intelligent, capable, generous, influential and, generally, oldest members." Usually only one nominee is named, but if two are put forward, a vote is taken.

A Hmong proverb captures this ancient form of government:

In the thick jungle, there is one tree that is highest;
In one group of cousins, there is one person who is smartest.
In the thick jungle, there is one tree that is biggest;
In one group of cousins, there is one person who is leader.[5]

T.V.'s father made the grade and became village chief in Khammouane Province, southeast of where Ly Vong lived in Xieng Khouang. "The villagers obey him, follow him, listen to him, and eighty or ninety percent of the time just ask for his advice, what to do or what not to do." In turn, T.V.'s father taught his older sons how to be leaders, and this elder team taught T.V. But young men also watched skilled leaders—they do it now in America, too—taking note of how the older ones handle situations and even memorizing the words used to solve a sticky problem. "You have to be smart and learn as much as you can so that you can show others that you are capable of leading them to a direction that is right."

The village headman is mayor, city planner, recreation head, hosteler, detective, judge, counselor, and economic consultant in one, although I assume only the rare person would excel at all duties. A leader is called on any time, day or night. He has a ceremonial role at births, marriages, funerals, and spirit ceremonies, and he organizes the New Year festivities. He advises quarreling couples and with the help of advisors picked from clan or family heads settles disputes between villagers. He both runs a bed and breakfast for friendly visitors, such as Hmong with no relatives in that village, and mobilizes armed villagers against interlopers. He pulls together work groups to maintain trails, construct wells or bamboo aqueducts, and build individual family homes. I observed the latter in Thailand, where a family was rebuilding a house over the same hard-packed earth floor where the previous one had stood, re-using some materials from the old house.

Although a man had the final say at home, and a gifted man like Ly Vong might grow accustomed to having his way, a leader's power was far from absolute. He would be followed only insofar as he showed results. Villagers could justly call a meeting any time to complain about the headman. Neatly capturing the Hmong character, historian Keith Quincy says, "The independent-spirited Hmong would never tolerate anyone, and especially a Hmong, exercising absolute power over them."[6]

One of the defining characteristics of traditional Hmong leadership is that it is largely a peacetime system. It is directed at undergirding agriculture and village life. But with the arrival of Westerners, and war, the shape of leadership began to evolve. By serving as intermediaries between their people and Lao, French, Vietnamese, and finally Americans, traditional leaders found themselves operating in unfamiliar spheres. Suddenly they were dealing with military structures, where leadership was designated from above, not chosen from below. They handled economic development programs. The new role might enhance the leader's standing because of his new-found access to salaries, supplies, and services such as hospitals, but it could also cause stress in social relationships, especially with old leaders who were being left behind. To some of those active in new spheres, the opportunities, ideas, and technologies were stimulating, but there was also a critical point where the newness could overwhelm.

With the advance of war in the 1950s, people were forced to flee from their homes. Talk to almost any Hmong leader and you will hear how a single leader bore the responsibility of getting twenty or fifty or seventy-five families out of their villages at night through enemy-peppered jungle. Using the ancient paths of tigers and elephants, the leader walked at the head of the line of frightened men, women, and children while another man brought up the rear. Both might make forays back and forth along the column to check on the weak and frightened and offer encouragement. Leaders moved hundreds undetected through the middle of villages at night and talked more than one terrified individual across rushing water.

The physical strain of such a task might trigger an older man's desire to cede leadership to a younger man. But there were cases in which a leader gave up his responsibility for less honorable reasons. In one instance, a clan chief, perhaps overpowered by the responsibility of evacuating an entire village, fled alone in the dark of night while his people waited to receive directions from him.

Leaders of each level — family, village, clan — while caring for their charges, also could look to the next level up for guidance and strength. Thus even the strongest community leader could say that, once Gen. Vang Pao left the country in May 1975, there was "no one left to protect us." They appear to have been right. After Vang Pao's departure, the Pathet Lao began rounding up Hmong leaders and forcing them to do demeaning work — pulling plows to break up soil and hauling the dirt to fill American bomb craters. Many died under the regimen.

As family and village groups fled to Thailand, some leaders found themselves dealing with the Thai government, United Nations refugee workers, and other nonprofit organizations to secure the basic necessities and, later, education and economic help for their people. Once again old leaders scrambled to adapt to a new situation.

It was in 1958 that Ly Vong was stationed in Lat Houang on the edge of the Plain of Jars, between his home district of Nong Het and Long Cheng, the isolated headquarters for the Royal Lao Army's Hmong division. As befits a people who measure distances in terms of experienced space rather than abstract numbers, Pao Chao explained that Lat Houang was as far from Long Cheng as Sacramento, their home at the time of my visit, is from Davis, about twenty miles. Pao Chao's knowledge of the distance must have come from a trip by foot, since there was no road into Long Cheng from that direction.

In 1961, Ly Vong claimed his bride. "They met," Katie said, "and five days later my dad just kidnapped her." Ly Vong, seizing her by both wrists, declared, "You're mine!" It's called a "catch-hand" marriage, in which the "captive" is nearly always a willing, if coy, participant.

But Pao Chao Lo truly didn't want to marry Ly Vong. He was over twenty and a soldier, and she was only fourteen. But Pao Chao's uncle, who was also the village headman, and her other relatives concluded that Ly Vong was a good man. Pao Chao should accept him.

The men had spoken, but Pao Chao's mother objected. I have heard Hmong women object. She probably howled.

Not only did fourteen-year-old Pao Chao not find Ly Vong to her liking. She also had not understood what marriage meant.

"That night my mom and he stayed in the bedroom, and the family left them for one night," Pada explained discreetly. The next morning, Pao Chao fled.

She went to the house of her uncle, the headman. With his distraught niece before him, he reconsidered. If she really didn't want to marry Ly Vong, they could reopen discussions. Still, he said, the old, the young, everyone listens to his advice, and Pao Chao should listen to him, too, and take his advice: Marry him. And so she did, on April 4, 1961.

The wedding would take days. It would focus not on the lovely bride in her silver neck ring and embroidered finery, nor on a romantic vision of living happily ever after. Rather, it focused on cementing mutual responsibility and solidarity between the Lys and the Los, a tricky proposition between two clans that harbored an old enmity. In one version of the tale, a split between the Ly and Lo clans originated in the 1920s when a daughter of the Lo chief committed suicide. She had been married to a Ly, who reportedly beat her. The son of this marriage was the renowned Touby Lyfoung, the prominent military and political leader. The rift was exacerbated in disputes over who rightly should head the administration of Nong Het. Many Hmong add a story of the theft of a horse. The rift took on deadly significance when the dead woman's brother, Faydang Lo, became prominent in the communist Pathet Lao. Maybe friction between Ly Vong and his Lo bride was foreordained.

Pada, the eldest, remembered how it went with her parents. "When I was younger back in Laos, he was very strict to her and to all of us children. He treat his children like we are his soldiers. He was very, very, very strict, and we used to hate that." Pada laughed. Later I learned that, during the time of chaotic evacuation from Laos when it was everyone for himself, the stern father had taught his children the techniques for squeezing onto the plane and then threatened them with an image of their fates if any of them failed. Left alone without mother and father, "You will have no food to eat and nothing to drink. No clothes to wear. ... You will cry all day, all day, all day, all day. Nobody will take care of you. You will die. ... When you die, the flies will eat you."[7] Pada, the oldest, twelve at the time, was responsible for carrying seven-month-old Cheuxysy onto the plane. If she dawdled and were left behind, he would become her responsibility. By instilling terror, the father sought to transform childhood irresponsibility into independent resolve.

But after moving to the United States the strict husband and father began to soften. He began to open himself to his family, the daughters said. Perhaps he had discovered how much he did not know. He still had his temper, to be sure. "I think his temper was a package deal," Katie said.

Catch-hand marriage riles the American sense of individual rights. But Hmong practices — they vary considerably — reflect the character of Hmong society. Hmong men run things, with certain hedges and constraints, and so they naturally consider themselves in charge of marriage, too. As boys are taught through childhood by precept and example to take the rights and responsibilities of leadership, girls are taught where they fit into that male world. But the catch-hand marriage is not necessarily what it appears. Should the marriage not go well for the wife, the "capture" allows her to say, "This marriage was not *my* idea." In a convoluted way, the practice provides her with leverage in resolving difficulties.

Ly Vong moved up in the Royal Lao Army, becoming an officer and taking more classes in Lat Houang. Pao Chao spoke for herself in English. "They told me not really many people [were] over there," indicating that he was one of an elite. For two years he taught artillery. Their first child, Pada, meaning flowers, was born in 1962 in Pha Khao, between Lat Houang and Long Cheng. Then he was transferred to Long Cheng. Pao Chao and their baby daughter went, too.

In Long Cheng, Ly Vong for two years supervised basic training for soldiers of all ethnic groups. He was a stern instructor. Recruits complained of his strictness, said his kinsman, Nom Npis Lis. But in the heat of battle they knew he had given them valuable, life-saving training. "So they know Ly Vong is a good man," Nom Npis told me. Some former soldiers, especially in the village militias, will tell you they had no training at all before being sent against the enemy.

But severe illness ended Ly Vong's assignment as a trainer, Pao Chao said, and ultimately meant that Ly Vong did not advance beyond the rank of captain in the Royal Lao Army. He had once listed his complaints for me, explaining, "I was artillery commander. We fought each other a lot. One day one hundred to two hundred shell, TNT, C-4 [plastic explosives], C-3 explosion, like that. So I don't know if that caused illness. Maybe bad food, because soldier not easy."

Ly Vong and Pao Chao had nine children. Their youngest, Noumoua — Katie — was conceived in a refugee camp in Thailand and born in Albuquerque, New Mexico. Her name means "every day she will always have more, more of love, more riches, more everything."

Besides giving his children unique names, Ly Vong had "interesting and very mysterious" dreams and foreknowledge. Katie said her brother Chysa also has it. Once Chysa told the family that someone close would die very soon. Shortly thereafter, an uncle died. This skill would soon prove invaluable to Ly Vong's family.

In May 1975, the Pathet Lao and North Vietnamese were approaching ever closer to the military center at Long Cheng. They captured the road junction at Sala Phou Koun to the northwest and began advancing on Long Cheng with tanks.[8]

Hmong numbering in the tens of thousands swarmed into Long Cheng hoping for evacuation. The mountains around the base were nearly devoid of roads — only the one along which the communists approached. No one now would be able to escape by truck, taxi, or motor bike. If one could not wedge one's body onto an airplane, the choices would be to stay in Long Cheng and hope to be peacefully absorbed by a communist regime, undertake a rebel's life in the mountains, or attempt to walk toward Thailand some seventy-five miles to the south.

At first, only the most important Hmong officers and their families were eligible for evacuation, conducted as secretly as possible to avoid panic. A few were airlifted out in two C-47 transport planes — twin engine DC3s — which could carry about thirty people. Then the larger C-46 was pressed into service, an aircraft that had never before taken off loaded from that runway and now began to do so heavily overloaded.

On Tuesday, May 13, at the behest of CIA officer Jerry Daniels, an American C-130 began making as many runs to Thailand as possible — three or four a day. The four-engine aircraft, piloted by a civilian Air America crew, was a more powerful plane than the others and would have had no trouble getting up and over the mountains if it, too, had not been overloaded. But five to six thousand Hmong had gathered, desperately hoping for a way out.

Ly Vong's family failed to push their way on the first four flights. Pao Chao prepared food, and the family again waited at the airstrip.

People around them cried in fear and desperation. Some forgot to go to the bathroom, a grandmother recounted. Mothers forgot to nurse their babies. When a plane came, people rushed to clamber up the side of the ramp instead of walking up it. Children were accidentally boarded without a parent. Women who had imprudently dressed in skirts had to be hauled up to preserve modesty. (As Ly Vong chided, "Each person must know by themselves!") One better-off family threw a bag of money onto the plane but could not themselves climb aboard. Someone dropped a suitcase on the runway and paper money blew all over. Jeeps stood about where officers had abandoned them.

"You look around the ramp here — abandoned suitcases, clothes all over, shoes, trash of all kinds. It's really a mess," said Jack Knotts, a helicopter pilot on the scene. "There's— I estimate — I don't know—five, six, or seven thousand people up there. All streaming toward the one C-130 — trucks, jeeps, and people walking, carrying all their personal possessions."[9]

Waiting that Tuesday, Ly Vong suddenly remembered a dream of several months before, picturing the airplane that would take his family to Thailand. He had dreamed that it would come to a stop not at the top of the runway where the thousands waited but at the bottom. Now alerted by God, he believed, Ly Vong remembered the dream and became certain that their plane was coming.

Using the need to go fix some food as a ruse, Ly Vong herded his family away from the crowd at the top of the airfield toward the other end. Two-thirds of the way down the field he told his family, "Stay right here; we're going to wait." As late afternoon turned into evening, relatives who were remaining behind stopped to talk, weeping over the realization that they might never see each other again.

Then the airplane came, landed, turned and taxied away from the crowd, as Ly Vong's dream had foretold, to the bottom of the airfield where a military truckload of colonels and families waited in hiding for the plane.

Chaos ensued. "When that plane lands," Katie translated for her mother, "you just run for your life. You push and shove. You step on people. You don't care. It's just like a swarm of bees."

Ly Vong and his family raced the short distance to the plane. They were among the first to reach it and were jammed into the front of the plane's cargo space. Ly Vong and Pao Chao tallied their family and came up lacking Chysa, the five year old. He must have fallen behind or, reputed to be hot-headed, perhaps had decided not to cooperate. Urged on by his wife, Ly Vong finally turned back and fought his way out of the plane to look for Chysa. The crowds continued to push on board. The airplane closed its doors, taxied down the concrete runway, and lumbered into the air — without Ly Vong.

Chysa, it turned out, had in fact boarded the airplane.

That night, with the Pathet Lao advancing, people waited all night for another airplane, crying.

By the next day, Wednesday, May 14, tension boiled. The C-130 pilot landed and taxied to where the crowd was huddled. Without stopping the plane, he dropped the ramp and kept rolling as people fought to climb aboard. The plane's crew member in back had to force the door shut against Hmong who were hoping, praying to be the last one to squeeze in.

Ly Vong did get onto a plane that day and was on his way to Thailand, to rejoin his family.

That was Wednesday, May 14. It was the last day of evacuations from Long Cheng.

7

An Argument with the Stone Age: Chamy Thor

The river never return.
— Chamy Thor

More than anything, going back to one's childhood home is about revisiting oneself.

I sensed this only dimly the day my family indulged me, after a Father's Day dinner, with a return pilgrimage to the house where I grew up. A crowd of us drove there, parked, and got out to walk around. Thanks to my mother's vow not to uproot her kids as she had been uprooted as a Navy child, I lived in the old two-story house from age six until I left for college.

I had not visited the neighborhood in decades. It had been the scene of pain and joy — the sweet scent of neighbors' lush flowers not so innocently plucked for a secret clubhouse, the crazy exhilaration of winning at dodge ball, the confusion of home, the comfort of school, all of them eventually absorbed more or less peaceably into my adult self. Now, family chattering around me, I walked the neatly sectioned sidewalk, climbed again the hilly route past the pepper trees to school, and stood again to gaze up past the languid deodar tree to the windows of the bedroom into which I was moved, unwillingly, after my brother left. Behind the flow of powerful feelings sprouted a desire to trace the effects of all that had occurred then.

In Laos, I saw, Chamy also revisited bruised memories and some scenes of delight.

The welcome was more than Chamy had expected. Besides the sister she had known would be there, other relatives had traveled miles to welcome her back to the land she had fled eighteen years before. Youngest sister, youngest sister's husband, mother's sister's son, children, and babies gathered around her. There would have been more, Chamy was told, but several relatives mistook the day and came yesterday. Chamy's youngest sister, Tooj, was red-faced and weeping, not with ritual tears but, it seemed, with the momentary laying down of some heavy burden. This was one of the younger siblings whom Chamy carried on her back while their parents farmed.

At last the greetings ran their course, and women wiped tears away with their sleeves. Chamy, as I've come to expect, had revealed little emotion, responding instead with her gentle, bubbling song-bird laugh. Now our knot of people, like many others around us in the baggage area and outside in front of the terminal, began to disperse in an assortment of dusty vehicles beneath the blue sky of a warm November afternoon.

A cousin of Nom Npis's had rented a passenger pickup truck and helped us load our personal luggage into the back. Five of Chamy's six giant suitcases were hoisted onto its roof. They were the biggest suitcases I have ever seen. This relative, on Nom Npis's side, is an employee of Vientiane's Wattay Airport, which occupies a piece of land about a mile north of the Mekong River. He was a valuable insider who knew how to get things done. A few days later, when we were back at the airport for a trip north, he stood beside the airline clerk and checked our pile of luggage free onto the tickets of unsuspecting passengers traveling light.

But right now, the cousin did not possess the magic to produce Chamy's sixth giant suitcase, the one that had traveled on my ticket. It was held up by customs. "Npis have to come for it later," Chamy said. I wondered what customs thought I might smuggle in — cartridges and clips for the guerrillas still operating in the mountains? In truth, Chamy had filled each of these bags with fifty or sixty pounds of used clothing from the Goodwill store in Sacramento, to be distributed to relatives.

"Come, Sue. We go now." I climbed after the nimble Chamy into the back of the pickup and sat crammed on a bench beside her. Jammed in with us were her youngest sister, a half dozen children, and other relatives who had waited all day for our flight. My head barely cleared the steel frame overhead, and my knees locked our smaller luggage into place against the opposite seat. We started down the airport's gravel road, past some employee's tidy vegetable garden. Suddenly I was aware of being out of my territory and in someone else's. But this was the land of my friends Chamy and Nom Npis, Mai Xiong, Ly Vong Lynaolu, the breast at which they fed, a country that taught them much but ill-prepared them for America.

With the sharpened senses of the just-arrived, I took in the square white buildings along Thanon Luang Prabang on the drive into town, the motorized bikes and tiny two-stroke, three-wheeled taxis with the onomatopoetic name of tuk-tuk, the odd-looking trees, the signs in a graceful alphabet peddling Laotian beer and Laotian cigarettes, and the small, slight pedestrians on the weedy sidewalks. The sun shone down. No need for sweaters.

Nom Npis sat in front with the ranking males. Around me, Chamy and the others chatted. Mostly, Chamy listened. Now one and then another spoke over the truck's noise. "What did they say?" I leaned toward Chamy. "Oh ...," she began in a promising tone but then returned to the others without finishing. The women, several with babies tied to their backs, looked tired and sweaty in their soiled skirts and blouses. The life of a young mother. Chamy, with her smooth paisley blouse, spotless black slacks, and careful makeup, looked in contrast like a visiting queen. I was eager to observe how my friend fit into her humble, old-style family.

Apparently no relatives lived in Vientiane with whom we could bunk, so we headed up a side street to a guesthouse. It occupied the second floor above a well-known French-Lao restaurant. We dragged gear up the outside concrete stairs, sweating, along an outside balcony, and into a pink-curtained room. It had one double bed, theirs, and one single bed, mine.

"You have that one," Chamy said, indicating the narrower bed with the sheet folded down.

Well, sure. I was here for the ride, but I hadn't anticipated sharing a room with somebody else's husband. Perhaps Chamy and Nom Npis didn't want to put me through the agony of sleeping alone. After all, we arranged our flight from Los Angeles so that we could travel with forty other Hmong instead of "alone," just the three of us.

"Cheaper this way," Chamy said, the more obvious explanation for the shared room. Still, I grew up the lone girl in my family, and I learned to think of a bedroom as private space, not an assembly space. Now in the pink bedroom at Santisouk Guest House, I saw that I had just been handed a priceless chance to get to know these two.

Through a door near the foot of my bed I found a sink, a toilet perched throne-like on a small platform, and a bathtub, where Chamy later showed me how to do laundry. I watched her stand in the tub and deftly work wet, soaped lumps of clothing with her short, broad feet as if they were hands kneading dough. My attempts were laughable.

Now after the dusty ride from the airport I sank down onto my sway-backed bed, thrilled with everything new to my eyes. Meanwhile Chamy, brows gathered in a managerial wrinkle, took charge of window opening and shutting, closet organizing, and locating the community clothes lines, which she found looped from wooden arms on the red concrete balcony outside our window. Laos at last, I sighed.

"Let's go," said Chamy brightly the next morning. I had already yielded up most of our three-week itinerary to Chamy and Nom Npis, curious as to what their priorities would be. As most of their planning took place in the abbreviated Hmong of old-marrieds, and as Chamy's habit of minimalist translation unfolded, I knew little of what was afoot. "Sure!" I replied. "Where?"

"We go see Vientiane," she announced. Apparently it would take a few days before we could receive permission and get tickets to fly north to see her mother. Driving there along the nation's main north-south highway, a back-country track of scary description due to guerrilla raids, was out of the question. After that first night's befuddled sleep, which began at five p.m., Chamy had arisen at eleven p.m. mistaking the hour for three in the morning. She was up, businesslike, turning on the overhead light and locating fresh clothes for the day. What was it she thought we might do at three a.m.? I wondered. When dawn finally broke we took off on foot for the market a mile away. Chamy led. This was her town. Her stride, toes out, was firm, like that of a school principal navigating her domain. Head up, her arms swung freely. Hers is not the kind of reserved, feminine walk I see in most Hmong women. Nom Npis, in a fresh white business shirt open at the collar, had selected for himself the position of porter. He paced behind Chamy with his still camera and video camera and Chamy's all-purpose shoulder bag. His shoulders were sloped but strong, and his head stood erect on a muscled neck. I trailed behind, checking for extra film and writing jiggly notes in my notebook.

We paused for street-side fruit and savory, pâté-stuffed French bread that is one of the positive legacies of colonialism. The Laotian woman spread on the meat filling and handed us the crunchy bread wrapped in recycled business flyers. "Eat!" sang Chamy, gesturing toward my sandwich with hers. "It's good! Make you strong!" She laughed.

Near the U.S. Embassy, four goats grazed around the base of an ancient, blackened stone tower. "I remember this very well," Chamy announced. Then I spotted someone I knew — Pao Vang, a community-active Hmong man from Sacramento whom I met while recruiting for a university leadership institute. A tuk-tuk steered around us as I introduced Pao to Chamy and Nom Npis. They had not met before. Chamy was polite but brief. "Oh, from Sacramento?" Then I remembered: I haven't noticed any Vangs in the Thor or Lee family tree. Pao Vang is not clan. Without the compulsion to discover common ancestors or relatives, they had little to say.

We walked on. Using my hand as a shield against the hot sun, I soaked up the sight of purple-flowering trees planted along the sidewalk, the mix of urban-French and rural–Lao architecture, and the short-statured Lao who passed us quietly on the sidewalk without glancing up. We climbed, sweating, up stairs to the top of Patuxai monument. This small-scale Arc de Triomphe stands grandly at the nexus of two Paris-sized boulevards. Peering out each of the four sides of the monument in turn, at first I saw only a handful of buildings edging a puffy, endless sea of deep green trees that stretched out on a plain as flat as a tray—palms and unfamiliar trees. The quiet was barely disturbed by the little bit of traffic directly below. Tuk tuks, a few smoking motorbikes announced by a brr-r-r-r-t , and bicycles with passengers sitting sidesaddle passed by on the street. Their passage had swept a pathway clean of the rust-red dust that covered the remainder of the paved surface. There were so few vehicles that I could count them.

Nothing worthy of comment presented itself to my eyes. Little of the city was visible beneath the jungle cover. No remarkable temples poked through. Only a few government buildings lined the avenue, most in need of paint. Overhead, the deep blue sky was cobbled with thin, cottony clouds, and a light breeze blew. A small, ex-colonial capital in a small, ex-colonial nation.

But my companions, silent, saw more. Nom Npis pointed to a white-colonnaded building below. "This building?" he said. "That is the Senate. Where uncle was senator. And back there, behind trees—" He pointed behind the Senate building to the compound, where we could just see vegetables growing in small plots. "That's where I stay. That's where I live." Suddenly I realized that this was the uncle he lived with in Long Cheng as a boy in order to go to school, the one whom he had to serve willingly day or night. Nom Npis continued to look, his face dark in the shadow of the monument's roof.

Chamy shook herself out of a reverie to direct my eyes to the left. "Right there," she said, "that's the lycée where I go to school." I recalled the stories she told me at her dining table back home, about her years of absence from the home village and her head-down doggedness to achieve. Behind tropical street trees with gaudy flowers I could see a two-story, mint-green building with two wings like arms flung wide before a large, yellowing grassy area. Half a dozen big, old trees grew in the lawn. They looked like elms. Imported from France, I guessed. More elms rose from behind the main building, where I glimpsed some long, low buildings.

Chamy said, "See the long white wall? with the gate at the end?" She frowned against the brilliant light. "That is the gate I use to go in and out." This scenery was far richer than I thought. I had overlooked the ghosts.

Back down on the street Chamy said, "Did you see the postcards with Hmong people on them?" Yes. They were on racks at the souvenir stands under the arch. "They not there before." In her time, such simple acknowledgment of a minority's existence did not happen. "The government makes people be nicer to Hmong now. Before, it was very segregated." But Nom Npis hastened to modify the rosy image. "Discrimination starts twenty-five kilometers outside Vientiane. Here, if they discriminate, go to jail." Of Laos's more than four and a half million people, Hmong still make up the third largest ethnic group. The Lao are most numerous, followed by the Khmu, who live below the Hmong on the slopes of mountains. The Khmu, the "laboring class," also apparently occupy a spot below the Hmong in the social hierarchy, but both rank beneath the Lao.

We walked onto the lycée grounds. Chamy maintained a breezy demeanor. The high, open-work facade was streaked with black tropical mildew. Leading up to the entrance was a broad, graveled driveway that divided around a carefully bordered, European-style island filled, I suddenly realized, with what I know as house plants. Someone, drunk or indifferent, had painted the curbing of the grand driveway a blinding, sloppy white. Circles of students in uniform sat quietly under the trees or strolled across the grounds. The girls' long black hair was uniformly pulled back into ponytails. An occasional pale butterfly flitted past. We walked through a passageway in the main building to find long sky-blue and white rows of classrooms, each room opening to the outdoors California-style.

"So this is where you studied." "This is where I study," Chamy said, affirming my statement by repeating it, in the Hmong way. Crowds of high school age boys and girls in navy blue were taking a break beneath unglazed, louvered windows. An army of bicycles had been herded into one courtyard corner. Chamy stood, one hand in her slacks pocket, and took it in. Her face revealed nothing. Perhaps she wondered at the chance events that directed her life.

We didn't leave by Chamy's gate — "I not supposed to use it when I go here, but I do it anyway," she said with a laugh — but back through the formal front entrance with the drunken curb painting. Then we walked as she once did to the last house she occupied as a student, after her twin uncles were killed in the war.

The road we walked was once paved. Now it featured big, lazy pot-holes. Grand old French colonial mansions showed the trademark streaks of tropical mildew. Some were occupied by multiple families. Others, Chamy said, had been torn down to eradicate reminders of colonialism.

"After 1975 the government close Laos. No foreigners, no outside goods. They say 'We can do it ourselves.' Since communist takeover, Laos have gone back to the old way of making fabric, like from silk, and every-body have to wear Laotian dress and go back to the old [ways].

"Only they don't manufacture machinery or lawnmowers or paint!" Chamy said in disgust. Vientiane, to her sorrow, was now dusty, unpainted, weedy. "It's like a ghost town," she said. Earlier we had walked by the Aus-tralian Embassy, freshly painted and with meticulous grounds. "That is how Vientiane used to look." Still, government authorities were beginning to see that the big two-story reminders of colonial humiliation could also fill the need for office space. And so on our walk we passed a few old houses caged in casual scaffolding and sporting a few workmen.

It was a long walk to Chamy's old place. The sun was bright and hot, and Chamy opened the black umbrella she had bought to provide some cool shade and to protect her skin from darkening. We came upon some heavy road repair equipment parked at the edge of a dirt road. I stopped to photograph a road grader for my grandson and only then noticed the driver seated in one of the cabs. He was motionless. It was siesta time.

We trudged on, finally arriving at the blackened, shuttered wooden building where Chamy lived with her younger brother and an uncle for her final eighteen months of school. The building was topped by a corru-gated metal roof and had five apartments in a row like motel rooms, with plywood doors and a minimum of framing. "This one on the end." We stopped there. It appeared to be boarded shut. "We cook in back," out-side the building, she said. Indeed, this must have been a big step down from the fine home Chamy's fighter pilot uncles had invited her to share. The road here was deeply rutted from the annual monsoon rains and dot-ted with litter. A few children from two apartments down paused to look at us and then resumed their play. Nom Npis and I studied the grim old building but then stepped away. Chamy lingered, one hand again in her slacks pocket, taking the time she needed to remember.

On the way back into the center of town, Nom Npis said, "We go to find rice noodles, my favorite." He had made a trip to Vientiane three years earlier, and we now benefited from his knowledge of the best places to eat. Leaving behind the racket of motorbikes that converged at the broad-roofed Morning Market, we wended our way past stands and open-fronted shops to a back alley with boards thrown down to save feet from mud. The shop Nom Npis chose was open-air but for a roof. We seated ourselves on plain wooden benches at a table covered with red and white oilcloth. The food Nom Npis ordered for me was *fawm*, Lao noodles in a hot, seasoned broth. "Do like this," Nom Npis encouraged, using his fingers to add fresh greens and slim, mild green onions to the broth and mixing everything together with a tablespoon. I already knew to go easy on dipping from the tiny dish of pepper sauce.

When we were sated, I turned to Chamy with a question. "Are you ever sorry you left Laos?"

"No!" she answered. "No. Never!"

Kilometer 52

We had one more day before our flight to Luang Prabang, the lovely ancient royal capital in northern Laos. "Today we go to Kilometre 52," Chamy said, giving "kilometre" her usual French pronunciation. "That is where I spend summer vacation with my uncle"—still another uncle besides the Vientiane uncles. It was too expensive and difficult to go home. Now Chamy's youngest sister, Tooj ("tong"), and a few of Tooj's children joined us for the day trip to visit relatives.

The surprisingly comfortable bus out of Vientiane bore a plaque over the driver's head announcing that it was part of a Laos/Japan "project for improving public transportation in Vientiane." This was not the only evidence of foreign assistance I would see in this poorest of poor countries where the average per-person earnings is three hundred fifty dollars a year. Other discreet signs on equipment or infrastructure named Australia, another important presence here. Somehow it had escaped my notice that Australia is a neighbor of Southeast Asia.

Suddenly the bus pulled to a stop beside an empty field, and riders in front of us began to laugh. The door swung open and a woman, in her thirties or forties, hopped out. She was laughing, too. Puzzled, I watched her head across the field to the far side, where bushes and tall grasses grew. She disappeared behind the growth for a minute, then reappeared and quickly made her way back to the bus, laughing as she approached.

"She have to go to the bathroom," Chamy explained, scarcely heeding the woman. The bus doors closed and we continued.

The episode put me in mind to ask Chamy about public health. "They don't have that. They don't know about that even in Vientiane.[1] People get sick and die, they don't care. Life is cheap. They're not nice. You struggle to live, so they're not nice to each other." Her tone of voice, though restrained, clearly proclaimed: This is no way for humans to live.

We were still on a paved surface as Highway 13 angled northwest across the flat plain of Vientiane. I noted signs that announced Pepsi, Toyota, and Shell Oil along with a haphazard dusting of trash and some foraging front-yard turkeys. I craned my neck to catch a glimpse of a water buffalo cow and calf. Chamy, however, was intent on the vegetation.

"Ohhh, this look more like it." The clusters of trees, the arched stands of giant bamboo, the big-leaved roadside plants, all these had laid hold on her heart. I thought about Chamy's garden with its rows and rows of vegetables and herbs and the special bamboos, the love and labor she lavishes upon it all. "Maybe I move back to Laos," she joked.

We arrived in Kilometer 52 after a brief, unseasonable rain and got off on the main street. The town clings closely to both sides of Highway 13 as to a source of life. Nom Npis strolled up to some Hmong men he didn't know and began to converse, one hand thrust deep in his slacks pocket. Nom Npis never met a stranger.

I observed the Laotians and Hmong stopping by to look at us and noticed a stark difference between them and the American Hmong with whom I was traveling. American Hmong are much better fed than most people in Laos. This came home vividly to Chamy, too. Before seeking out the relatives, Chamy crossed to the market and bought a length of Lao fabric. She always has an eye out for textiles and needlework to add to her collection. At a muddy spot where we turned off the main road to find the relatives, a tailor, a friendly woman, ran a small shop — a shed, really, open to the road. A treadle sewing machine half swathed in a stitching project stood on a table positioned to catch daylight. Chamy left the fabric there for the tailor to stitch together, a simple seam joining the two raw edges to form the Lao sarong-style skirt. A few hours later, when we returned to collect it, the woman unfolded the skirt and showed us the extra material she had been obliged to add to accommodate Chamy's rounded figure.

"She say I am too fat for Lao skirt." Chamy made a wry face. Although pudginess is desirable in Laos — a sign of prosperity — Chamy is American enough to be self-conscious about this. "I try to lose weight," she said, voice trailing off in the classic American complaint.

Straddling muddy gashes in the narrow wet road, I followed the others to our first family visit. This household belongs to Tooj's husband's nephew. It was my first taste of traditional Hmong life, and I was eager. Children, the youngest conveniently naked, played outside. Inside, light filtering through the loosely fitted wall boards brightened the cool darkness. Chamy and the others sat and chatted quietly while I gazed about the wooden interior, thrilled to be at a relative's home at last. From pictures I had seen, I recognized an occasional pot or tool hanging on a wall or resting on the dirt floor. But, being a child of the city, I was not prepared for the killing of the dinner chicken, its wings spread in Tooj's hands as if in flight and its life's blood dropping into a metal basin.

Before taking the afternoon bus back to Vientiane, we stopped at a house close beside the highway that belongs to Nom Npis's clan relative, a cousin of Ly Vong Lynaolu's. Along with teaching college classes at a row of classrooms built by Americans in 1973 a short distance from the highway, this middle-aged man teaches some seventy teenagers at his home. More accurately, under his home. Underneath his Lao-style house on posts, twenty students gather at a time on benches and at desks. A sentence on the chalkboard read, "Lesson five. When you visit Lao textiles, you'll see something." Elsewhere in Southeast Asia people are scrambling to learn English, but it surprised me to find it here in this deliberately isolated country.

We sat just behind the teaching area and drank coconut milk drinks, chatting with the cousin. The immaculate floor under our feet was concrete, Nom Npis pointed out, lifting his eyebrows knowingly at me. Nom Npis had stayed at this house for several weeks on his previous trip to Laos and, he was pleased to say, helped with the two hundred dollar cost of the floor.

This cousin has given up the thatched-roof, dirt-floor Hmong house of his heritage. Well-educated, he is part of the tiny Hmong elite, a few of whom have adopted Lao dress and housing. In this he's symbolic of Kilometer 52. Although founded in 1968 for Hmong by a Hmong man, Nom Npis told me, Kilometer 52 is now half ethnic Lao. And more than a few of the Hmong have adopted Lao ways.

The man who founded Kilometer 52 was the older brother of Ly Vong Lynaolu and another of the Hmong elite. I glanced up the street, with its numerous sturdy wood houses and big covered market. This was a far cry from the romantic mountainside Hmong villages I'd seen in photographs. "Ly Vong's brother owned it all?" I asked Nom Npis.

"He own it all. He planted thousands, thousands fruit trees." This brother of Ly Vong's also reportedly owned another village east of Vientiane, similarly subdividing it for small businesses and homes. This brother had come to the United States in 1988.

"They garden in our back yard," Chamy added, hoping I could remember which family she meant. Unfortunately I could not sort him out from the dozens of others I've met within her sphere.

Family

At last we were on a prop jet bound for Luang Prabang.

"Now we see the real people!" Chamy said. I didn't understand what she meant. I had thought those relatives in the thatched-roof house in Kilometer 52, the ones with the bleeding chicken, were real Hmong. But she was teaching me distinctions. Before we arrived in Laos, I assumed *Laos* was Chamy's world, the Hmong's world. But it isn't. Even Vientiane, where Chamy lived for years, belonged to the French and Lao.

Even in Kilometer 52, home of many hundreds of Hmong, we had not yet entered the pure, remembered Hmong world, where things went unquestioned and you behaved like everyone else. Details of family life in Kilometer 52 might seem the same — the foods set before us in common bowls, the house, the little kids running bare-bottomed outside — but the setting had changed. Kilometer 52 sits on a major highway far from the Hmong's mountains, with buses and taxi trucks that offer a stunning alternative to foot travel on steep paths and a market that provides vegetables and meat over which one did not personally labor.

Chamy had taken refuge in Kilometer 52 years before, no doubt a welcome break from the onslaught of new thoughts and demands imposed upon her in the French school. This outpost of the Hmong world offered a safe haven, but for us on our journey backward in her personal time, we were not there yet.

The isolation of our destination was impressive. Though the trip by air cost precious money, it was the only sensible option for travel to Luang Prabang. Only the bold drive Highway 13. Not many miles past Kilometer 52, the French-built highway reverts to a dirt road threading through jungle, where tenacious guerrillas keep alive the hope of wresting a homeland from the Laotian government. There is no train in Laos.

By now I was getting into the Hmong swing of things. We had awakened this morning about four thirty so we could arrive at the airport at eight for a ten-thirty flight actually scheduled for eleven thirty that finally left at twelve thirty. I could only be amused by the Hmong's abhorrence of being merely on time. In the morning, if it's light enough to see, you're late! Chamy and Nom Npis do not have this habit through individual quirk, as I once thought. Rising early, in the dark, was how one kept the food coming.

Now in the air, we left the table-flat plain around Vientiane with its tan, wintering rice fields and tracings of roads and began to see a pebbling of lush hills. Soon green mountains rose wave after wave under a sky made more blue by the pure white of cumulus clouds to the northeast. Then steep, rocky mountains rose around us, standing guard over an ancient landscape stark in its green emptiness. Rivers sent glinting strands through valleys unmarred by human improvement. Occasionally we spotted farmers' fields like squares of rough cloth between the trees. Chamy had already told me that in places like Luang Prabang, away from the Vietnamese war front and contact with Westerners, more Hmong men and women wear the traditional black pants and shirts. I saw them in the picture postcards at the Patuxai monument, dressed in black clothing spiced with brilliant red sashes, and, for the women, long aprons and embroidered collars like the one I had stitched. This, too, signals "real people" to Chamy. Elsewhere, in the areas of greater contact, Hmong had traded traditional dress for Lao or Western styles.

From the airplane window, Chamy quietly took it all in, her dark hair neatly combed, pearl earrings in place. I was eager to meet Chamy's mother. Would she be the same cool number as Chamy, in full possession of herself here in home territory? On our arrival in Laos I had watched in amazement as Chamy remained dry-eyed while weeping relatives poured out their emotions to her. Would she be equally composed with her mother?

The plane dropped down and taxied near to a small, once-white terminal building. As we descended the wheeled stairs, clumps of people glanced our way but no one showed signs of greeting. Chamy ignored them. "We have to wait to see my mom. They not come today." The village was still far away. "One brother in Sayaboury Province — I don't know if he'll come. Too far. His family, they won't come." But when we drew close, one of the knots attracted Chamy's attention, and she veered toward them.

"Oh, they come!" Chamy exclaimed with a thrill in her voice. It was her family. Oldest brother, second brother, wives with their arms and environs full of children, cousins, and Mom. Nearly twenty people had come. Even the brother from the next province had come, complete with his family. Chamy greeted her brothers reservedly and then placed an arm around her mother's shoulders. Chamy's mother began to weep and reached up to stroke her daughter's hair as the others stood close. Then tears streamed down Chamy's face, too. Her people had made difficult, expensive trips to meet her.

I wanted to study each face, each person, but my attention fixed on Chamy's mother. She was two or three inches shorter than her daughter, putting her at about four ten, I guessed. Nobody hugged. That's not Hmong. Rather, women will caress the back of the other's head, place a hand lightly on a shoulder, and engulf each other with words rendered

Chamy Thor (center) and her mother (right) at a market, Laos, December, 1994.

soft and wavering by crying. I was much included in this welcome, as one after another of Chamy's relatives smiled warmly into my face, patted my arm, and said, "*Kos tuaj los*," "You've come!" Letters Chamy sent to her mother via family in Luang Prabang had told them of my coming.

Later Chamy said to me, "They didn't recognize me." That was why they had not stepped forward as soon as she came down the steps. Small wonder. The last time they saw her, she was as gaunt as they.

While we stood at the edge of the runway and the first news was exchanged, I got a chance to observe the family. Chamy's mother — her name is Kia Lis — was dressed in a pair of black slacks and a purple-flowered black shirt topped by a sweater that hung from straight, wide shoulders. Her head was nearly engulfed by a big cuffed cap of fuzzy black material, despite mild weather. She seemed to disappear inside her heavy clothes. Standing on either side of her, the young wives of the family in contrast wore short-sleeved blouses and light Lao skirts. Several had babies tucked into sash slings on one hip. One of the babies continually reached out a small hand toward Kia's arm and looked into her face. I guessed that Kia was the child's babysitter. Kia's face, like that of her first-born son who stood a few steps behind her, was dominated by high round cheekbones that tilted her deep-set, modest brown eyes upward at the corner. What startled me through all this was that her face was virtually free of motion, thin lips moving as little as possible as she spoke her few words to Chamy.

Slowly we moved toward a muddy, banged-up Toyota pickup truck to drive the mile or two into town. Nom Npis, the second brother, and a tall man who turned out to be the head man of Chestnut Mountain, the home village, lifted our bags on top of the pickup. The giant suitcases now numbered only four since Chamy had left two with Tooj. We clambered inside the truck, and I smacked my head on the overhead frame. "Ohh, Sue!" Chamy made a motherly face at me. "Be careful!" During the short trip, Chamy, her brows now drawn closer in a slight, constant frown, placed a gentle hand on a child's small back and listened to his mother weep and talk: I want to see my mother, too, this smooth-skinned woman said, unconsciously massaging her little one's hand and intermittently wiping tears off her face with her wrist. But America, where her mother has gone to live with a son, is too far away and there is no money. Kia sat across from Chamy, hands at rest in her lap.

In Luang Prabang, the bags were deposited at a relative's house, and we were deposited at a big central market. It was time to shop. This caught me by surprise, but the clues had been there all along had I read them. Preparing for the trip, I had asked Chamy about money. "How much are you bringing?" "Oh, three or four thousand." I had thought Laos was inexpensive, but I took her information into account. Now I was to discover the mathematics of the visit.

Luang Prabang's market is an extensive indoor market with a crosshatching of aisles that offer clothing, jewelry, and household goods. As we walked through it I noticed items stacked in neat piles on tables or dangled at a height of eight or ten feet at the front of each shop. It had the earmarks of capitalism. Later I asked Nom Npis if they were state-run shops. "No, private. Only manufacture is state[-owned]."

We moved up one crowded aisle and down another — Chamy and I and five of her female relatives. In a strange city amid people I had only just met, I felt at ease and included. Several of the young women watched over their shoulders or touched my elbow so I wouldn't become separated. As we wended through the market, I was intrigued by the goods, familiar categories like towels and blouses but in unfamiliar patterns, fabrics, and shapes. Studying all this I failed to comprehend what was going on with Chamy and her women. Moving along the market aisles like a ball team, the women were pointing out what they needed. "I buy for them," was Chamy's report later.

After a good half hour and apparently a satiety of purchasing, one of the more outgoing young women addressed me with a warm smile. On her head she wore the thick French-blue scarf favored by Hmong, tied at the back under a knot of black hair. "You buy a bed quilt?" This was conveyed to me in Hmong but mostly through our location beside a bedding shop and by pointing, first to me and then to my green shoulder bag, which she correctly assumed harbored my money. The other women, smiling and laughing, gathered and nodded. I thought, What do I want with a bed quilt? These are a current favorite in Hmong circles and as I learned later are rolled at the head of the bed each morning. Chamy spoke firmly to the woman, whose happy face showed no alteration. "She want you to buy her a bed quilt, but I told her no."

"Is there any problem with buying her one?" I asked. "No, it's OK," said Chamy. With our small, approving audience of the other women, the woman picked out a quilt in primary colors and I handed over some kip to the hovering clerk.

The transaction was wholly cheerful. The only one discomfited was Chamy, who knew that such "begging" would be awkward in the United States. But to the women the situation was simple. I, clearly, had money, and they, clearly, had needs they could not fill. The solution was obvious.

I continued to be drawn to Chamy's mother. It was this woman who had tied a baby onto little Chamy's back and had come to nurse it in the field when Chamy called. It was Kia who tended Chamy through her difficult first pregnancy and assisted in the emergency roadside delivery of the baby. The truth is I am awed by all these tough Hmong women of the mountains who for generations have worked from dark to dark raising and preparing food, have endured frequent births, and still possess a warm and companionable quality. It's not that they are superhuman. Hmong can be harsh on each other, harboring animosities for decades like the Hatfields and McCoys, and tipping the balance of power heavily, sometimes dangerously, on the side of males. But their habit of no-fuss, openhanded welcome, tucking you under a wing as if you were one more relative, captures the heart. Kia showed this quality, too, but she was nearly invisible about it. She seemed so timid and yet had been willing to fly on an airplane to America, alone, to see her daughter. Now, the immobility of her face and its small, wrinkled eyes reminded me of an aged tortoise. But my sense was that the face concealed much story.

Amid a family of black-haired people, Kia Lis, who was probably about sixty years old, has brown hair, smoothed back and fastened at the neck with a big plain barrette. Chamy doesn't have the brown hair, but she resembles her mother in the rise of cheekbone and bas-relief profile. Chamy is the fourth child of Kia Lis and Txhiaj Lis Thoj but, as in so many

families, Kia isn't certain of the year of the birth. Kia's first children are
the two older brothers who met us at the airport. Next was a daughter,
shot and killed escaping across the Mekong in 1979 with her son on her
back. (I later uncovered a similar story among friends in Santa Ana. Such
stories hang like a pall over many families, like the families of massacre
victims in the U.S.) Next in line came Chamy. A younger brother died of
illness in Laos in 1984, and the youngest brother, with his wife and children age two to sixteen, share a house with Kia, as is the duty of the
youngest son. I almost missed meeting this brother. He was attending
truck-driving school while we were in Laos, and only toward the end of
the trip did he have time off to visit us. Chamy's youngest sister, Tooj, a
seamstress, I knew from our arrival in Vientiane.

After these seven children, Chamy's father got sick.

"When I was probably five or six years old, my father died. Then they
make my mom marry with my uncle," who lived nearby — "really good
friends, good older brothers."

"At that time my uncle have nine children [and a wife], and my mom
with seven children, so we have a lot of people living in the same house."
To this union was born just one child, a daughter, who lives in Appleton,
Wisconsin.

It was while she was living in this crowded house that Chamy, her
older step-sister Mai, and a young aunt were picked to go to Vientiane to
school. Had Chamy's mother not married into that household, it is unlikely
that Chamy would have gone.

Soon, Kia found the house too crowded. "Too many kids there, so
they don't have enough food. They are starving," Chamy said. So her
mother made the decision to move out and live by herself again, with her
children. Her eldest was fifteen or sixteen years old, the son she once fastened to a house post in his baby carrier for lack of a babysitter. Her
youngest was still a baby. Then in 1965, her new husband was shot in the
neck by communists and killed.

Once our shopping at the big market was completed, we three travelers, the welcoming party, and the mountain of luggage were piled into
a big passenger truck. This vehicle was put at our service by another relative, complete with a nineteen-year-old driver. At last, we were on our
way to Roob Ntsej, Chestnut Mountain, Chamy's mother's village. Outside Luang Prabang we stopped before a police station set back in an overgrown yard. Nom Npis asked for my passport and some kip to facilitate
the granting of permission to stay in the village. He headed off with Chestnut Mountain's head man. Kia trailed inconspicuously behind.

Here, I learned later, was what happened: The request was presented to the police. Two Hmong from America and a friend are outside, and they want to stay in Chestnut Mountain with the mother — this lady here. They have come a long way for this visit. The request was discussed in a back room, and, when they emerged, the verdict was returned. No go. Chamy's mother began to cry and then to wail, and the police chiefs began to laugh. I have already bought a cow and paid three hundred dollars for it, Kia cried. OK, OK, the police conceded, shushing her. They can stay for one night, but you must guarantee their safety.

I was so amused by this tale of Kia and the police chiefs that I did not notice an extra man, taller, tidier, sleeker than the others, climbing into the cab of the truck as we took off along unpaved Highway 13 toward Chestnut Mountain. Actually Chamy had mentioned it months before the trip, but my personal experience didn't provide a mental slot for the information.

Chestnut Mountain

After more than an hour's drive uphill out of Luang Prabang on graded dirt that shaded flesh-like from red to purple, our truck pulled off and parked in a flat area. A big, faded-red hydraulic shovel occupied part of the turnout. A few hundred yards farther along the highway, workers blasted rock to widen the road.

Above the turnout, several Hmong houses roosted on the ground like large brown hens. Children telegraphed our arrival, and a scattering of grownups appeared. "We're here," Chamy said. We were indeed. Chestnut Mountain. This was what I had come to Laos for, to see the kind of world that nurtured Chamy, the kind of life she would now be living but for an uncle.

Chamy had never seen this particular village. Her mother moved here after Chamy left Laos. We walked a quarter mile up a six-foot-wide, hand-cut road to a cluster of houses. With their big brooding roofs that extend nearly to the ground, they give an appearance of solidity. But closer inspection showed that they had loosely fitted bamboo and plank walls to allow smoke to filter out from the indoor cooking fires.

Kia's house was third or fourth in. Like the others, it rested on a level pad against the hillside, the soil retained both above and below by logs. In front, an open area clean of vegetation was alive with children, dogs, and a few men who chatted. Not far away, a serious-looking girl of about ten stood with hands quiet at her sides watching us. She reminded me of Chamy.

Hmong build their homes from materials around them. Here, cleared fields are visible on distant hillsides. Chestnut Mountain, Laos, December 1994.

The wooden door to Kia's house stood open. Chamy, Nom Npis, and I stepped over the big hewn doorsill and made our way through the house's twilight to the bamboo guest platform. Houses like this, I thought, are the antecedent to Hmong homes I have visited in California that are kept darkened by drawn curtains: Perhaps the dark interiors in California bring comforting memories of former homes. Chamy set down her bag on the platform and pushed it neatly against the wall. I sat and eased my backpack off my shoulders. Kia spoke brief words to Chamy: We are family, and so we would not sleep on the guest bed. Instead, we would occupy one of the three beds in the family bedroom, displacing the usual occupants.

I sat on the platform and looked around. Walls, packed dirt floor, framing logs, thatch above, the small loft toward the back of the house — everything was in soft shades of gray and brown. No wonder Hmong festival dress is highly colored.

Against the rectangle of bright daylight that was the front door, strings of adults and children stepped in to talk or just look, occasionally followed by one of the village dogs, which someone promptly chased back out. I was eager to ask about the village and about the house in which Chamy now held court. Chamy as usual was eager to explain Hmong ways to me, the good and the bad, as she saw them.

This house was built for Kia by one of the brothers, she told me. The land was neither leased nor bought, simply occupied. "How was it built?," I asked. "Probably after you get all the material together [from the forest], the village men will help you put it up, probably one or two days. Everything would be fastened together with strips of bamboo. "No hammer. No nails." Chamy said with pride.

From my spot on the guest platform I could see the small fire ring near the middle of Kia's house. It was into a *qhov cub* such as this that the absent-minded babysitter Chamy saw her baby brother fall, scarring his body and her memory.

Inside the family bedroom, sectioned off from the main room by bamboo walls, the giant suitcases were opened and Chamy helped family members choose clothes, lifting items in her hands and turning them this way and that. Wads of money were quietly pressed into calloused hands. From my backpack-suitcase I pulled a warm sweater bought in Los Angeles's Chinatown for Kia. She accepted it with minimum comment — good Hmong manners — and hid it away.

Seated again on the guest platform, I looked more closely at the interior of the house. On an earlier trip to Thailand I had noted the daily ritual of Hmong women sweeping a packed dirt floor like this one with a short-handled broom, removing dust and the other debris of living. Such a floor gives the feel of linoleum underfoot. Of course it's harder to keep one's clothes and one's children clean with a dirt floor, even packed as hard as it is, but it's a forgiving medium for kids who spill.

I could see Kia's water containers, not the traditional wooden ones but big multi-gallon plastic ones, in the corner by the big stove. Made aware by a city manager friend back home who was always on the look-out for wires and other evidence of utilities in back-country photos, I asked about what I didn't see around the village as well as what I saw. No, Chamy said, there was no running water anywhere in Chestnut Mountain. Water was hauled uphill from a pond the men dug near a creek a mile away. For laundry you carried your load down to the creek, washed it on the rocks, and spread it to dry on bushes. Chamy once showed me the dark wrinkled nut the size of a walnut that women gather, split, and rub on their laundry for suds. Then she told me about coming home after four years at school, wanting to help her hard-working, widowed mother. "I see that they don't have any water, and I pick up one [carrying] barrel. It's been a long time that I didn't do that. And I went to the stream, and I start to do like they did [shouldering an adult-size container]. And I'm [bent] very, very close to the ground...." She was laughing. "My uncle wife saw me and she laugh at me. She say, 'Ohh, look at you, you don't have to do that if you don't know how.'"[2]

Neither is there electricity in Chestnut Mountain. A project to string power lines along the highway was under way at the time of our visit. A few well-off villagers owned kerosene lamps to provide light, and Kia had borrowed one for our visit. "When we got there they sent somebody over to borrow," Chamy said. "But it smells bad, so I don't care for that." She laughed. "They treat us special. That's why they borrow the kerosene [lamp].

"But actually, the kerosene [lamp] have to use a certain type of fuel, and they don't have money to buy that. So it's best to raise pigs and get the oil from the pigs."

Chamy described this pig-oil lamp. "They build a small metal [receptacle], and then they put pig oil in it. They use the piece of fabric, long fabric, and they braid the cloth and they put it in the oil so the end of the cloth will come out of the little pan to put the flame on. In the old day we used to have that." Such lamps have been a universal of human life, from pottery lamps that burned olive oil in ancient Rome to recent Alaskan native stone lamps that burn whale oil. "Very few people have the kerosene, even now." Later, on returning home, I stood in astonishment before the light switch in our kitchen, flipping it on and off. Same with the faucet. It registered that the absence of such utilities means trips up a steep path carrying twenty or thirty pounds of water, hours spent collecting wood and tending a fire, and bending over to catch light from a lamp for which you've boiled pig fat. It means more dirt, less food storage, less information. It means less time to maintain schools, to study, to write or produce books.

Centuries of isolation made the Hmong infinitely self-reliant. Chamy remembers the recipe for making paper after having watched her mother do it once. The paper was probably put to ceremonial use on family altars. From the forest Kia selected young bamboo, Chamy said, boiled the bamboo heart for hours with ash, pounded the pulp, mixed it with glue made from bark, and spread it to dry on a cloth tied by the corners to trees. On a later visit to a Hmong community in Thailand, I watched a relative of Chamy's quickly create a length of string by rolling three strands of plant fiber along his bare thigh, as easily as if he were fishing it out of the center of a shrink-wrapped ball from the hardware store.

Each of these skills—making paper or string plus innumerable other skills related to food, house, clothes, health, and arts—represented hundreds of bits of knowledge passed down from parent to child woven together with movements of hand, back, leg, and arm, and practiced, practiced over years.

Everyone in Kia's main room stood up. "We go for walk around the village," Chamy said. Outside Kia's back door we stepped onto another clean, flat space fenced on the downhill side and watched over by a ten-foot-tall poinsettia. Beyond this back area lay an exquisite panorama, a quiet green valley surrounded by mountains that wore clouds like necklaces.

Chamy and Nom Npis led the way up the easy hill, a royal procession. I comfortably fell in with the children, who were entertained by my efforts at Hmong and bounced along with me cheerfully. Children such as these, especially the girls, loved to look at the family photos I brought of grandchildren and a daughter in her wedding dress. "*Kuv tus ntxhais, kuv tus vauv,*" I pointed out my daughter and son-in-law. "*Koj tus ntxhais, koj tus vauv,*" they repeated meticulously.

The village was steep in places, with graded and fenced trails that traversed the hillside between rows of houses. A brown and white dog with a curled tail accompanied us for a distance and then returned in the direction of the house. More giant poinsettias stood out like flaming torches against the brown of soil and thatched roofs.

We arrived in a level open area like a small town square between the houses and grain storage sheds. Three elderly men gathered at the bottom of some stairs leading to a home's rare second story. One small old man in black jacket held a staff and stepped carefully up onto the stairs' footing to talk to the camera. I caught words I understood: "plant rice," "don't have money." Beside him in dusty black shirt and pants stood a man with tousled gray hair and another man with a puffy red nose. In their genuine dignity, the three might have been posing for Mount Rushmore. Men like these were important fixtures in Chamy's girlhood, clan elders whose words carried weight. They were the ones with the most common sense and wisdom. But outside the Hmong world, their knowledge meant little.

Men such as these three and the younger headman would have kept such order as was necessary in the Phou Lac of Chamy's childhood, where everybody knew everybody. They were the law, albeit only by the villagers' leave. Even today, no external laws reach Chestnut Mountain. No taxes are levied in the village, and no fees are charged to hunt or fish. It is the same through much of Laos, not just in the Hmong villages. For example, no driver's license is required outside of Vientiane or Kilometer 52.

"That's why when they have [a vehicle] accident?" Chamy said, "the two people just keep fighting, arguing to see who is at fault. There's no rule, no sign, no whatever.

"When there is a big problem, big killer or something in the village, then they just take that person and lock him in a jail in a city until people get money and just bail that person out. But very few, very few reach the city like that. Mostly the killing is free."

It was about then that I finally noticed the sleek, tall man in the tidy olive shirt and pants, who had joined us in the truck and now accompanied us on this walk. By lifting my camera toward him I asked if I might take his picture. He nodded, and I clicked, before returning my attention to the three old men.

We continued our tour of the village, with stops at a three-room school house, one of whose teachers is married to a friend of Chamy's from her girlhood in Kilometer 52. And we paid a call at the home of Chamy's second brother, who has a problem wife. Finally Chamy took me to visit a man who was sick. The man, middle-aged, lay on a low bamboo bed. Chamy spoke to him and he pulled up his shirt. From a hole in his abdomen, plastic tubing ran down to the dirt floor, draining some unknown fluid. I winced at the septic scene and steered my mind away from how the incision might have been made. He lived for several more weeks, Chamy later told me. I saw that she liked to show me these primitive conditions. She wanted me to see just how bleak traditional life could be.

Back at the house the busyness at the *qhov cub* was diminishing, and Kia scooped rice into big bowls with a palm-sized paddle. The younger women carried these and bowls of greens to the table near the wall.

Kia stepped quietly toward us. "*Noj!*" she said just audibly, simultaneously giving a nod of her head and gesturing us to come. It is exactly how I have been invited to every Hmong American table to dine. We took places at the full-size Western-height table, brought in for tomorrow's feast. Chamy heaped steaming rice in my bowl, and then we dipped our spoons, politely, into the steaming vegetables. Water in cups was passed last, and we retired from the table, to my dismay leaving the clean-up to Kia and her crew.

After the evening meal Chamy said, "Come on." I followed her out of the house by the back door, next to which I earlier saw the ten-foot-tall poinsettia in brilliant bloom. "You can go over there," she said, indicating a trail that traversed the mountainside through dense trees and shrubs. I was glad for the density, since this was our "outhouse." Chamy said nothing, allowing the third-worldness of the experience to register on me without comment. Beneath her polite exterior I suspected that she was engaged in the classic inner battle of those who have come up from poor beginnings:

Two of Chestnut Mountain's elders give a State of the Village report for visitors, December 1994.

batted between reminiscences that strengthen the tenuous link to her past and a growing distaste for the poverty in which her family still lives.

Hands rinsed off in a pan of water poured out for the purpose, we headed for bed. Ours was constructed of split bamboo at a comfortable sitting height. The bed was walled on three sides and filled the entire end of the tiny room. It was reached by a two-foot-wide walkway between our bed and the next one. That bed was already occupied by maybe five children, two of whom were still wide-eyed and watching. Nom Npis graciously took the space next to the farthest wall, with Chamy beside him and me on the outside. In the privacy provided by the dark, I slipped into sweat pants and a T-shirt. Suitcases and extra pillows and blankets were piled at our feet, preventing me from straightening my legs.

Kia was the last to fasten the wood doors and crawl into bed between a few more grandchildren at the far end of our shared sleeping room. All was silent. Lying on my back in a roomful of family, in a village of family and clan and partner clans, I was reminded of a biblical image that always fascinated me: "And Jesus said to them, 'Imagine this situation: You have a neighbor and you go to him in the middle of the night and say to him, "Lend me three loaves of bread. A friend of mine has showed up, and I don't have anything to feed him." And the neighbor answers, "Don't bother me. The house is locked up, and my children are with me in bed. I can't get up to give you anything." I tell you, even if he won't get up and give it to you because of friendship, he will get up and give you as much as you need to save face.'"[3]

Fortunately, in the dark of that Chestnut Mountain night, I was still unaware that the tall, tidy stranger who slipped into the truck at the police station and whom I had photographed was our official military escort. Ostensibly he was there to protect us, Nom Npis informed me later. "They afraid somebody in the village will hurt us." But was he in fact protecting Laos against us? The Hmong did, after all, inflict great damage on the communists in the war, many of whom had then fled to America.

That night, when Chamy's oldest brother had seen the government escort, he asked two of his sons to stay awake and keep watch outside the wall at my feet, to protect us. Another man from the village also came, with his rifle, to watch. It was a silent cat-and-mouse drama there in the black mountain night, guarding against the guard. Nom Npis, of course, looked characteristically relaxed reporting all this to me later. "Don't worry" was his creed. Indeed, I already felt sure that little could catch Nom Npis unprepared.

In a house filled with people, darkness affords the only privacy. Darkness and wordless communication. At night in a village where houses are close and the walls are slight, sound carries. There is little sound in a sleeping Hmong village. Babies cuddle next to their mothers. The village dogs don't bark. No radios blare, no television. No refrigerators hum. Only the roosters make their predawn statements, calling the day.

So when a funeral drum sounds all night, everyone hears. During our stay later in a Hmong community in Thailand, I heard such a drum. It was driving Chamy crazy. "I hate the drum," she said. "It reminds me of dead people." In fact a boy had died, an eight-year-old who had stood too close to a kerosene lamp when his father tried to light it. It took days for the boy to die. By the time we arrived, the boy's body had been tied up to the wall as is the custom and the funeral drum had sounded without let-up for several days. When it was time for the burial, the dead boy was carried on a stretcher by a half dozen men past the house where we were staying to the burial ground. He was dressed in embroidered garments, and his skin was purple, almost black. This, I learned, is what happens in the tropics. The body was laid in the ground and covered with dirt and then stones. Sticks were laid in a pattern on top. Chanting accompanied the procedure. A few feet from this grave was another filled only a few weeks earlier by a young woman who had died in childbirth.

Death is omnipresent in the villages. Kia Lis told Chamy about an eerie occurrence. Kia's sister, whom she had visited in the United States, appeared to her in a dream and said, "Are you coming back to U.S.? No? Then let's go back together to the old village." "No, there's nothing left there," Kia had replied in the dream. Several days later, Kia learned that her sister in the U.S. had died. Immediately Kia went to her rice field and cried all day. At the end of the day she was weeding at the top, and a bird came near, not flying and not leaving, but staying close. Kia said to the bird, "If you are my sister, take me with you." Several days later, Kia got sick and nearly died. Kia Lis wept and wept as she told this story to Chamy.

The Rice Field

After the roosters delivered their call in the village, grownups in our household rose, straightened their clothing, dabbed eyes with water, and began the day. It was still pitch black. Nom Npis had gracefully levitated his way over Chamy and me, but we waited for some promise of light before we got up.

It was the hour of personal needs. Chamy said, "We can go change and brush teeth or whatever." That meant the jungle again. It had rained lightly during the night — this was supposed to be the dry season — but we

Nom Npis Lis with Chamy Thor's niece, Chestnut Mountain, Laos, December 1994.

were not troubled by leeches. Blessedly. Also blessedly, no children came to monitor us. I balanced fresh clothes on the driest rock I could find and brushed my teeth in my trail cup. I moved a few yards farther along the trail and informed my body that it was now or never. Successful but stiff in the knees, I promised myself a blue ribbon when I got back to the states. I gave my face and underarms quick dabs with a wet bandana as I wriggled into clean clothes and that was it. Ready for the day.

A small army of women and children had assembled downhill from Kia Lis's house. An immaculate twelve-year-old nephew of Chamy's wore a new lined windbreaker and exercise pants. Something out of one of Chamy's suitcases? "We go for a walk," Chamy announced. The girl with the intelligent eyes was there, too, this time in the company of another girl, arms entwined. I never saw the one smile. She turned out to be Chamy's niece.

The morning scene from our mountainside was stunning. Mist had wreathed the houses just below us and dressed with gauze the green valleys and mountains that stretched as far as I could see. In the distance I could easily pick out both current and abandoned fields. The crowd of women and children, patient, paused with me. They, along with the houses emitting wisps of smoke, were a part of the vision, which was not some idealized picture of coffee-table-book photography, I reminded myself, but one of human persistence.

We headed down the road and off to the left, dropping down through a grove of banana trees to one of Kia Lis's fields. Except for our voices, the only sound was the chirping of crickets. The field was several acres and had a slope of about thirty degrees. Stubble was all that was left of this year's rice crop. This was the site of so much of Kia Lis's daily labor and the place where she grieved over her dead sister. Clambering down the steep slope below the trail, Chamy's youngest sister-in-law dug up ten huge cucumbers stored under ground and carved two of them with an eight-inch curved knife. With this she also gestured freely as she talked. This sister-in-law had an unusual beauty, with wax-smooth skin, even white teeth and a fine-boned, slim nose. Her straight hair was knotted at the crown of her head. We stood around eating slabs of cucumber while Chamy videotaped several of the women, weeping as they spoke messages in soprano voices for family members in the U.S. "*Kuv nia-a-a-m,*" wavered one, a small somber child leaning hard against her and finally hiding behind her away from the camera's eye. "My mama-a-a-a ...," the last syllable spoken with an almost ritualistic cry.

The ritual of the videotaped messages intrigued me — how much communication these unlettered persons packed into their high-tech moments. Chamy eventually persuaded her mother, who until then had consistently dodged all cameras, to record a message. In her roughened alto voice, with her lips scarcely opening, Kia spoke into the video camera. Throughout her spoken message, she shifted weight, fiddled with her hands, and looked about like an uneasy fifth grader giving a report.

> This is your daughter-in-law Kia Lis. Sir [Nom Npis] brought the clothes to us. They ... went through the luggage and they found ... five scarves and two shirts with shiny collars. It might be this one I'm wearing now.

She patted her left sleeve with a vague, feathery motion.

"Yes, it's the one you're wearing now," Chamy said from behind the camera.

> I kept one, and Daughter-in-law kept one. Daughter-in-law got the green one and I took the blue one. And I'm already wearing it right now, Aunt Yer. I have worn it and it makes me miss you a lot.
> You live in a country that has much, so love us, too. And I say this to you, OK? I say these couple of words to you so that you know.

When the gentleman [Nom Npis] brings the tape back to America, he'll send it to you and you watch it so you can see me.

I wish that you will eat well and live well, you and your children. And see if you have time to come and see us. Others have come from France and others from America, so see if Yawg Pog and you have time, then come and see us. We live in this country in suffering and poverty. I came back from there, and this is what I look like.

And so I've worn your shirt right now to be videotaped for you to see.

Throughout our visit Kia Lis had carried her face and body, even her spirit, as if to occupy the least space possible. Struck by her manner, I later commented on it to Pang Foua Yang Rhodes, who translated Kia's message for me. "Her style is very typical [of women]," Pang told me, "the words, the intonation, even her hands." What a contrast to Chamy, whom I had watched motioning Nom Npis this way or that from behind her camera like a polite traffic cop or snapping water off her hands after washing dishes. During several sightseeing visits I had seen her standing on some monument, elbows poked out, feet apart, her face up like a banner. The daughter so different from the mother. Probably endowed from the start with a different personality, Chamy was set on a path completely foreign to her mother's by leaving the village. The daughter questions all, turns a matter over in her mind, and then acts boldly. The mother lives the old ways, a submissiveness that seemed to aggravate Chamy. Yet Kia Lis successfully raised eight children, much of the time as a widow. She had her own resilience.

Returning to the village, we passed a corn mill where a child was pulling and pushing the heavy cross-piece to drive the millstone while her mother, baby tied with a purple sash to her back, dropped a few kernels of corn at a time onto the bottom stone. Chamy negotiated taking a turn with the woman, then pressed the video camera into my hands. Working the corn mill takes skill. If you don't exert the right pressure at the right time, the thing stops. Chamy, in blue satin blouse, shoved with all her weight against the wooden crossbar. It was decades since she had done this. Quickly, she had the stone moving round and round. Wood rubbed against wood with a sound like a dog yelping.

"I got it!" she yelled to me, her white-toothed grin announcing her glee. She was proving to the voices lurking in her head that the *school* girl had not impaired the *village* girl. And, it seemed, she was gathering both of those aspects of herself, as if with a mother's arms, into the woman she was now.

A village mother and her daughter (behind the millstone) grind corn to feed livestock, Chestnut Mountain, Laos, December 1994.

While we were gone, Kia Lis's three-hundred-dollar cow had been dispatched by someone with an ax, and a team of men set about butchering it on a large wooden platform built for the occasion. Large hanks of meat were draped over an upright pole until they could be further cut up and cooked for the "guest party" to follow. Smoke rose in calm air from the men's cooking fires, and dogs with stiff ears ventured as close as they dared.

All the village was invited. Only the second brother's problem wife would not come. I never got her side of the story, but apparently she is "hard lady to get along with," as Chamy described her.

For the others gathered around the house — there were perhaps a hundred — a festive mood prevailed. Meat is as much a rarity as visitors. Nom Npis had brought a Polaroid camera as well as the video camera and a regular camera and delighted a few with instant photos. Chamy videotaped a phalanx of girls and boys as their mothers named them one by one. "*Tus no hu ua ...*" touching each one. Then I asked if I might take some family portraits. Besides the pleasure I find in images of families, this would also help me connect Chamy's brothers — two of whom were there — to

Hardier than she appears, this relative (left) of Chamy's is mother to six childen and helps farm the family's fields.

their children. There was another woman I wanted to photograph, too. I first saw her at the airport in Luang Prabang. She was gorgeous, with a round, childlike face, sweet laugh and perfect skin. She wore a fine blue scarf over her hair that emphasized her features. She looked about fourteen years old and reminded me of a Vermeer painting. But when her husband and family assembled for a photograph, I saw six children through my lens. A seasoned mother!

This woman was Chamy's great-uncle's daughter. Mentally, I threw up my hands. Myself the product of a number of two-children families, I have never been at ease with the terminology of kinship. On our way to Laos, Chamy had sketched out her family tree on my notepad. Eight children. Then she added her mother's generation (five siblings) and her father's (seventeen siblings). Since many of these produced their own large households, sometimes including multiple wives, the count would grow exponentially. (I asked Nom Npis why a man would take a second wife. "To grow the population. If you grow the population [of your family, I understood him to mean], more important." I also understood that raising a flock of field hands translated into abundance.)

I have tried valiantly to keep track of all this, who belongs with whom, where they live, and when it was that Chamy says I met them. It means everything to them — family. This swirl of relatives is their home town, their neighborhood. Their life insurance. Their air, sunshine, soil, and water. Their story. But at that moment in Chestnut Mountain I gave up. They knew who they were, and that would have to do.

Stools and benches had been gathered from neighbors and placed around the table of honor inside Kia's house. Chamy, Nom Npis, and I were seated near the center. Before we dipped from the bowls of rice and platters of meat, it was time for *khi tes* ("tie the hand"), a Lao custom that seems made to order for the Hmong. A hive of men surrounded us where we sat. Boiled eggs and then big silver French piasters were placed in our palms. One by one the men leaned over each of us to tie a soft white string around our wrists, at the same time intoning quietly, "Ahhhh [on a descending note], today is a special day, a special night," as Nom Npis later translated the hum of words, "that you come back to see us. And I'm going to tie this string for you and you will be healthy, won't have sickness. You will have luck. You can do what you wanted. You'll live for a hundred years and never be sick." "You'll live until your hair is gray," Chamy added, "past a hundred years and never die."

It had started to rain, and the ever-wary mountain dwellers knew we would have to rush to get down the road before it became impassable. Goodbyes were not difficult this time, as Chamy's family was returning to Luang Prabang with us in the truck, to do some more Chamy-sponsored shopping. It troubled me that Kia Lis climbed into the back of the truck, which, even with side flaps, was open to the rain, while Chamy and I were ushered into the cab. "It's OK," Chamy replied briefly to my protest.

Very soon I had other concerns. We had just passed a cluster of men contemplating a huge construction truck that had slid halfway off the slick road, and from my seat in the cab I could see why. The road ran red with mud. I glanced across Chamy at our nineteen-year-old driver, who was going too fast and fish-tailing. He slowed and regained control, only to begin another slide. Beside the road, the hill dropped away at a steep grade.

I changed my mind about the window that wouldn't close, dumping rain on my slacks: This would be my escape route. I said to the handsome young driver, "If we're going to tip over, let's tip over on your side. That way you'll be on the bottom and Chamy and I will be on top!" Chamy thought this was immensely funny and translated it for the nineteen-year-old. In the meantime, the driver absorbed the translation, laughed, and relaxed into the job of staying aboard the slippery road.

Chamy grew pensive. Finally, she spoke through the growl of the truck. "I worry about my oldest brother. He is sick with dry lung. He work hard to be able to leave home to come to visit. He have a lot of coughing." He had looked nearly skeletal to me, in his black business suit. "Dry lung" is what killed Chamy's father.

Chamy also felt bad about her second oldest brother, the one whose oval face and squared chin most closely matched hers—the one with the difficult wife. This one has six children, ages two to seven. "Did you see his bedroom? Nothing in it. I didn't know how poor he was. No pillow. No mat. I looked at each bed and only a tiny blanket on each bed.

"They are poor because his wife not working very hard and my brother gets sick very easy. Sometimes they have no rice, and my mother has to give. When the wife is sick, he takes care of her, but not the other way. He thinks she doesn't give him enough attention. She's quiet, not outgoing around the village. He says because of her they don't have relatives in the village being loving and caring." This wife was the only person in the village who did not come to the feast. "I asked why everybody have an OK life but they are so poor. That's what I found out.

"You see the kids don't have enough to eat? They have meat like that once a year, and not fruit." Of course Chamy had been made aware through letters from Laos and first-hand reports that times were hard. So she had already mulled over possible solutions, such as trading mountain dry-land farming for irrigated low-land farming. With irrigated land, she reasoned, the rice output would more than double, and with animal fertilizer a farmer could stay put. As it turned out, the oldest brother already had such a field but no equipment or animal to build dikes. His children were too young and he was too weak to do it alone.

"The youngest brother asked me to help him buy a truck like this one so he can be a taxi and make money so my mother doesn't have to work so hard. Now she goes to the field every day." Two thousand dollars for diking, a portion of five thousand for a truck.

As they had for our arrival, Chamy's family gathered at the small, pleasant airport in Luang Prabang for our departure. Since we arrived very early — of course — there was plenty of time for photographs and video-taping more messages for folks back home. After the grown-ups had their fill of talking to the video recorder, they decided to put Nou, the huggable two-year-old son of Chamy's youngest brother, in front of the camera, to show off how well-spoken he was for one so young. Grandmother Kia Lis hovered behind and coached him as he spoke bravely in a small voice. How old are you? he was asked. "I am two and some." What's your name?

"Name? Nou." And what is your father's name? "My dad? He is called Dad." Everyone laughed and cooed.

Goodbyes grew more intense and the weeping began. A ten-year-old niece with a baby on her back stood before Chamy and cried, wiping her face with the end of the shawl that held the baby. Chamy stroked her head and tucked the girl's hair behind her ears. Chamy patted her brother's head while he too wiped his eyes. Everyone was milling past Chamy. Standing before her daughter, Kia sobbed with a jerky intake of breath, like a child. She wiped her tears with the lapel of her jacket and then completely hid her face in the jacket as Chamy stroked her head.

New Year

Back in Vientiane, we headed again to Kilometer 52 for Laos's largest Hmong New Year gathering, where young women wore the latest Hmong fashions from China and the U.S. A reporter interviewed Chamy and Nom Npis about their return to the homeland. Then Chamy and I walked a mile up the highway to the spot where three uncles had houses and where she stayed during vacations from school. Stepping into an overgrown field, Chamy walked to a tree shaped like a lumpy balloon on a stick. "Right here, this the place." Chamy stood quietly. A bit of her soul was here, somewhere.

Later Chamy said, "I miss my garden, I miss my children. I want to go home." There was more quiet as she negotiated the tricky waters between a past that left her hungry and the tough, tiring present. Then she took a breath and said, "The river never return."

Back in Vientiane I saw a tuk-tuk, the small pickup taxi, from which the company name Daihatsu on the rear panel had been obliterated. In its place was painted: Sometime.

I made a side trip, alone, to see the Plain of Jars, the heartland of the Hmong in Laos. Here Ly Vong Lynaolu and Chamy and Nom Npis had been born and raised, and Mai Xiong received her call to be a shaman. Nom Npis had relatives there, so he could not go. He would need to give them money.

I made the hazardous flight, spotted Long Cheng from the air, and, with nobody there to guide me, got myself violently ill on food. There was no electricity to ease my difficult night.

With an Australian couple I bought a tour of the unexplained giant stone jars on the plain, some taller than a man. These stood or lay on the ground near a twenty-foot crater marked by the sign "Bom U.S.A."

Back in Vientiane, the three of us together again in our familiar guest house, I posed a question to my friends. "If you ruled the country, what would you do?" Nom Npis gave his reasonable answer: "I'm not in the position." Chamy, on the other hand, had no such qualms. She was ready with a full program.

"I would turn country into democracy, give everyone equal chance to compete with each other. I would let foreign people travel, and send people to educate with other modern country so have modern idea. I would provide a better standard of living for old people or handicap."

And farming would be modernized.

"Horse or cow manure [is used for fertilizer close to Vientiane], but in the country, nothing. They have no project to teach people new techniques. They plant too many plants. They are healthy plants but they don't produce, so have to plant a lot and go every day to pull the weeds. If go to school, they learn to use more productive strain.

"When Hmong plant corn, they plant very far apart. Type of seed doesn't produce much corn. They plant far apart so have enough soil to feed that plant. It makes just one ear per stalk." Did she learn this from her husband?

And another problem: "Farming can feed them but need money to buy clothing. Used to have way to buy — opium — but government stop that. That's the worst problem Hmong people have right now: No cash."

Spurred by her family's poverty, there was a lot of energy in Chamy's make-over of her native country. It issued from impatience with things done ineffectively. She wanted things to be better for her mother, brothers, and sister — the one whom she had carried on her back. But in part it also seemed a wish to ameliorate the world in which she had grown up.

On our last day in Vientiane Chamy and I went for a walk along the Mekong. She wanted to show me something. We enjoyed the shade trees along Thanon Fa Ngum and a striking white Buddhist temple with double, softly concave roofs and crimson and gold trim. At last we came to a spot where a few outdoor tables marked a snack shop that sold tiny sweet bananas and other items. Chamy marched ahead of me to the edge of the riverbank where she could look down at the brown Mekong, a river that rises twenty-six hundred miles away on the Tibetan plateau. She frowned through the bright sun, traveling back to the time when she was thirteen years old.

"This is the place where I almost drowned." I recalled the story of her attempt to swim and the fearful realization that she could not lift her head above water. Here, at the spot where we stood, she had seen that her mantra, her byword, "I can do anything," did not always hold, that there were, indeed, things she couldn't do.

"So, what's the verdict? Do you want to move back?" We were on the airplane home. Nom Npis had ironed Chamy's slacks one last time with the electric iron he had carried everywhere, and she looked lovely. The question unleashed a torrent.

"People there are rude. They push their papers ahead of yours when trying to get plane tickets. Charge too much to foreigners—for taxi, for food. That's why if I didn't have relatives, especially my mom, I wouldn't come back here." She went on to describe how nothing gets done without bribes or connections.

"You can get a good job or education only if you've got a friend or relative. Like Npis Xiong at airport, he put us through first because connections. Hmong supposed to be able to open business but in fact they can't get permission. Big important people won't answer you but only look at the sky as if you are invisible. In America, bosses are nice, friendly; even if you go higher up, they smile and speak to you.

"In Laos you can't wait politely in line for things, like at the gate from Bangkok to Vientiane." It reminded Chamy and Nom Npis of Long Cheng, where he had dragged her over people's heads to get onto a helicopter to go to Vientiane. Once it took her two months to get from Xieng Khouang to Vientiane, an hour's trip by air. Planes, and the money to pay for a flight, were scarce. She had missed one month of school.

"I don't like to stay in Stone Age. Too hard," Chamy continued. "Women work very hard. You have a baby, you carry it in front and also a basket full of crops from the farm attached to your back.

"If can go and help, yes. Wouldn't go and live like them. They have very old-style life. From generation to generation, never change, like people who stay in a cave."

Besides, "Too hard taking care of personal needs in the wet forest, with everybody watching or wanting to. And in the house, someone always asking for something. [One night] was enough." Chamy and Nom Npis, they confessed, like a hot shower and soft bed.

And one thing more. "I feel I lose power over here. I'll wait until they treat women better before I go home. Like I said, the river never return."

More had happened here than criticism of a style of life. Chamy had come face to face with the depth of the disconnect from her own childhood. The gilded outsider, the educated, big-city daughter, she no longer belonged in the world in which she grew up. But she let me know that she also no longer wanted to belong. At least not to that life. Anger over the life her family was forced — or chose — to live powerfully stoked her desire for change. The attitudes, understandings, and behaviors of her relatives defined what she wished to escape.

We dropped down into Seoul, Korea, for a one-hour lay-over. Waiting in the lounge, Chamy and Nom Npis spoke together in Hmong while they took furtive glances at a passenger from first class leaning against a plate-glass window. Chamy bent toward me. "You know the movie 'Killing Fields'? That's him over there. The star." I thought they must be mistaken, but they weren't. "That's a good movie," Chamy said.

"Well, why not go over and tell him so." They laughed as if I were crazy. "OK," I said. "I will." I did, meeting Haing Ngor, the gracious Oscar winner, who freely gave me his address and invited me to contact him if I wanted to talk about the Southeast Asian experience.[4] I explained about my shy friends, and we motioned them over. Shaking hands with Haing Ngor, Chamy and Nom Npis wore warm smiles. They had seen his film more than once.

Then I understood. Ngor's story of the Khmer Rouge excesses in Cambodia helped to tell their story of war, too.

Back on the plane for the last leg home I asked Chamy, "Were there surprises for you on this trip?" It took her a while to answer.

"It's like a dream," Chamy said. "It's not real, because we only see them a short time. You don't really have time to think about something you should have said." She had wanted to see her family, she said. To see the change, to see if she could help.

But surprised? She had been surprised by her family's warm welcome. "I felt welcomed home when we reached Vientiane. Everybody came to wait for people from America and made narrow walkway. I was surprised."

She continued. "I never seen my second brother cry at me, and he cried a lot." Her mother cried. Chamy had cried, too. It seemed that they were remembering how deeply they belong to each other.

"I didn't think they would come to get us but they all came. I was surprised my older brother came all the way from Sayaboury to wait for me.

"They hired the car and driver to come down from the mountain. They came from a long way. They could just stay in the village and wait. But probably," she said quietly, "they couldn't wait."

Part III

NEW WORLD: AMERICA THE DIFFICULT

Kev ceeblaj: Trouble
(*ceeb*: to be tense, frightened, startled)

8

A Death: Ly Vong Lynaolu

Cross the river, you'll take off your shoes;
Flee from your country, you'll lose your status.
— Hmong proverb[1]

Ly Vong Lynaolu came to the United States in 1976. With his family he settled in Albuquerque, New Mexico, sponsored by an American family. There, Ly Vong, military officer, a leader of his clan, and father of nine, took a job at Levi Strauss. He sat at a sewing machine and made pockets.

And he couldn't get the seams right. He couldn't do the corners. If he sewed the minimum number of pockets, he earned $360 per month for his family. If he sewed more, he would earn more. His widow, Pao Chao Lo, bypassing the interpreter's services of her youngest child, Katie, told the story herself in English:

"They give him pocket. Have the three corners, like this." She showed me on her blouse. "He cannot do the corner. He do no good. If he do better, he got more money. He try to do more and more, more and more. But he cannot do it.

"The machine is old. Machine is all broken. They come to fix the machine. And he get mad and he ask them, 'If you get a gun for me, I know how to fix it.' He get mad. 'I do very bad, [I want] a hammer to broke your machine.' They told him, 'You must, uh, what do I say? value this.'" Pao Chao, the master seamstress, laughed. "He always get mad."

After six months of sewing, Ly Vong went to work interpreting for a Vietnamese physician, a more dignified job, for another six months. Then in June 1977, the family moved to Southern California to help Gen. Vang

Pao start a Hmong-Lao mutual assistance association and to rejoin family, always a strong reason to relocate. Pao Chao had other reasons to move as well. Chinese medicine for her debilitating headaches was readily available in Southern California, and escaping from the cold winters of New Mexico to a milder climate would surely help them, too.

Snow held another problem for Pao Chao. Katie interpreted this time: "My mom said that it was one fear after another when my father was in Laos. All he'd do is, he'd go and take off to the war, and she wouldn't know if he'd come back or not. So every day she'd pray. But then now here in the States she has to pray again because, like what if he doesn't make it through the bad weather and come home or not?" Ah, yes. As I had been told, not to have the father is like living in an unfinished house, open to wind and rain.

In Southern California, Ly Vong went to work for a company that made car batteries but soon left and went to work full time in Santa Ana for the newly formed association.

After several years, in January 1981, Ly Vong and his family moved about seventy miles northeast of Santa Ana to Banning. There Gen. Vang Pao sought to establish a Hmong community where housing was cheaper and families might farm again. Ly Vong continued commuting to Santa Ana to work at the refugee center, but, perhaps due to his habit of losing his temper, he lost his job.

As at the Levi Strauss factory, Ly Vong's work life again became frustrating and demeaning; indeed, it grew worse. Before his death, Ly Vong described to me what happened while he was working as a teacher's aide in a high school. His voice had risen.

> Before San Bernardino I live in Banning. Three American ladies discriminate me. Make me very angry. Act as if more smart than me. I don't want them to stay and gobble [chatter]. They don't know how we fight.
>
> One lady I went to work for at school, she wants my daughter for her son to f---! I want to kill her! Mrs. I---. One American lady work with me, too, knew Mrs. I--- was bad. The principal moved me another school. An American lady there discriminate, too.
>
> A human being should not do that way. I told them, but they try to look the Asian down. It made me very bad headache, that situation. Before that we were officers, not babies for American lady to treat like that. Now if I stay home, headache, too.
>
> Sometimes I go out to cut weed to reduce anger and high blood pressure.

During that period, Katie and some of the other children attended a small church-related school in Banning. (A number of churches both sponsored Hmong families and made scholarships available to their children.) She was miserable. As Katie talked about it, her voice dropped from her usual chatty pace to a halting, subdued tone.

"I went to a private school from second grade to sixth grade, and I was one of the only Asians in the whole school. I went the longest. My two brothers went, too, but they got out and went to a public school after a while.

"We were going to the Seventh-day Adventist Church at the time, and in fact most of the kids who went to the church went to the school. And you know, I had such a hard time. Now I say I'm never going to send my kids to a private school. It's like you just isolate them from so much. I think my worst years were private school."

Katie said she learned much more from being in public school. "I think there was a more normal atmosphere, where there were a lot of kids. I mean that school was so little. We only had two classrooms. And it was smaller and smaller every year."

For Ly Vong, the final straw came during an exchange at a roadside spring in the mountains above Banning. This spring is very popular in the area; people drive some distance with gallon jugs to take home pure spring water at no cost. At the request of Pao Chao, who could not drink the tap water, Ly Vong drew water at the spring, too.

One day, as Ly Vong himself told the story, he and a Hmong friend agreed to get water for Pao Chao. They parked and got out with their hands full of empty plastic jugs. Two American men were there already. One said to Ly Vong that he could not have water without paying. Ly Vong went along with the joke, only to discover that the man was serious. The man fully intended to bar Ly Vong, who was obviously a "foreigner." In a rage, and mortified in front of his Hmong companion, Ly Vong drove empty-handed back down the mountain. The man who once trained the entire Hmong army, a leader of his clan and his people in Laos, descendant of kings, could no longer provide the smallest thing for his wife.

In September 1990, the family moved to Sacramento, where their sons worked as interpreters. Ly Vong focused his leadership on the Hmong arts organization founded by Nom Npis Lis and on Chao Fa, a quasi-religious movement that in this country seeks cultural preservation and the reestablishment of the Hmong in Laos. (In Laos, Chao Fa is said to carry on guerrilla efforts to bring down the communist government.)

Though failing in the world of American employment, Ly Vong still exercised the broad-ranging, old-style leadership. His leadership was described this way by fellow clansman Nom Npis Lis: "His opponents didn't like him. He strong, defend what he wants. But he a *good* man."

A leader like that might spend thousands of dollars to help others with food, clothing, and housing. Nom Npis continued, "So the people if not safe in the United States, [the leader] must help them, make them survive, make them happy. And Ly Vong still do it [here]."

Did Ly Vong ever accept America?

"My dad was never thrilled about being here," Katie said, seated in the family living room with her mother. "I don't think the U.S. was what he expected at all, you know, with all the push and shove. And especially in New Mexico there was not a lot of Asians, and I don't think that he got a very good vibe racially, or politically. He always said that this is a break, that he was always going to go back to Laos and live again. But he never made it."

Pao Chao dabbed at moisture in her eyes. What did she think about being in America?

"I think that probably I got headache. I don't want to stay in the U.S.A. In my country I have many children but I don't got headache."

The voice slowed and moved to some interior place.

"Too many bill and too much money for everything. And my husband and me, we think the same. We have to go back to my country. In my country, only my husband working, but we have money to support the children and buy the clothes. We have the garden, we have vegetable and lots for eat and my husband working just for money for buy clothes or go somewhere. And like we live together in that house. If I don't like my house, whole the town of men come to help I make my house. [Everyone comes to help take down the old house and build a new one.] And if you need house they whole help you to do it. You don't have to pay, and we think it's better.

"And after my husband got laid off at Lao Family"—the association he helped found—"and he don't do at school, he working with the Chao Fa. We think we have to go back [to Laos]. We think the god know how the Hmong people look like and give the land for us and we must go back.

"And now my husband pass away. But I still remember over there."

Ly Vong died suddenly at home. The local newspaper gave his age as fifty-five.

The funeral was held at the handsome Sacramento Memorial Lawn, apparently the only mortuary in Sacramento willing to accommodate the lengthy Hmong funerals. I did not know of Ly Vong's death until after the ceremony, but I later attended segments of a funeral for a member of Chamy Thor's clan at the same mortuary.

Though traditional village Hmong funerals have been altered to fit urban America, they remain nothing like mainstream American ceremonies. They are longer, more comprehensive, and more dramatic. Since my own father had died ten months before, attending gave me an opportunity to consider what funerals accomplish.

The well-kept mortuary is at a major intersection in Asian-American Sacramento — Stockton Boulevard and Lemon Hill Avenue — opposite the popular New Paris restaurant. Arriving early on the fourth or fifth day of the funeral, Chamy, Nom Npis, and I found a parking place in the large lot — a hopeless task later when we returned in the evening. We walked along a breeze-way between wall memorials and into a canopied, concrete courtyard busy with people. Tables were set up, some with covered dishes of rice. A portable trailer kitchen with a glass front revealed men at work over big pots on a stove. Beef was being carried in and cut up next to the kitchen to feed the arriving mobs.

At the far end of the courtyard the double doors to a large activity room stood open. The doorway was jammed with mourners. Between announcements on a loudspeaker I heard the wail of the kheng, the big bamboo flute with curved pipes, and the brrrum, bum, brrrum, bum of a drum. The stately rhythm reminded me of the funeral procession of President Kennedy. Inside the asphalt-tile room, a big barrel-shaped drum hung suspended from a tall, freshly constructed tripod of two-by-fours. The player struck the instrument with two drumsticks, first in the center of the cowhide head and then at opposite points on the rim, in steady alternation. The two khengs' whining sound reminded me of Scottish bagpipes but quieter. The kheng players simultaneously played and executed dance-like steps, occasionally crouching a bit to move under the long front leg of the drum's tripod, as if weaving the instruments together. Kheng players learn not music but words, since the instrument duplicates the natural music of the tonal Hmong language. Drumming and kheng-playing by a succession of men continues around the clock until the last day of the funeral. I watched an older man walk among the drummer and kheng players, stopping to pour a ceremonial drink of beer for each.

Male and female mourners sat separately on folding chairs or stood clustered in separate halves of the low, acoustic-tile-ceilinged room. Against the far wall stood the open casket, surrounded by a crowd of mourners. Along with groups of mourners who came and then drifted away, others — women — pressed against the casket, leaning over the beloved with kisses and caresses. They would keep twenty-four-hour watch lest an enemy place something under the body, such as a bone, that might cause trouble in the deceased's next incarnation.

Family members were identified by a nametag or headband, except for married daughters, who no longer belong to the family in the same way. The families gathered in groups in the courtyard and, having been officially invited in, were piped into the room. They carried baskets with meat, wine, ceremonial money to be hung on the wall in bunches, and real money. The gifts were handed over as they entered. The food would later be distributed to all those who worked on the funeral as the "last meat." As Chamy described it, the meal means, "That's it. You never see him any-more." As I watched, each group proceeded to the casket, crying openly and speaking aloud about their loss, "Now we don't have a father. Now we don't have a son." This procession of mourners continued until the room was filled with hundreds of people.

I commented to Chamy about the open crying, even by men. It seemed so reasonable. I asked Chamy and Nom Npis if they had watched the funeral procession of Princess Diana. Yes, they had. And did they notice that Prince Charles and the two boys and the princess's brother, walking behind the casket, never broke down and cried? Indeed they had. "We think they don't care," Chamy said. I explained that the British and American way is to keep one's composure. Anything else is considered weakness.

To be sure, there is as much a ritual quality in Hmong crying as there is in American composure. In each culture, some individuals are bound not to fit in. What happens to a Hmong relative who, given the choice, would not feel like crying? Chamy replied, "You make the sound — and the tears come."

On the final day of the funeral, which began after we left that morn-ing, the kheng players and drummers were replaced by chanters, whose role it is to thank the families who have brought gifts and pass on instruc-tion to the younger generations. When we returned later in the day, the room was jammed. In the center was a table with drinks and a cooked pig on it. Eight or ten men sat around it, including two or three men who rose in turn, took the microphone, and in the ritualized, regular beat of Hmong chanting repeated from memory the required text that would bring the funeral to a close. All the while, a knot of women, talking quietly, con-tinued to huddle around the casket.

At Ly Vong's funeral and burial, members of Chao Fa, clad in bright red shirts with the organization's round emblem on the back, participated in their leader's last rites. The funeral lasted five days.

Ly Vong was buried on a grassy hill in Vallejo, California, in sight of the ocean across which lay the land of his birth. The refugee's yearning for the past was materially formalized.

Some said that Ly Vong died because he left the Christian faith and returned to the healing ways of his ancestors.

As Katie explained on behalf of her mother, for years he relied on Christian prayer and Western scientific medicine to improve his health. He could not understand why he only became sicker. Finally he gave up going to church. Occasionally, at Pao Chao's urging, he would go, complaining, but only so that she would stop badgering him.

A month before he died, Pao Chao said to him, "OK, if you want to do the curing process, then let's do it." So they called a shaman to come and perform the ancient rituals.

In honor of Ly Vong's return to the old ways, the family has ceased attending church since his death.

Ly Vong's family maintains a place-holding leadership role in Chao Fa, but the Hmong arts organization, in which he took the role of elder statesman, had to be disbanded. According to Nom Npis, its former project director, Ly Vong left a vacuum that the younger Nom Npis cannot fill.

"If we, at that time, this small organization, if we did not let Ly Vong to be the chairman, so everybody else have laughing and yelling. If they know you are the young generation and doesn't have any experience and if you talk to the elder people, they say, 'You are too young to do good. [You are] just *cheating* us.'

"If Ly Vong go there, everybody keep quiet. If somebody big mouth, Ly Vong say, 'You are big mouth. Can you raise your hand to the god before you say anything?'

"So everybody keep quiet! They say, 'Yes, sir.'"

The old leaders are dying, as they always have. But now they are dying in a different land, and they are not being replaced. Different leaders are required.

Nouzong Lynaolu, Ly Vong's second daughter, not only helped organize the New Year's gathering in Sacramento at which her father got up and danced so regally. She also chaired the 1996 Hmong National Education Conference in Sacramento. She has served as chair of the board of the Hmong National Development, Inc., Washington, D.C., and president of Hmong Higher Education Network, San Francisco.

Completing a circle begun more than a century ago when her ancestors left China, Nouzong traveled as a delegate in 1995 to the United Nations' Fourth World Conference on Women in Beijing. She went with a small group of Hmong women. One of their goals was to connect with other Hmong women, especially those from China, their sisters. They succeeded in their goal.

9

Ties That Bind:
Hmongtown, U.S.A.

Open your door to everyone, you'll never be poor.
Shut your door, you'll never be rich.
— Hmong mother's saying

It was snowing an April shower when I bought a van ticket at the airport for the run to downtown Denver. My hope in coming to the fourth Hmong National Development Conference was to get a glimpse of Hmong America outside my usual circles. I was looking for anything that would show me how Hmong were adjusting to America.

I took a seat in the airport van. As it filled, a woman clambered past me toward the back whose long hair, clothes, and round face looked Hmong to me. After most of the passengers were deposited at their destinations, I asked if she was going to the conference. She was, she assured me as her sober face thawed into a relieved grin. She was evidently tired of going solo.

I didn't know what to expect of the conference accommodations. They turned out to be as luxurious as any conference I've attended. The hotel's chandeliers and plush carpet were grand, and the Hmong at the registration table were dressed in business best and spoke perfect English. They did have a glitch in their system, however, that left lines of people snaking down the broad hallway. As it turned out, organizers were swamped by hundreds of last-minute registrations that brought the attendance close to six hundred. This didn't surprise me. The Hmong readily undertake even the biggest events, including weddings, at the last minute.

In the same cavernous ballroom where I later watched, fascinated, as Tou Ger Xiong summarized his culture under ten brisk headings, participants stood as their states were called. California, Colorado, Massachusetts, Montana, Oregon, Washington — maybe two dozen states were represented, all of them home to significant Hmong populations. The four women college students at my table looked fresh enough but confessed that they had driven all night from Minnesota to get here. One was studying marketing and another history and China, where she hoped to study soon. One of them was responsible for taking notes so as to report back to their sending group. I wondered how alert she could possibly be.

A cheery woman emcee with red-dyed hair, white mini suit, and perfect diction spoke into the microphone to introduce my former language teacher, Dr. Lue Vang, the harried but ever-joking chair of the conference. ("The weather is very nice!" he quipped about the snow and cold.)

Then a kind of State of the People address was offered by Mai Zong Vue, one of the competent, personable new women leaders, president of the group organizing the conference, Hmong National Development Inc. Most Hmong live in Minnesota, Wisconsin, and California, Vue confirmed. Nearly half, I knew, lived in California. Forty million dollars worth of produce is grown by California Hmong farmers, she continued. Nationwide, there are sixteen lawyers, half of them women, she ticked off encouraging numbers. More than a hundred Thai restaurants are owned and run by Hmong. (I decided to take a closer look next time I go out for Thai food.) But Vue also had a problems list. Too many Hmong are extremely poor, divorce is on the rise, some individuals are slow to apply democratic principles to daily personal life. Clearly, issues of the community were not going to be whitewashed at this conference.

Dr. Yang Dao, educated in France and the Hmong's first Ph.D., walked to the microphone amid applause. He is the stately senior scholar who later at the banquet shed the intimidating sternness of his book-jacket photo to laugh and beam at Ms. Vue as he guided her across the dance floor to big-band music. He added his scholar's angle to the picture: There are eighty-five Ph.D.s including seventeen women, one hundred seventy master's degrees, engineers, doctors, a dentist, a school supervisor, professors, CEOs, and a few members of school boards and city councils. I had seen one of the physicians pictured in another conference brochure, a tiny woman in traditional Hmong dress who is a wife and mother of three. Not someone you'd guess to be a doctor at first glance.

I tried to keep my eyes on the speaker and my notepad, but couldn't help sneaking looks at the elegantly groomed people around me. Many of them were students, but the older elite were here, too. Business suits, tasteful dresses, perfect makeup. I had a sudden flashback to Chamy's underfed family and happily dirty children in Chestnut Mountain.

Later I dug some more statistics about the Hmong from folders in my filing cabinet.[1] Estimates of total Hmong population in the U.S. range from about 98,000 in the 1990 Census through the 130,000 official estimate for half a dozen years later, to the 200,000 to 300,000 suggested by Hmong social service people and others. Worldwide there are at least seven million Hmong, including (around 1990) 200,000 in Laos, 400,000 in Vietnam, 140,000 in Thailand, and 10,000 in France. The remainder, the bulk of the seven million, are in China. For years, Fresno, California, had the largest Hmong population outside Asia, but it has recently lost numbers to St. Paul, Minnesota, as a result of fear of gangs and worries about welfare reform. The 2000 U.S. Census indicates St. Paul's Hmong population had risen to 25,000 while Fresno's was about 19,200. As to states, Minnesota, with 60,000 in the 2000 Census, still trails California's 67,150.

The Hmong median age is a little under thirteen years. It's thirty-three years among Americans who are not of Asian background. The obvious reason is that Hmong women give birth to an average of about six children, three times as many as non–Asians. More than three-quarters of Hmong households have five or more people, compared to a mere one-tenth of non–Asian households.

Given the houses bursting with kids, it's not surprising that nearly half the Hmong population is in school. Their average income per household is about $14,276, half that of non–Asians. Less than a third of Hmong are in the labor force, compared to nearly two-thirds of non–Asians, the difference again partly a result of the high proportion of children. These are 1990 Census figures.

Hmong as a group have a hard road before they reach economic independence. Many agency officials, academics, and casual observers are persuaded that no immigrant group has arrived in America less prepared. The title of the Denver conference, "Living the Dream," with its inescapable reference to the mythic "American dream," acknowledged the salience of the issue for the Hmong community. Hmong face innumerable hurdles. Some non–Hmong I talk to, the outspoken ones, express impatience. "Why don't they learn English?" "Why do they have so many children?" "Why don't they just get a job?"

Dr. Mymee Her, the first Hmong woman psychologist, suggested that some Hmong need to overcome the hurdle of memory before the more manifest needs of language and employment can be addressed effectively.

Hoping aloud that her newly weaned three-year-old would not wander up to the front as she gave her keynote address, Her probed behind statistics to describe what she had learned about the Hmong, including herself. Even the normal chattering along the fringes of the crowd quieted as she spoke. She offered insights worth quoting at length.

> When I was asked to deliver a keynote address for this year's Hmong National Development conference, I was told that the conference theme was Living the American Dream. I was ecstatic, relieved that for once I did not have to talk about the struggles and suffering of the Hmong people. I was going to be able to talk about something more positive, more upbeat. But as I sat down to think about what I was going to say, I was confronted by my ... responsibilities as a psychologist. Years of training as a student of psychology and a practitioner have taught me the importance of integrating human experiences, past, present, and future. If one is to adequately live and move on with his life, he must examine his past, come to terms with it, and then move on. Thus it becomes impossible to talk about our people living the American dream without talking about the history that has brought us to America, including the struggles and sufferings every Hmong must endure....
>
> So what is the American Dream? Some say that it is having a family and living in a brick house with a white picket fence. Others say it is having money.... Yet others say it is having power and influence. Whatever the definition may be, it implies being able to fully participate in the economy of the United States: being able to work, provide for one's family, and sustain some financial independence.
>
> What, then, does living the American Dream entail for the Hmong? If we are to adequately address the Hmong's adaptation to life in America, we must examine the political history of our entrance to the United States. The Hmong are classified as refugees.... Due to their involvement with the United States during the Vietnam War, the Hmong were in immediate danger of being exterminated....
>
> Hmong refugees came to the United States *wounded*. Most have been beaten up physically and emotionally. We sought out shelter [in] whatever country would offer us safety. We had no anticipation of what life held for us in the country of refuge. We were in a state of shock, not realizing what had just happened to us....
>
> As a little Hmong girl, living in the mountains of Laos, I had no concept of what America was. My world was small and did not expand beyond my mother's farm. I never ventured into the jungle because my mother warned that tigers and [other] wild animals would eat me, should I wander too far....
>
> I had heard of Thailand because my mother raised the famous *qab thaib* (Thai chicken). In my four-year-old mind, Thai people looked like the chickens in our front yard. I had heard of America

from the American missionaries that came to spread Christianity to our villages. I thought Americans were giant Godlike creatures that only ate bread....

I came to the United States scared and in a state of shock. When helicopters flew over my head, I wanted to run for shelter, because I feared they were going to drop a bomb on top of me. Loud popping noises made me think I was being shot at. Horrified as I was, I was to attend school. Imagine what I must have been thinking when my teachers asked, "What do you want to be when you grow up?" ...

What *are* the Hmong's American dreams? ... Hmong's dreams don't fit their American reality. For most Hmong, their dreams are simple. It is to harvest enough food and raise enough [live]stock to feed their family for the year. In a world whose technologies are centuries ahead of theirs, how could they even begin to imagine the possibilities ...? One must have enough exposure to the American way of life to even begin dreaming....

The Hmong, therefore face many challenges in their conceptualization of the American Dream. First and foremost, they are faced with a devastatingly *cruel* past that has robbed them of any self-worth and dignity which might have existed prior to the war. Secondly, they are now living in a land whose life and technology is beyond their understanding. Living the American Dream for the Hmong, then, involves more than simply coming up with a wish.... It involves healing. The kind of healing that consists of painfully digging into their hearts and their souls through layers of trauma and hurt to find any traces of hope that is left to believe that they indeed deserve a better life....

I think what we often do as professionals helping the Hmong, or as Hmong survivors of a war ourselves, is that we forget to allow time for healing. For many of us, we haven't stopped running since the time our villages were bombed in the mountains of Laos. With repeated exposure to terror, we are conditioned to instinctively run from any situation which we perceived as threatening. We ran ... to anything or anyone which we think is safe. Running. Running. To Thailand. To the United States. One step away from death, and one step short of safety. And we kept on running. Refusing to look back. Wanting to forget. Needing to forget.... Even years after the war, we find ourselves running, not really knowing where safety lies.

When I was completing my doctorate to become a clinical psychologist, I was required to undergo 40 sessions of psychological therapy. Prior to attending the weekly one-hour sessions with a psychoanalyst, I did not think I needed help. I was angry at the requirement. I have already dealt with the war and was tired of being reminded of it. I was even more angry at the cost.... But I needed my degree, so I complied. To my surprise, I found myself in tears in my first session. I started my therapy with: "I am Hmong, and I am a refugee from Laos."

Suddenly, memories and visions of communist soldiers marching the streets and bombs bursting in the distance filled the therapy room.... Intense fear penetrated every fiber of my being. The fear that any moment I would die! The fear that did not end when the war ended. The fear that continued to be interwoven into every experience of my life — when I was nervous about a test, when I did not understand materials I read for a class, when I interacted with my teachers and co-workers— always fearing that if I did not do or say what others expected of me, a bomb would go off....

There, in that therapy room, I began my road to understanding my hopes and dreams and motivations behind my ambition to succeed. I had been determined to prove that no one could ever hurt me again, the way that I was hurt as a seven-year-old running for her life from communist soldiers. I was going to become somebody ... building a life where we would be respected, and a life where no one would dare to walk all over us.

What I have learned over the years ... [is] that we all experience different levels of trauma from the war. My immediate exposure to war lasted two weeks. Others' experiences lasted years.... Not only were we as Hmong exposed to war, [but] our children who are born in the United States, far away from the killing fields, are exposed to war through our experiences. I am convinced that many problems we have in our community today with gang[s] and juvenile delinquency are a direct result of Hmong parents' inability to function in their parenting roles. They are too overwhelmed coping with their own experiences of war. They cannot be physically or psychologically available to their children, because they are drowned in their own experiences....

Recently, I started to work with a Hmong family who has been involved with Child Protective Services. Their eight children have been removed from their home due to physical abuse of the youngest child and father's drug abuse....

As this family began therapy with me, it was discovered that the father had been abusing opium to deal with his post-traumatic experiences of war. He had been hearing and seeing things.... He was actively reliving scenes from his war experience of 15 years. He had chronic pain in his head, back, and legs from having been wounded as a soldier. Opium helped him cope with these experiences....

When he was not using opium, he was irritable, angry, and violent. He often hit his eight children and his wife. His children started rebelling, believing that they are not loved. The oldest son and daughter (ages 17 and 16) started hanging with gangs and began abusing drugs. Indeed, there is a lot of healing to be done with this family.... [2]

I was moved by Her's description of the psychic cost of displacement and understood for the first time how many there are like Ly Vong Lynaolu.

In the hall outside the ballroom, people consulted their programs to choose workshops. Walking through the press of people, I began to realize what was feeling so strange to me: Many of the young Hmong were five feet six, eight, or ten inches tall. One or two of the young men must have been six feet. ("Good fertilizer," a Hmong woman told me.) I wondered what this culture was making of its reverence for the tall now that the young were becoming giants. Several wore a T-shirt on sale that proclaimed, "I is a Hmong man" and on the back "Hmong men are sexy."

On my way to an economics workshop I bumped into my friend from the airport van. Spilling out to her my previous evening's call to the hotel plumber about my lack of hot water — which, I remembered, did not faze me in Laos — she immediately invited me to move in with her. That sounded wonderful, and over the next few days I got to know a remarkable Hmong, head of a successful women's outreach program. I was amused to watch her staying up late every night and then sleeping in — what would a mother-in-law have said back in Laos! She frequently called home and visited local relatives, and she consumed vast quantities of chocolate. We talked endless girl talk, and she treated me as if we'd known each other for decades.

Living the American dream has irresistible appeal for Hmong. But they are having a tough time of it. More than sixty percent of Hmong families in the 1990 Census had incomes below the poverty level.[3] Welfare rates in the late 1990s showed a high of sixty to seventy percent receiving government assistance in Fresno, where employment opportunities are limited. The welfare picture is far different for Hmong in Colorado. The director of the Colorado Refugee Department told the conference that of the five thousand Hmong in the state, less than one percent receive welfare (two-parent families are not eligible), and the majority of those are disabled or over sixty-five. Ninety percent own homes and some own businesses. The director attributed the success story to some vigorous, culture-sensitive programming plus Hmong pride and the tradition of family self-sufficiency. "The Hmong had to be tough to get here," she said. "They just needed a little money."

Hmong hate economic dependence. Independence, of any kind, is sweet to the taste. If only we had a piece of land, they say, we could support ourselves as we did back home. At first, Hmong did not regard government assistance as demeaning but as a reward or payment for having suffered and fought and died in Laos on behalf of America. Even now, when most have begun to understand the stigma attached to welfare, they have not forgotten the promise of help given by CIA individuals. The promise pledged that, should they lose the war, America would take care of the Hmong.[4] It was a contract the Hmong could understand. Such agreements were made between brothers and between clans at a wedding. Mutual responsibility was at the core of their society. Anyone might need help at any time. Nor would you have to report for a humiliating appointment at a welfare office and submit to medical tests and demands that you go to school.

Regardless, most Hmong have put their disillusionment behind them. They value success, working hard, getting an education, becoming a doctor or teacher. Admirable aspirations, except that there is an edge of desperate bravado about their goals, revealing a conviction that their survival remains fragile. Despite their Great Depression-style frugality, the five- and six-dollar-an-hour jobs that most of them can get with limited English and few skills are inadequate to support a household of ten, even when both parents work. I had sensed a hint of panic in Chamy when she recounted her struggles to get into and through college.

That is why welfare reform and the loss of food stamps in 1997 struck such fear into more vulnerable older Hmong, triggering three suicides. "It's not because you didn't love or support me," one woman in her fifties spoke in Hmong into a tape recorder before hanging herself in the garage. "My sadness over the American system and my health problems drove me over the edge." (Suicide by hanging is deplored by the Hmong, who believe that one forfeits reincarnation by doing so, but hanging also carries the message, "I'm not mad at you, just troubled by my problems.") Thirty-six hundred Hmong in California alone appealed for waivers to the cutoff of food stamps. Food stamp benefits were restored about ten months later.

For all the differences of custom and style between the old village life such as I saw in Laos and the new one, the biggest difference is a sleeper: It is not the language or the foods but the alien economic system. Many Hmong are as lost in their attempts to fathom the subtle techniques of survival here as I would be if deposited on a Laotian mountaintop and told to farm. That system did not depend on money, and ours does—a vast difference. One Hmong woman said, "I feel so helpless. I never felt helpless back in Laos."

The way people make a living is a powerful engine that drives how their relationships function. Change one and it throws the other out of whack. Where Hmong admonished each other to "stick together like the chickens" to survive, now individuals need to be ready to cut ties and go where the jobs are. The value is no longer to do as the ancestors did but forever to be open to something never done before. That threatens family cohesiveness.

It is an emotional leap from old to new ways. One Hmong man could not answer his college son's question about his view of life in the United

States. He was too humiliated by his work as a dishwasher. Only women wash dishes. How could he face this in front of his son?

The adjustments are exhausting, as Chamy let me know one day when I picked her up after work. Still decades from retiring, she nonetheless dreamed of it. She said: "I open the mailbox, and there are many bills. We didn't have that in Laos. You found a good place where soil is good, built house, and raised vegetables and hunted wild animals. You didn't have to pay. Here, you pay for everything." For the first time I understood how different it is for her. Then I recalled that land on this continent was once "free," too.

Chamy discovered another economic reality by coming here. In the shift away from family farming, she and Nom Npis acquired a houseful of what could be seen as laid-off workers—their children. In the mountains, their children would have spent the better part of their waking hours directly contributing to the family economy, not going to school. Even after having been fed, clothed, and housed through the school years, most American children are not expected to reciprocate immediately by helping to support their parents as they are in Hmong society. The new system can make a Hmong parent feel used up. As Chamy sighed to me one day over the telephone, "I feel seventy years old!"

Still, Hmong have one economic tool not generally used in the American mainstream. They often rely on uncles, brothers, and cousins to tell them about job openings and help out with a car, food, and sleeping space if the family has to relocate. "Their society is built in such a way as to be self-sustaining," a Catholic Social Services worker told me when I was first learning about the Hmong, "but it does not encourage them to go out and mix."

Mid-afternoon on Saturday at the conference in Denver, eleven Hmong men, some young, some old, with a couple of wives, occupied a small fraction of the chairs in a workshop room to learn about microenterprise. The workshop was billed as "Financing Self-Employment." When the Anglo presenter asked how many were currently in business, two raised their hands. Providing goods and services to Hmong seems the easiest, though not the only, businesses to envision. Hmong businesses that I've run into include video stores, insurance companies, travel agencies, and a security guard service, the latter a nice segue from military duty. A relative of Chamy's owns a grocery and dry goods store in Fresno. At a summer arts fair at Lake Tahoe, I found not one but three Hmong booths featuring embroidery. The operators—invariably cheerful—had driven into the mountains from three Central Valley towns, Stockton, Merced, and Fresno. I decided that the fair with its outdoor booths was much like the Laotian markets I had seen. This was an echo of the old country for them.

Hmong lack long-term experience as entrepreneurs—and even as customers. Beginning when the political leader Touby Lyfoung made his foray into the lowlands in 1960, Hmong have tiptoed into this unfamiliar occupation. In May 2000, a Public Broadcasting Service segment airing during the twenty-fifth anniversary of the fall of Saigon stated that there are more than eight hundred Hmong businesses in Minnesota's Twin Cities, a number whose impact will build exponentially in following generations. The banquet speaker Saturday night in Denver pushed small business, stating that "business and enterprise are the means that will give us resources to rebuild our people." But there is still much to learn, and businesses tend to be fragile.

Farming is another story, an occupation far more familiar to the Hmong than business. Even though the system is vastly different, Hmong at least feel some confidence in growing things, if only as hired landscapers. A *Los Angeles Times* article depicted Hmong as the best strawberry growers in Fresno, where they also do ninety percent of the work of picking tomatoes and strawberries. A Denver conference speaker from the U.S. Department of Agriculture, who described programs in credit and marketing and thrilled the audience by speaking a little Hmong, said that six hundred Hmong families farm thirty-five hundred acres around Fresno. About half that number farm in Wisconsin and Massachusetts, some owning land and some renting.

Marketing techniques can be a blend of old and new. Outside Mai Xiong's apartment building one day, I saw an old white pickup truck parked under a Chinese elm, its bed filled with boxes of fruit. The arrangement was not so different from the mats stacked with produce in the market in Kilometer 52. But then a woman named Xai handed me a flyer that said, "Asian pear for sale. Yes! Asian pear for sale. Our Asian pear are now ripening and we are selling them at our farm. How? You will bring your own bucket…. If you enjoy fruit farm environment, come to enjoy the day at our farm."

Hmong also seem drawn to raising chickens, as much out of the need for birds that meet ritual standards as from know-how. Nom Npis owned a chicken operation for a time, but it was hundreds of miles from home and became too difficult to supervise at a distance.

Farming has also taken some distinctive turns, such as the raising of ginseng in Wisconsin. It turns out that Asians consider Wisconsin ginseng to be the best, better than that grown in Korea or China. Another activity is the gathering of matsutake mushrooms by Hmong in the Oregon woods.

Old-time American mushroomers grew disgruntled at the Hmong hunters with their efficient family teams and willingness to work endless hours.

While only a smattering of conference goers chose the money-related workshops—I was reminded later that the few there would spread the information efficiently—the room was packed for "The Forbidden Discussion: Sex, Dating, Marriage and Gender in the '90s." Such a workshop must surely shock the elders, a few of whom attended, like reluctant chaperones, looking a bit hurt and angry. The subject seems to be a touchstone of the trauma of adapting from the old culture to the new. About 150 mostly college students jammed the room, plus a number of the fifty or so non–Hmong at the conference. When the chairs ran out, kids stood or sat on the floor. The workshop was presented by the same funny guy who explained what makes the Hmong Hmong. Public discussion of sex was not on his earlier list characterizing the Hmong.

The subject extended over two workshops, and I suppose the second session included some affirmation of Hmong traditions. But this one seemed to be mostly a tough look at gender inequality and the strict ban on talking about sex. Tou Ger Xiong got laughs when he described some of the elders' circumlocutions, such as "your red grandmother is visiting" for menstruation and the Hmong version of the stork story: "There was a knock on the door, and there you were!" Tou Ger's eyebrows, arms, body, feet, and elbows in constant motion, he used his considerable skills to draw individuals into the talk. But despite a list of his credentials in conflict resolution, only one side of the matter was voiced: unwanted parental limits on male-female behavior, limits that these students know are not imposed in the mainstream culture. It was a venting session that probably established a sense of community among the young. The only voice from the other side, pointing out that sex is an adult activity that demands responsibility, came from a white middle-aged woman. None of the older Hmong men present spoke. Perhaps they were saving their words for later.

Hmong rules are strict. Young Hmong are not supposed to date. A "date" equals engagement. One workshop student told about a guy who took a girl to Burger King for ninety minutes, and when she returned home her parents said, "That's your man. You're not welcome here anymore." So the two married and have three kids and no college education. Tou Ger added this tale of his own: He was hanging out with a group of Hmong friends at White Castle, a hamburger shop, when the girls stated that they had to go home. The parents of one of them wouldn't let her in the house, however, so she went to a pay phone and called Tou Ger. Visions of what life had in store for him passed through his head. "I felt very weak," he said. He was sixteen. Then his friend on the other end of the phone said, "I'm just kidding!"

A recurring theme in all the talk was the strictness of parental authority, which everyone soon recognized was largely a function of the community's standards: "The culture is based on family unity, not the individual; maybe that's why parents are so strict about it," as one younger male said. Tou Ger followed up: "My father told me, 'Son, don't do this [go out with Hmong girls], because I can't help you if you cross a certain line.' It's the community understanding of harmony."

I began to see that the Hmong choice of the community's well-being instead of the individual's was on full display before me. A male-based community. Every culture has to rein in the power of sexual energy or society unravels. How they deal with it reflects what and who they value. Apparently Hmong response to the power of sex — like that of our culture for much of our history — is to pretend it doesn't exist. If the young learn about it, it's assumed, they'll do it. And any procreation that undercuts the carefully preserved male lineages could destroy the structure built on those lineages. The integrity of a family would weaken, and with it the tight bonds of mutual responsibility that ensure survival in a tough environment. So sex is one of those things, as Tou Ger's father said, that is "not meant to be verbalized."

The energy was high in this room throughout. I could imagine, as the young generation flailed about finding their footing, that the older ones experienced an array of emotions: anger, frustration, horror, panic. Perhaps panic most of all. I like to think that the young won't give up all the values of family and stability that they've inherited.

Back in my room just before the conference's big banquet, my sociable roommate was emerging from a nap. She had, however, taken in one workshop that I missed, "Dress for Success." As she poked through the closet she told me that the workshop had caused her to change her mind about what to wear that evening. The workshop presenter, Maykou Margaret Vang, had convinced her that the long skirts so favored in America by modest Hmong make them look shorter. And it's true. I had often noted how wonderful a Hmong woman can look in traditional fancy dress with its knee-length skirt, and now I realized that the traditional design suits Hmong stature perfectly.

Lots went on in the hallways of the conference during the day, and I found myself chatting with complete strangers. It's easy with the Hmong. One of these was a man named Chee Yang, who followed me out of a workshop on politics—another event that drew only a few. Yang wanted me to meet another "American," a former helicopter pilot from the Vietnam War.

We found Dennis McCormack in one of the meeting rooms, a fellow of medium height, one of those human beings who is completely at ease with himself. I took a liking to him right away. He had already given a workshop describing the work of the Lao-Hmong American Coalition, of which he was chief financial officer and Chee Yang was president. The coalition's goals, McCormack said, are to bring the Hmong to the attention of the American public and, second, to improve their situation, for example through ESL and citizenship classes. We talked briefly before he replayed a video about an event that clearly made both McCormack and Yang extremely proud.

McCormack had served three tours of duty in Vietnam between 1967 and 1972, but during that time he knew nothing of the Hmong, he said. Only years later did he come upon them in the course of doing research on prisoners of war and those missing in action.

He told me: "I became interested in Hmong history because of MIAs in Laos, and I studied the structure of the war. It was an eye opener for me. It was a secret even from us in Vietnam. We had crews that went there and never returned." These were the Ravens, who fought the Secret War in Laos alongside the Hmong, dressed like cowboys in plain clothes and flying beat-up planes. The story is vividly told by Christopher Robbins in *The Ravens*.

"The history is just fascinating," McCormack said. "They oughta make a movie out of this—it's just incredible."

The more McCormack learned about the Hmong, he told me, the greater grew his respect for them, their culture, and their military contribution. He was a key player in a committee to organize an American tribute to them in 1995, twenty years after the fall of Vietnam and Laos. Another military man, Bill Bilodeaux, who was wounded while serving in Vietnam, is executive vice president of the Lao-Hmong American Coalition.

Yang got the video rolling, and I kept one ear on it and the other on McCormack's commentary. This was the *first* tribute to the Hmong, McCormack emphasized. I had seen a video of another commemoration, at the Vietnam Veterans' Memorial in Washington, D.C., in 1997. That one, attended by congressmen and military figures and a senator, had brought tears to my eyes. Watching it, I had been captured by the sight of Hmong men dressed in jungle camouflage and Hmong women in their glittering green, pink, and blue garb passing in front of the black of the memorial's marble that lists the names of the American dead. I was overwhelmed by the cultural richness as well as the somber story of America.

McCormack's video, on the other hand, documented the twentieth-anniversary recognition by the United States government of the Hmong military contribution to the war. The ceremony took place under blue skies at the Colorado School of Mines in Golden. Hmong men in their fifties and sixties donned uniforms and basked in long-delayed honor. Each man received a congressionally authorized medal. On hand to honor the Hmong were a row of American military dignitaries, including Gen. Art Cornelius, a Raven who flew with the no-fear Hmong pilot Lee Lue, and Brig. Gen. H.C. "Heinie" Aderholt, a veteran of World War II and Korea who started the air and CIA operation in Laos in 1960.

A few old friendships were renewed at the ceremony, McCormack told me as the video ran. For the first time in twenty years, Cornelius met his "backseater" Peter Vang. "[Peter's] hands are all scarred and twisted from being shot up," McCormack said. A backseater, as Robbins describes in his book, was one of the elite corps of Hmong officers who sat in the back seat of small, vulnerable spotter planes and, as Laotian nationals, were legally able to validate targets via radio and authorize fighter planes to strike.

The ceremony unrolling on the video closed with eight veterans' organizations placing wreaths in memory of Hmong dead. These organizations included the American Legion, Raven Pilots Association, and the Veterans of Foreign Wars. "The Hmong were thrilled," McCormack said.

I was struck by this military man's quiet passion for the Hmong. McCormack explained. "I've been involved with mountain people in various settings, Montagnards [in Vietnam], Northern Iraq with Kurds. Mountain people always fascinate me because they are independent. We had Long Range Reconnaissance Patrols but had more than fifty percent casualty rate. Hmong seemed to survive better — they were better able to live off the land, and that made them more invisible."

McCormack observed that whereas the Viet Cong fought a guerrilla war in South Vietnam, in Laos they functioned as a conventional army, with long, vulnerable "logistical tails." Hmong were good at hit-and-run harassment. "They tied down ten North Vietnamese Army divisions we would have had to deal with.

"They're tenacious, honest, and loyal," McCormack said, relaxed in his fold-up conference chair. "They saved several hundred American airmen." And here in Colorado? "They are extremely industrious. They're a good model."

McCormack was sympathetic to the fractures he has observed within the Hmong community. "Basically, it's the old guard against the new guard." He sees three generations. The "old soldiers" who were in their forties and fifties when Laos fell lost all their status and find it tough to learn English. "It's extremely hard to lose all their prestige. They're still head of household but don't command respect." These are the ones most bent on mounting a military offensive to retake Laos.

The middle group includes people like Chee Yang, the coalition's president. "They have a foot in both worlds. They were involved in the war but were young. Yang went to the University of Colorado and got a degree in communication. They still have a strong bond to Laos—the Hmong have an extreme attachment to the land that's hard for us to understand—but see the future is here."

Meanwhile the young, the college generation, have little or no memory of Laos. "They have a strong attachment to their families, but they're Westernized. They say, 'I honor my parents, but going to fight in the resistance is baloney.'" Their attachment to Laos comes through their grandparents, who stay home in isolation and talk to the young. But "the old are passing on. Kids aren't going to learn Hmong and Hmong culture. They'll be strangers to Laos."

The younger Hmong around us at the conference illustrated his point. From the brash, American way they used their bodies, calling attention to themselves, to the skits spoofing their parents and traditional rituals, the twentysomethings have made a break. They act in Hmong theater groups, read romance novels, and build jazzy personal home pages on the World Wide Web. They learn computers instead of reverse appliqué, play boom boxes instead of the kheng. The conference itself was an example of the new thing, a place where young people stepped outside the ancient circle of farm, family, and village and discussed the unspoken.

Yet these same ones retain many marks of the Hmong. They cheered the few young men who, dressed in traditional black, paraded onto the ballroom floor and executed the intricate kheng dancing. And in their homes they are still strongly imprinted with family. Over lunch one mother described her fourteen-year-old daughter's subterfuges to wangle human company at night. She begs to sleep in her parents' bed, pleading a headache, or pays her disgusted younger brother to sleep in her room. A man with us at lunch leaned forward to explain to me, "Hmong culture is about relationship." He repeated it, drawing concentric circles with his finger on the place mat: You take care of the community first, the family next, and the individual last.

The young people I was seeing at the conference live in both worlds and have absorbed this discrepancy into their psyches where it is a prescription for turmoil.

I needed to visit Fresno, long the largest settlement of Hmong outside Asia and a community where Hmong have had both success and difficulty. I knew that Hmong live in every region of the U.S., from Boston to San Diego and from Seattle to North Carolina. They have settled in Billings, Montana; Philadelphia and Pittsburgh, Pennsylvania; and Grand Prairie, Texas, between Dallas and Fort Worth. Minneapolis–St. Paul, Minnesota, was home to about thirty-five thousand Hmong in the 2000 Census, and the old Yankee-German-Polish immigrant city of Wausau, Wisconsin, where my Irish-American mother grew up, is struggling with an eleven percent new immigrant population — many of them Hmong. My young friend Pang Foua Yang Rhodes grew up in a small town of eighty-five hundred in Iowa.

Fresno is the southernmost of a string of Central Valley towns on Highway 99 with good-size Hmong communities, which include Merced, Modesto, Stockton, Sacramento, Yuba City/Marysville, and Chico. The lure of agriculture in this barely undulating valley was a strong one for the Hmong, despite roaring hot summer temperatures and paltry rain — quite different from the weather in Laos. Driving north from Los Angeles to Fresno, I passed through miles of four-foot-high grape vines growing out of beige, sandy soil before my first sighting of Fresno. Silvery water towers and grain elevators share the horizon with a few sophisticated, medium-rise commercial buildings. But the agribusiness wealth on display in the endless fields and in the designer city hall belies the weak economics of individual households in the region. Out of a hundred metropolitan areas surveyed nationwide recently, Fresno ranked ninety-ninth in personal savings and income. A graph spanning 1969 to 1993 shows Fresno County personal income well below the California average, with U.S. personal income marching in the space between them. Fresno didn't drop below the national average until refugees from the Vietnam War arrived in large numbers.

Fresno has a typical population mix for California, which is home to more than a third of America's immigrants. The entertainer Cher hails from Fresno, a product of the Armenian immigrants who came here early in the twentieth century fleeing massacres and deportations. Fresno County has a population that is just over half white, more than a third Hispanic, over eight percent Asian, and a little less than five percent African American. In 1990 it was listed as the fourth largest California county in numbers of Southeast Asian refugees, behind two other major sites of Hmong settlement: the county that contains Stockton, and, in second place, Merced County.

The first Hmong family showed up in Fresno in 1977, according to an article by Kou Yang in the December 1990 *Fresno County Hmong Newsletter*. In the early years Hmong had a welfare rate over eighty percent, a measure of a stunned population.

Despite the powerful pull of community in general for the Hmong and Fresno's long-standing status as home of the largest Hmong-American population, there is little in the city that could be called "Hmongtown" in the geographic sense that there are Chinatowns, Little Tokyos, or Koreatowns elsewhere. Rather, there are two major clusters of Hmong some distance apart, with numerous families scattered elsewhere. The same is true in Sacramento, where knots of Hmong occupy apartment buildings in low-income portions of the city or in lower middle and middle class neighborhoods. Perhaps the scattering is a legacy of their history of living in villages dispersed throughout a jungle. Mark the spread-out locations of Hmong businesses, agencies, and institutions on a Fresno map, and it is evident that Hmong Americans don't feel compelled to huddle in one place.

In Fresno a cluster of Hmong live in low-cost apartments near California State University that are traditionally rented by students. More nearly a "Hmongtown" in the sense of clustered shops and offices is a community known as Asian Village, a short distance from the fairgrounds where thousands of Hmong converge every December for the world's biggest Hmong New Year celebration. But Cambodians, Vietnamese, Lao, and Thai also live here. All are served by grocery stores, a pharmacy, clothing shops, travel agency, video store, and a mutual-assistance association. Much of this is located in one mini-mall.

On the other hand, "Hmongtown" in the sense of an identifiable network of people is very real, nurtured by the liberal use of automobiles, telephones, and the Internet. It is their Hmongness that binds them, not geography.

Chamy had prepared me for the visit to Fresno by giving me the name of a relative who had beaten the California odds and appeared to be economically successful. I wanted to meet him. Talking to Chafong Lee first over the telephone, I quickly discovered that he was not eager to talk to someone who was writing about the Hmong. An ill-conceived, demeaning article had recently appeared in a national auto club magazine, and many Hmong felt angry and humiliated. But finally he granted permission, and I drove to Asia Super Market on Tulare Street. His business, which includes supplying Hmong stores across the U.S. as well as this retail enterprise, occupies a recycled supermarket of 1970s vintage. In the parking lot a woman was unloading fresh cilantro, green onions, and more from her covered-bed Toyota pickup.

Inside, the cavernous space was divided between food and dry goods and seemed to offer about anything a Southeast Asian could want. Here were 409 cleaner, Listerine, and the green-wrapped soap I had carried to Laos. Foods ranged from six-foot-long sugar cane and beautiful ginger root to Cheerios, instant coffee, baby food, and peanut butter but no plain Hershey bars. Four forty-foot shelves were devoted to noodles, rice stick, spring roll pastry and the like. I looked for rice but couldn't find any. I had walked past it coming in — big sacks stacked on pallets by the front door.

Between the food and a display of Asian-style clothing I found the candles, paper money, plain paper decorated with painted red squares, and gold-stamped paper that I had seen on family altars. I also saw huge soup pots two and a half feet in diameter along with the portable gas burners and propane tanks to fire them up for community gatherings. Against the back wall I counted forty-two bolts of black velvet, all but three of them printed with designs in silver glitter or iridescent purple, pink, green, or turquoise.

At the front corner opposite the entrance were displayed Hmong dolls, clothes in which to bury the dead, and elaborate women's hats for New Year festivities featuring lace and yarn puffs with sparkles. I saw pre-wrapped purple turbans and ready-made jackets and dress aprons such as I had labored over, one of which was backed with a fabric printed with the Denver Broncos logo. It seemed that the store not only employed tai-lors to make the Hmong clothes but also offered classes where Hmong women could gather around tables to create whatever fancy-dress designs their imaginations suggested. The evolution of "Hmong dress" continues.

I joined Chafong Lee and one of his daughters at a folding table near the ready-made clothes, and his son brought us cans of Sprite. Lee proved to be appealing, with a fine, open face, a genuine smile, and a tendency to put his fingers on his lips as he talked. His eldest daughter was on duty in customer service, and his wife, an outgoing woman with perfect business manners who first directed me to her husband, is vice president of Asia Super Market and Hmong Union Trading, Inc., the dual family business.

This store, Lee said, was his fifth. In the process of developing a work-able plan, he moved between three cities. He started in 1984 with a land-scaping, house-cleaning, and hauling service, followed by a video store that folded after a year, then a video and clothing store that lasted three years.

"After that, not quit yet, try one more," he said, laughing. That one wasn't what he wanted either, and he sold it to a brother-in-law and moved, eventually, to Fresno, where he expanded from a small store to the present one. "Someone else might give up, but I didn't." I couldn't help but reflect on the solid business lessons he was passing on to his children.

Lee quickly named Hmong-owned stores up and down California and in Oregon, North Carolina, Minnesota, Wisconsin, Detroit, Denver, Seattle, and on Long Island.

His daughter said, "He does business there, so he knows."

"I send catalog and go there. I working seven day a week, twenty-five hour a day." He laughed with a certain delight, perhaps enjoying his stamina. Suddenly he apologized. "Sorry my English! I came November 26, 1979, I have no English. Go to adult school, learn ABC, sit down with book and chair. My dream is come true — this." He gestured over his shoulder.

Given that few Hmong run such ample operations, I was curious to know how he learned to do it. Apparently he was not practiced at explaining, so his daughter helped out.

He said, "I have little bit of knowledge [from] my family, old generation. I see older people in Laos do it [selling goods]." He had relatives who sold clothes in Long Cheng. "I see Lao, Chinese, Vietnamese. Shopping eyes."

Shopping eyes? His daughter said, "He went around and just studied" what shopkeepers were doing. He was learning as Hmong have always learned, by watching. She continued: "Foreigners came in and did business. He saw that was where the money was going." He had been gifted, as Chamy was, by older relatives who had forged a new path in which he could walk.

"Come USA, Hmong people don't think how to do business, just working farm. But Chinese, Vietnamese doing business. We have to do that way. We cannot live by farming anymore, by waiting for someone to give." In fact, Lee never lived on a farm. When war displaced his family from the mountains, they chose to live in town, and that's where he was born.

Lee has two brothers and a sister who own businesses, in Yuba City, Sacramento, and Stockton. His eldest daughter, the one at the customer service counter, was studying business management, and Kao, our interpreter, was pursuing business law, but the dad has no guarantee they'll take over his business. "They don't follow the parent," he said with the usual laugh. "They go their own way." If they do, they will take with them their experiences in their father's store.

Along with their fledgling economic skills, Hmong are turning to social and political organizing to protect their culture and advance their well-being. They study unfamiliar mainstream organizations, much as Chafong Lee used his "shopping eyes" to learn the retail business, and adopt and reshape them to further the Hmong cause. Education and women's organizations push learning and empowerment. College students organize for action as well as fun, continuing a Hmong student tradition begun in Vientiane, Laos. Hmong radio, TV, and newspapers, some more long-lived than others, spread the word in both English and Hmong.

Relying on their long-time practice of village government — and under the gaze of photos of Touby Lyfoung looking down from everybody's living room walls to prod them into the mainstream — Hmong have begun to serve in positions in local governments. The first Hmong to serve was, perhaps not so remarkably, a woman, Choua Lee. She was elected to the school board in St. Paul, Minnesota, and was followed by another Hmong, Neal Thao. Lormong L. Lo of Omaha, Nebraska, was appointed to the city human relations board before being elected to the Omaha City Council in 1994. He was chosen the council's president. Joe Bee Xiong was elected in 1996 to the Eau Claire, Wisconsin, City Council on the momentum of many non–Hmong votes, and Bon Xiong was likewise elected to the Appleton, Wisconsin, City Council.

Hmong increasingly understand that by such means they can improve their welfare and help shape their surroundings, and not only by electing individuals from among their number. Hmong showed up en masse before a Minnesota city council to have a say in the matter of a Hmong–owned custom slaughtering operation that became engulfed by suburban growth.

I believe that Hmong communitarian structures combined with a determination to make a place for themselves whether in a jungle or a country of strangers has fitted them for political effectiveness. For what is politics intended to be if not people coming together to make things better? As a zealous Hmong woman attorney and activist at the Denver conference suggested, corral all your relatives and send them out to leaflet neighborhoods and you can get your person elected.

One organization with over ten thousand members took its case to Congress and won. Based in Fresno but with a non–Hmong director and lobbyist in Washington, D.C., Lao Veterans of America Inc. persuaded Congress and President Clinton to make citizenship a little easier for Hmong who fought during the Vietnam War. It was a ten-year effort. On a June day in 1998, a crowd of Hmong men in military camouflage filled the House Judiciary Committee's meeting room and cheered the yes vote that paved the way for the cause. The bill, signed into law on May 26, 2000, waives the English language requirement for up to 45,000 Hmong veterans, their spouses, and widows to become citizens. With citizenship, Hmong who fought on America's behalf but couldn't learn English can take an important step toward belonging.

Hmong pursue economic advantage vigorously. But I don't think it's the money they want, beyond enough to live decently. What they crave, as they have throughout generations of unwanted migrations in China and Laos, I suggest, is the security that will allow them to be who they are.

And they crave respect.

10

Kids Astray: Sai Sue Lor

It takes a whole life to be a good person,
But the blink of an eye to be bad.
— Hmong saying

As businessman Chafong Lee had done, it looked as if Doc might one day make a success of himself. As his nickname suggested, the youngster was on track to become a physician.

It's the number one Hmong dream. Doc's school attendance had been perfect. He was getting nearly all A's. A penciled note pinned to the wall of his parents' front room in Fresno said, "I want to be a doctor when I grow up."[1]

But then Doc entered adolescence. His family moved to Sacramento, and, at the age of twelve, he traded in the academic life for membership in a gang. His group was one of the deadliest in the Sacramento Hmong community, Masters of Destruction. Ironically, most of these gangs had been imported from Fresno, the town he had just left. Gangs were known to reproduce themselves when some youthful visitor boasted of his exciting gang experience back home and awe-struck cousins created a copy in the new community.

When the Hmong writer was gathering information for an article, he went to talk to Doc and his gang buddies. They wore baggy pants and slouched a lot. He concluded that these young men had no pride in being Hmong Americans. He believes they formed groups "to feel like they belong and to build strength against bullies."

To Doc and his friends in MOD, however, it was about having fun. MOD members and the wannabe group called Little Rascals mostly drank, smoked, and talked. Some boasted of ganging up on a prostitute in a motel. They also used rock cocaine, marijuana, and opium. One of Doc's friends, more talkative than Doc, was given a car and money by his parents. It was their desperate attempt to win him back from his rebellion. This buddy is called Johnny in the article. All the names are fictitious. Johnny said he prefers just smoking cigarettes and "hang[ing] around with my home boys" somewhere safe. But he's also stolen cars and car stereos and sold drugs when he needed money. And sometimes he and the rest fought against rival gangs.

Johnny told the writer, "We don't just beat [them] up for nothing." Only if the others give them a hard look. Then they fight with fists. Guns are brought out only for revenge or "backup." Doc had made a trip to juvenile hall for carrying a loaded .22. Johnny was sent away for aiming a loaded shotgun at a police officer. He acknowledged he liked "playing" with guns and aiming at people. He said he's never shot at anyone. "You kill somebody, you pay for it, man." Not long before, a MOD member in Fresno shot at a couple of gangsters. Then he got into his buddy's car. At the same moment, someone fired an Uzi and blew away the back of his skull.

But it was another story that got to Johnny, about gang buddy Jimmy. The article explains:

> Jimmy was chatting with five of his buddies on a front lawn near Martin Luther King and Franklin Boulevard one day as several Laotian gangsters walked by. One of them called out, "This is Lao," showing his pride at belonging to a Laotian gang.
>
> "This is Hmong," responded Jimmy. "Fuck padet." Attaching "padet" (an unusual Laotian fish dish) to a Laotian is an insult, like attaching enchiladas to a Mexican.
>
> So the Laotian guys responded: "This is Lao, whacha gonna do 'bout it?" As the argument intensified, a Laotian gang member pulled out a 9mm handgun and aimed it at Jimmy. Sonny — the buddy nearest to Jimmy — pulled him down as the others fell to the ground. But for some reason, Jimmy stumbled back onto his feet.
>
> A shot went off.
>
> A bullet caught Jimmy on the forehead and exited at the back of his skull. Several more shots followed and, within seconds, the Laotian gangsters where nowhere to be seen.
>
> Jimmy dropped into Sonny's arms.
>
> "Don't tell my girlfriend," Jimmy managed to cough out as the rest of the gang gathered around him and cried.

"Everybody is getting shot left and right, man," Johnny sobbed while telling this story to the Hmong writer. "You might die one day. You never know."

Doc added, "If I [had] a job or something, I might just go to work and stay home. But I have nothing to do, so when my home boys pick me up, I just go."

Around the end of the 1980s, something caused a rise in the number of Southeast Asian gangs in the U.S. The Hmong community was not immune. During the same period, the number of gang drive-by shootings in Los Angeles County climbed from fifty-seven in 1987 to 110 by 1992. In Wausau, Wisconsin, with a population of fewer than forty thousand, an influx of Hmong and other Southeast Asians in the 1980s was accompanied by an increase in ethnic tensions. Both Asian and white youth gangs appeared, transplanted from St. Paul and Milwaukee.

In Sacramento, gang activity became more organized and violent. A former Hmong gang member told me that the 1988 film "Colors," which featured Los Angeles's Bloods and Crips, offered a model that Sacramento Hmong youth emulated, cranking up the intensity of its own gang culture. By 1997 Chamy would tell me that there were "lots of Hmong gangsters in the south area. Many families that have more than ten kids, fifty percent of them are gangsters." She mentioned car jackings, home invasion robberies, and killings. "Hmong gangster kill other Hmong gangster and rob their own people, not American, because they know where they keep money."

Fresno has had a reputation as the cradle of Hmong youth gangs. The number of street gangs of all ethnicities in Fresno jumped in one year from thirty-five in 1990 to sixty-one in 1991. Of those, African American gangs went from fifteen to twenty, with an increase of members from four hundred to five hundred. There were fewer Hispanic gangs but the rate of increase was comparable. The number of Southeast Asian gangs, however, more than doubled, from ten to twenty-three. Membership likewise burgeoned, from about three hundred to six hundred fifty. Hmong figured prominently in that number. (The California Bureau of Criminal Statistics and Special Services, Fresno Police Department, also listed a rise of "white" gangs from two to six, but with a loss of membership, from fifty to forty.)

By 1998, Fresno County had assembled an impressive array of crime fighters in one building to fight the cancer—from California Highway Patrol and the FBI to officers from the county's police departments. Murders by gang members had become the leading category of homicide.

Even without the murders, Hmong members of street gangs who steal, stay out late partying, consume drugs and alcohol, and engage in premarital sex are the grief of their parents. These distraught elders are sometimes the first to ask police for help with the children they can no longer manage. One mother from the town of Sanger in Fresno County said:

> I hope my children will never associate with such bad [Hmong] children.... I pray that they do not befriend such bad people, as I would fear for their safety.... Some of my relatives' children have become gang members in Fresno. They steal stereos and cars and demand money from old folks. They rob people's houses and minimarkets.... I wish the police would catch them and put all of them in jail.[2]

What's the appeal of gang life? These kids scare us. Gangs make a mess of communities. They leave mothers and fathers dismayed and despairing. They represent a failure of the hope parents attach to kids.

I asked Chamy why she thought Hmong kids were going astray. She had already thought it out. "They could be influenced by Southeast Asian gangsters. Gangster activities were never known to Hmong young people before. Once they learn something bad, they're expert in bad." She went on, "You don't understand why they do it." But she had a sense that the change to a new culture was behind it.

"Back home there was no law, no crime, because you don't want bad reputation. Here, there is law, there is crime. Reputation? Who cares." She became heated as she spoke.

"I can blame the system here because it protect young bad people. Steal a car? They go to jail [only] two or three nights. Back there, nobody steal anything. My mom and dad had silver bar under the bed. They go to farm and come back and nobody even open your door. Even a pig or dog could open it." I understood that in tight village communities the consequences of stealing would be severe.

I had already gone to visit a police community service officer in another town — a woman — to get her take on what was going wrong. She is Hmong, outgoing and voluble. We walked together to the break room, with leafy trees shading the windows.

Why Hmong gangs? I asked. Her reply was heated: "We oughta shoot 'em!" That off her chest, she returned to her professional self.

"I don't really know why they join. They say it's peer pressure, lack of love and trust in family." She gripped one of the two cans of Pepsi she had brought from a machine and looked squarely at me. "My opinion is it's just because they want to be in gangs. I grew up poor, never had money in my pocket, but I wanted to be better. Everybody has inner strength. It's yourself that makes the decision to join."

I asked her to describe her family. She is the fourth of four boys and three girls. "Not rich, not poor, just middle," she said. Her mother died while the family was still young, and thereafter her father maintained strict control over the children.

"Every three days Father would sit us down and lecture us. We had to turn off the TV and radio. He'd"—she pantomimed shaking someone's shoulder—"if we fell asleep."

"The boys' rules: Go to school, get a degree, work, don't get a girl pregnant. Girls' rules: No makeup, no boyfriend until we were old enough, which is when he says. Each kid who graduates from high school will have a working car—not a new car—to go to college." Girls had extra restrictions, such as no short haircuts, no showing lots of skin, no unsupervised time.

"Boys in Hmong culture have it very lenient. If I was out of class at two thirty, my father was outside waiting. When I interviewed here, he was outside waiting." It was a fear of unwed pregnancy, she explained. Such a girl could not expect a good marriage. A girlfriend fell into the trap and was reduced to marrying a widower with ten kids.

"My dad would starve himself to give his kids what they needed."

All the exhortation, sacrifice, and material encouragement kept her steered in the right direction. She graduated from community college, married, and, with the tacit assent of forward-looking men in her community, joined the police department.

Next I went in search of someone with a view from inside a Hmong gang. At a backyard picnic on a summer evening in Sacramento, I heard about a young man, Sai Sue Lor. Another guest was Sai Sue's supervisor at a company that makes exercise equipment. "He likes to tell his story," I was assured. Later, I telephoned Sai Sue at his parents' home. (His name is pronounced "sigh su" with the "u" like the "oo" in took.) I arranged to meet him and his new wife a few days later at a croissant shop in a mixed residential and light industry area in southeast Sacramento. We set the time for "late"—10 a.m.—since they would be getting up early to cook for a wedding.

At the shop, I got myself some hot tea, sat in one of the anchored plastic chairs, and waited. I watched each car that pulled in. Several of them looked likely, older Toyotas, a van, and a black sports car, but none of them produced Sai Sue and his wife, Ge Vang. A steady rain was falling. I dismissed the brown 1980s Cadillac Coupe de Ville, since I'd never seen Hmong driving Cadillacs. But the couple that emerged from the Cadillac—

handsome, confident in an American way, bending their heads against the rain — looked likely to be my pair. Once inside, they wiped hands dry and extended them to shake mine. It was a sure sign, if I needed another, that they moved easily in the mainstream.

Sai Sue, in a dark jacket glistening with the rain, asked Ge what she wanted and then returned to the table with coffee and muffins to share. It turned out that the wedding feast had been postponed because of the rain.

Sai Sue's supervisor was right. He is a talker, and so is Ge, who explained that she was a financial aid technician at Sacramento City College, reviewing files and making money awards to students. Through my habit of opening interviews by mentioning the Hmong people I know, I learned that Ge calls my shaman-friend Mai Xiong her grandmother, though she is more a cousin-grandmother, and that she considers Ly Vong Lynaolu grandfather.

I told Sai Sue that I was surprised to see a Hmong drive a Cadillac. It turned out that this was his third. "I'm a Cadillac man," he said with a grin that crinkled his handsome face. "When I got this, I gave my old one to Ge."

Sai Sue has nicely proportioned features and an open, confident demeanor. He claimed Ge was better at English than he — she arrived in the country at age four while he did not encounter America until he was nine — but I rarely missed his meaning. Now he settled back into his café chair and began his story.

Sai Sue's association with a gang, just a group of guys, he said, started innocently. But that casual group was a seed that, in their encounters with others, bloomed into death.

"In high school my hair was shoulder length in back. In the Hmong community, if you wear your hair long, it's bad. So my parents and my uncle complained."

His wife, sitting beside me, added, "They assumed he was in a gang."

"And if you shave your head, they complain, so you have to have a certain length, and your shirt has to be tucked in. I told my parents it's the style [to wear long hair and baggy pants]. You can't just wear tight jeans. You have to go along. My father cut my hair all the time. I told him, No more. My friends trimmed the top, and I let it grow behind.

"To my parents I said, 'I'm a good person. Don't assume I'm not.' I attended school — every class. I was taking something in zero and first to seventh periods, eight classes a day. My father was drilling, drilling: I should attend school so I can be smart and help my cousins, my relatives, not so to be smart for myself. I planned everything ahead for five years, what I was going to achieve. But there was always the pressure, 'You failed,

failed, failed.' He was always putting you down, never satisfied, to the point of breaking.

"With my father I got into fights. They don't like my friends. Even three blocks down I can't go [visit them]. I should stay home and study. 'Why you not have homework?' 'Lunchtime I do homework.' I'm the kind who wants to finish at school. At home, I have just a little bit of homework and then relax. My sister collects homework all day [and brings it home]. My goal is to try to finish everything there. A boy going to high school is different from a girl — they're more focused on education. At the teenage stage, the boy wants to go out and explore. Parents say no, can't go to friend's house. I have to lie to them. A typical thing" — he grinned — "to trick your parent.

"Finally I told my parents, 'I quit. I'm not listening to you anymore.'

"I got into a lot of trouble. My uncles, my aunt came to lecture me, to tell me to be good. Twice a year they did this." But their flawed knowledge of America broke the chain of passing values down between generations. And without a father and uncles who knew the ropes, Sai Sue was floundering. "I was a black sheep. When I reached the junior year, that was the crucial point. I told my aunt and uncle, 'I see myself as a bright kid. I have everything planned ahead. There's a plate for every year'" — Sai Sue set down his coffee and placed imaginary plates vertically in a row to show what he meant. "I know what I'm going to do. For each year I planned this class, this class. I wash the dishes, one each year.

"At Burbank [High School] I was one of the best math students. Father was proud, but it was not good enough. I want to be an engineer or mechanic. They want me to be a doctor or pilot." The elders' heroes.

Sai Sue ran with friends, mainly relatives his age — "people I attended school with. We'd just dress weird. I was in trouble once, for theft of speakers from cars. It was hard to ask parents for money because they say, 'What do you want it for?'"

At this moment the Anglo owner of the company where Sai Sue was working stepped in to get coffee. Ge hailed him and he came over. The small factory, I learned, with its twenty-six workers, was only a mile or so away. The owner was working on Saturday. His sober face told me he might be the kind who worked every day. With Sai Sue and Ge looking on, I asked what kind of worker Sai Sue was.

"He's a great worker. One of the most reliable guys I've got!" And he went briskly on his way. I knew he meant it.

After this brief break, I realized how captured I was by Sai Sue's comfortable presence. He had charisma. Twenty-four years old, newly married, his wife pregnant, eager to be a good man and a good Hmong, so open to an outsider—he was living on all cylinders.

Earlier I had asked him about his family, and he began in a distinctively Hmong way.

"I'm the seventh generation. The first great-great-great grandfather was Giatou Qai Se." Descendants of such an ancestor defines the scope of "family" for Hmong. His immediate family includes twelve children, six boys and six girls, all living in Sacramento. "I'm the oldest son of all my relatives." His father had been an officer in the Hmong army and was wounded. His mother stayed home and farmed. Sai Sue was born in Long Cheng, and the family came to the U.S. in 1981.

"Growing up in the U.S., we kind of put feet in both sides. Sometimes it drives us nuts." Sai Sue grasped his cup and leaned forward. "Parents expect a lot. You try hard to achieve in school but they expect more and more. They want you to become a doctor or teacher, but they don't help you that much, because they don't speak English."

Sai Sue didn't speak English either when he entered third grade as a nine year old.

"Our relatives said we would be poor, because there are a lot of us. So my parents said to us, Be good, try your hardest. Remember what your relatives have said." The children had taken the challenge to heart. Five of them were now in college. His two older sisters, one of whom had married a Hmong high school teacher, would finish shortly, and two younger brothers were a few years behind them. A younger sister was just entering college, and Sai Sue himself was about to start a college math class.

"Now, our relatives, if they need money, they come to us." He looked at me and grinned. "We throw the most parties, for example for graduation or when our parents are sick and we call a shaman." All Hmong are aware that such events are expensive. "We do it all the time. My mother said, 'If you open your door to everyone, you'll never be poor. If you shut your door, you'll never be rich.' [So we give parties and feed everyone.] And they wonder where we got the money."

I had more questions about how a gang worked. Did the gang have a name? No. Was there a leader? No, "everybody just ran." Were there drugs or alcohol? Maybe marijuana?

"Weed wasn't a hot item. Hmong didn't know about it until the nineties. In the nineties, everything change. Kids started to drop out of high school, smoke, drink, smoke weed. When I was growing up, parents were strict. Now they don't listen to their parents."

Ge turned to me. "This is the group that was raised in America."

"In the eighties, all the Asians got along—Vietnamese, Hmong, Mien.

In the nineties everybody started to split up. [Now] there are lots of gangs [only] for Hmong. Sacramento has at least ten gangs." The same gangs are found in Los Angeles, Denver, Wisconsin, Minnesota, South Carolina and North Carolina, he said. "If I belonged to a gang and a cousin came to visit from Nebraska, he'd join my group and start the same one when he went back."

I asked him to name the gangs. He began, looking at Ge as if at a list. There is MOD, for Masters of Destruction. "MOD — they don't listen to nobody." I couldn't unscramble the intricate history that Sai Sue then gave, but the group apparently originated in Fresno. ("Is Fresno the worst?" I asked. "You may hear more stories because there are a lot more Hmong there.") MOD's history involves Peace MOD (M plus a peace sign plus D) and MBS, which later sloughed off ORB. At least one of the splits was precipitated by two friends fighting over a girl. "That's what I heard," Sai Sue said.

TRG, for Tiny Rascal Gang, he told me, originated with Cambodians in Orange County and then branched out to include Vietnamese and Chinese. Finally it metamorphosed into a Hmong and Lao gang. USC — Sai Sue didn't know what some of the gangs' initials stood for — is mainly Hmong, who claim the Crips' blue color. AC is Asian Crip, all Hmong. Interestingly, it cuts across clan lines. Sacramento Bad Boys — SBB — began with Hmong, Mien, Vietnamese, Chinese, and Lao, but "there was a fight between girls and it broke into groups." Now its just Mien, as is ATL, Above the Law, a child of SBB.

Tiny Little Rascals — TLR — is a feeder group for MOD. "They're a junior group within MOD, sixth graders. Once they reach a certain stage, they become MODs. In the '80s it started in high school. Now it's fourth to sixth grade smoking weed and belonging to a group."

Ge broke in. "The younger see the older kids and say, 'That's my brother. He's cool.'"

Marysville Boys Crop — MBC — started about 1994 in Marysville and was transplanted to Sacramento. "Then there's HNS, Hmong something Society, and King Cobra. That's for everybody. There's a lot of other gangs. I just can't think of them now."

It was Sai Sue who told me the effect of the film "Colors" on Hmong gang culture.

"Before the '90s they would still listen to their parents and try to go to school. Then after the movie about the Crips and Bloods, everybody started to pick colors. MOD is Blood and Crip together. They don't listen to nobody. They start dating at an early age."

I asked how many in Sacramento belonged to gangs. His picture outdid Chamy's. "In South Sacramento, everybody is [involved]. If you don't belong to MOD or TLR, it's hard for you. It would be hard for them to go to school. For example, somebody would jump them and get into fights. Southside, the parties are all MOD; no other group can come. Even if you don't belong, if you wear baggy clothes, a beany, Nikes, and dye your hair, you're considered part of the group.

"Parents don't really know about it. They don't want to believe it. There's not a lot out there [in the open] about gang culture except at New Year's. At New Year's there's lots of fights, even in Sacramento. Otherwise in high school they try to keep it quiet. Unless you jump me."

I wanted details about joining and getting out. "They don't say, 'I want you to be in our group.' It's your own will." The routine is a thirty-second or one-minute "jump," a beating. It's referred to as jumping some-one in. "If a person has been with a group a long time" — in an informal way, I understood — "maybe two or three years, it's just thirty seconds. If they don't believe or trust him, it's longer and more people attack him. For some, they just walk in, talk, and everybody says Aye, Aye, Aye. It depends on how the person carries himself. If there's a fight and he sup-ports the group, then they'll say, 'Well, just become one.' He earned his stripe."

Getting out is tougher. "It's really hard to get out. If you were initi-ated and then they jump you out, the other group still considers you a member. They'll say, 'In the past you did this and this.'" The best oppor-tunity to get out, which most seem to take, comes when a member mar-ries. "You can walk away and start a new life or stay in. It's mainly upon you. Some [still involved] are close to thirty and have kids in school. They don't participate but tell people to carry out a plan." It occurred to me that Sai Sue had been married only for a few months, and yet he talked as if he had left the gang life long ago. I made a mental note to get back to the question, after his description of gang activities.

I asked if Asians fought only Asians. He sat forward and his right hand played across the table top as if it were a map.

"In Meadowview, Detroit Boulevard is a dead-end street. It used to be African American Bloods [in control there.] Then Hmong moved in, and it became MOD and TLR. Sometimes Bloods are all mouth, just talk. Asians are small. African Americans are big, but when it comes down to it, they're afraid to get killed. They learned, Don't mess with Asian gangs because they would kill them.

"Black will help Asian. If another group comes in, black will help. They respect them, because if they don't, Asians know where the blacks live. Asians believe an eye for an eye; you kill, and a week or two later, three or four are killed in retaliation." Sai Sue was rotating his plastic coffee cup in place on the table.

"But Mexican is second hardest [after Asian]. It's very rare for Asian to go against Mexican. If Mexican and Asian gangs conflict, it would be very tragic. Remembering my history, I have to take a deep breath." He paused. "I have a lot of friends who still belong. I don't want them to continue." He looked down at his empty cup.

I wanted to know what was so volatile about Mexican-Asian encounters.

"If it comes to a conflict, it takes a long period to die down. Mexicans don't want to give it up. They're very true to a group. Mexicans don't really back off. If they say they will fight, they will fight. If they say one-to-one fight, they do. Blacks are not true to their word. They don't just come out one-to-one, squash, and be done with it. They see you, they jump you."

Are drugs involved? "Nope. Gangs don't fight over drugs."

Ge: "Because drugs were for medicine." It's a cultural thing.

Sai Sue again: "Opium was grown because it was the only crop they could sell [in Laos]. Things don't get solved because they can't let it go, [not because of drugs]. 'My friend got shot,' and it's just stacked higher and higher. In the past seven or eight years— so many deaths. They just can't let it go." Sai Sue frowned.

How many deaths?

"Drive-bys in one year, maybe twenty to forty incidents. Maybe two or three a year die. It's very scary.

"Hmong kill each other. Since 1989–90 there have been deaths caused by Hmong. Drive bys. Parents don't understand why there's that much conflict. They don't understand how hard it is. They say, 'Bad kid, let him die.' If they understood more about gangs, they could learn how to stop it. Parents know not even a little tiny bit."

Ge added: "Parents just say, 'Look at that bad kid.' They assume their kid is an angel."

"I want them to use me as an example. There's a Hmong saying, 'It takes a whole life to be a good person, but only the blink of an eye to be bad.'"

We had been sitting at the little table for nearly two hours. Sai Sue suggested we go find some lunch. The rain had stopped. I climbed into my car and followed the brown Cadillac to New Paris Restaurant, the popular Vietnamese spot, which is across the street from the mortuary where Ly Vong's funeral had been held and not far from Mai Xiong's apartment. The waitress spoke with familiarity to Sai Sue. Sai Sue ordered salty deep fried shrimp with their heads on, sauteed half quail — "The state bird," Ge said — and clams on the half shell with onion chunks and black bean sauce. "He likes seafood," Ge observed.

We returned to the subject of gangs. I asked why kids joined now, hoping I'd get an answer free of economic and sociological theories. Sai Sue's answer spoke volumes.

"Why? They want protection, they want to get girls, they want to make a name for themselves."

So plain. So complicated. So revealing. They want protection from the warfare they and their older siblings helped create. They want to be adults, to be big, to shed the restricting, humbling status of little kid, to have a woman and a name, to wield adult weapons. They want to seize the dignity of maturity by ducking through a shortcut. They want respect. "Don't overlook me. Don't cut me with your eyes," a young Hmong actor at the Denver conference had said. They want to be men, to be masters. They can do it, they decide, with the support of their peers.

Interestingly, the gangs of Sai Sue and Doc are a perversion of a normal part of Hmong village life. A California Hmong woman in her late twenties had recalled her village girlhood for me.

"We played in the mountains all day until sunset. We would just show up [at home] at night, and my parents didn't have to worry at all. We could just roam around. You assumed that the neighbors would look out for your kids. We would go find fallen trees and jump on them. Or we would play jump rope with rubber bands tied together. That was very popular. Or we would hang out by the ponds. It was a carefree time." What was safe and nurturing in the mountains had become a disease in America.

As an adult, Sai Sue now sees that there is no shortcut to maturity. Rather, a good deal of learning and empathy is required all around if young people are to escape the sucking quicksand that adolescence here can be.

"I have a lot of friends who belong to gangs. Since I'm older, I'm asked for advice. I'm trying to help people. I tell them education is number one. Just attend school, have one or two friends, be a bookworm, and don't go to parties. The most important thing is how you dress. Dress decent. You don't need to join a group."

He advises self-control in the face of challenges. "You really have to discipline yourself and stay calm. You can't just strike back." Wind down your temper, and "maybe later will come an apology."

As Sai Sue had mentioned, girls are less likely to get distracted from school. Still, I knew a Hmong daughter who ran away from home for some weeks, scaring her parents silly. And, according to Sai Sue's description of gang history, girls are involved as girlfriends.

And the pressures, though different for girls, are just as great. Because of frequent moves—from a town in Nebraska, where they were the sole Hmong family, to Denver to Alabama and finally to California, Ge didn't have time to make friends. In high school she went through a stage of self-hate, she said. "Asians were projected to be this or that way, so I would try to be as American as I could be." There were very few Hmong or Asians of any kind at the school. "I was all closed up. I never raised my hand. I was scared. I felt this tension. I just kept quiet and studied." She was an A student. "I never missed a day even if I was sick, because I didn't want to fall behind."

And she was under pressure from her mother, the outspoken parent. "Be a nurse, be a doctor," her mother would insist. Her father, a former sergeant, "doesn't speak," Ge said. "He's not very family-oriented. He was a soldier, and she had to be mother and father, make sure we did everything right."

Ge's mother also insisted that her daughter stay close to home. Too risky to be unsupervised. But Ge didn't settle for that.

"I took Mom to school meetings. I took her everywhere. I explained to her what I was doing, and she let me go to the first annual Hmong conference in Minnesota as representative for the club. Because I took Mom everywhere, she was more trusting. But even with that she still said, 'You can't go late. You can't date.'"

"Her mom never knew we dated," Sai Sue admitted. "When she heard, she was real upset."

"She expected me to marry a Ph.D. He was a disappointment."

When she was accepted to colleges in other parts of the state, another glitch surfaced. "Parents want you to go to college but stay home." Sai Sue commented, "It's like a string attached to you." Then, too, Ge admitted that she was scared to go "out there" on her own.

At the local city college she quickly discovered that she didn't like nursing, but instead wanted to pursue sociology and ethnic studies. It was tough explaining that to her parents. Although Ge's mother has given up badgering her about becoming a doctor or nurse, she continues to say, "You still going to school to get degree?"

Ge wants to become a counselor. "People our age should be able to understand the difference between elders and those causing trouble. Maybe we can be a bridge." There was a moment of quiet. "I want to help parents understand how hard it is, that growing up here is different."

Lots of words have been written to explain gangs. No lone theory can cover anything as complex as human behavior, but several pieces from

Doc's and Sai Sue's stories seemed to converge on one element that resonated.

First, the gang names struck me with their mixed claims: Sacramento Bad Boys, Above the Law, Tiny Little Rascals and Tiny Rascal Gang, King Cobra, Masters of Destruction. Names like these veer drunkenly between images of absolute, fear-evoking dominance (Above the Law) and kid-talk (Bad Boys, Tiny Little Rascals).[3] It's a potent brew, as if to keep the hearer off balance. Are these just harmless young people or are they brutally powerful? Gang members even scare themselves with their claims to potency, as attested by Jimmy's buddies weeping over his death.

Something else that struck me was the image of two packs of boys trading taunts. "This is Lao!" "This is Hmong!" It seemed that they were after something more critical than a territorial claim or a chance to fight. Behind the words hovers a demand for respect. One can see the young men figuratively sticking out their chests and brandishing their identity. I *demand* respect! They are adolescents teetering on the boundary between childhood, when one takes food and orders from others, and adulthood, when one feeds and directs others. The scene brought to mind the whimsical T-shirts worn by gangly youths at the Hmong conference that proclaimed, "I is a Hmong man/Hmong men are sexy," a more benign claim to a longed-for state.

The hunger for respect — or is it self-respect? — was also evident in a comment of Doc's: "I have nothing to do," he said by way of explaining his gang involvement. The words are striking because the sentiment never would have, never *could* have been voiced in traditional Hmong society. Even as adolescents their fathers and grandfathers were crucial workers on the family farm. Being needed is a special badge of honor. Now kids like Doc and Sai Sue are not only economically useless. They represent a financial drain, someone for whom food must be bought. They are dependents.

Older Hmong in America are baffled by their wayward children. No wonder, given that this system is nothing like the one that produced good behavior in the old country. Right behavior is pounded in by means of lectures and proverbs. For example, the saying "Disobey your parents, and your children will disobey you" works almost like a curse, according to one elder. The father of the female police officer and the aunt and uncle of Sai Sue delivered stern lectures to their young. Even at New Year's celebrations, with their emphasis on good times, songs commonly exhort listeners to be good, respect parents, and work hard.

Rules protect the honor of family, clan, and community. Codes prohibiting murder, thievery, neglect of duties, marital trouble-making, and sexual immorality haven't changed in generations. What was required of great-grandparents in their young years, the old system says, is what is required now. The idea of changing the rules is unsettling.[4]

There are other means in the traditional arsenal besides lectures and proverbs to ensure good behavior. Chamy explained that the Hmong belief in reincarnation deters wrong behavior. "If they're bad now, they will suffer in a future life. Nom Npis's step-brother killed a couple in a past life." So in this life, two daughters died as babies with a "stroke-like handicap." After the first one became sick, a shaman told them about the past murder and said two must die. Chamy concluded, "We didn't believe it until the second one died."

Another Hmong belief has caused a flurry in several U.S. courtrooms. Dissatisfied with American justice, complainants have demanded that all parties drink specially prepared spirit water to discover who is lying. The one who lies will suffer, perhaps even die, according to Hmong belief, and his descendants may pay a price as well. In Hmong society, the guilty frequently confess at the mere threat of spirit water.

For all its imperfections, the Hmong system worked pretty well in the past. But here it doesn't. For one thing, the system is adapted to communities where people know each other, around a hundred fifty people. Above that number, academics have discovered, a formal criminal justice hierarchy and professional police become necessary. So older Hmong struggle with the transition to a system of anonymous legislators, police, lawyers, and judges—people they don't even know! And these strangers are promulgating disturbing ideas. Kids can't be forced to obey parents anymore. Parents, told to adopt new techniques to control their kids, have no idea where to begin. Kids don't look, act, or sound the way *they* did. Parents often throw up their hands.

The stress for parents is huge. But kids may have it tougher. Young people with little traditional encouragement to think for themselves are suddenly asked to exercise self-control, and this in a society that allows for a lot of variety. They grapple with conflicting messages. From America they hear, "Be yourself, all you can be," and at home they hear, "Live for us, not yourself." As I sat with Sai Sue and Ge in the restaurant finishing my lunch, I contemplated Sai Sue. Here was a thoughtful, egalitarian husband, interested in material possessions, unafraid as a young man to take a leadership role—pretty American. He had told me tales of his days as an American-style street tough, talking back to his parents. Through it all I had sensed a young man flailing about to create a personal identity, a uniquely American rite of passage. It looked as if the American Sai Sue had won.

But to my surprise it was Hmong culture, alone, that rescued him from the maw of gang life, and I had to acknowledge that he is still very Hmong. When I first contacted him I learned that he and Ge live with his parents—the traditional son's role. Later, at the cafe, he told me that he has embraced traditional Hmong religion "one hundred percent." He is learning the graceful, specialized language of religious rituals and prides himself on being conversant in the "flowery" language of the elders, rich in words and circumlocutions and tenderness.

So, what was it that sprang him from the gang trap? He had abandoned that life well before getting married. I had to ask twice, because I didn't understand enough to get it the first time. His parents and sister had gone to a shaman "to look at my sister." She had kidney problems. (His sister has had a transplant.) In the course of the visit, the shaman mentioned the family's first son — Sai Sue, then named Xeng ("seng"). "The Hmong shaman or palm reader said I was acting that way because my name was wrong. They should call me Sai Sue. So it was done.

"Once my parents changed my name, it made a big difference. I changed my whole life. It turned me around." Though I pushed a bit, his only explanation for the transformation was, "The shaman said the name given to me was wrong." Significantly, the new name he received was not another child's name but a two-syllable man's name, such as is given when a man marries and becomes a father. It marks the transition to adulthood.

By this simple act, Sai Sue became a man. Others assumed he was married and treated him with due respect. And in gang circles it was understood that now he could separate himself if he chose, with no penalty.

In a stroke, he was deemed a fully competent adult, a gift from his people.

Part IV

MIDDLE WORLD: BEING HMONG IN AMERICA

Kho kom raws: To adapt
(Lit., to arrange so as to agree with)

11

A Change of Mind: Lue Vang, Pang Foua Yang Rhodes

... a future different from the past, but not separate from it.
— Lue Vang

The Hmong are a sober people. They take challenges encountered by their culture with utmost seriousness.

Even without a written language, a country of their own, or a unified government, the Hmong have kept the heart of their culture intact, scholars say, for at least a century. This cultural core includes those things that Tou Ger Xiong wheedled out of polite conference goers in Denver: speaking the Hmong language, eating Hmong foods, and knowing the Hmong thing to do. Indeed, they've apparently kept their ways intact not just for one century but for many, while they were resisting Chinese efforts at assimilation.

Onto this durable core, some alien elements such as new words, new building styles, or new clothes have always attached themselves like barnacles. In America, away from their isolated mountains, Hmong have adopted everything from business suits to purses to VCRs.

But now two powerful institutions are poised to make big changes in the way Hmong think—formal education and the Christian church. Both school and church lead people to see the world in new ways. Both are having profound and sometimes unexpected effects on the Hmong.

215

Dr. Lue Vang, Rancho Cordova, California, 1990.

Oddly, certain traditions lead Hmong to embrace both these institutions.

Lue Vang wasn't born Hmong but Khmu. He became Hmong by adoption. The Khmu are descended from the oldest inhabitants of Laos, and are looked down upon by Hmong and Lao. But that was secondary to the Hmong couple who adopted him. They had no son to take care of them when they grew old. The daughter still at home would soon marry and leave. Hmong say, "Raise crops to prepare for famine, raise a son to prepare for old age." A son would also improve their status in the village.

Lue had been born in a Khmu village in eastern Xieng Khouang Province, where war would soon be played out. His new parents paid one bar of silver for him. Lue was a toddler and has no memory of the adoption. "I seem to have, I don't know why, I have some feeling toward someone other than my adoptive parents. But I always see that my adoptive parents are my parents." We sat in a corner of the school district trailer that was Lue's office in a town adjoining Sacramento. Around us on shelves were books and videos for and about the Hmong. Dressed in relaxed business clothes, Lue talked in his headlong, wordy, enthusiastic manner, phrase piled on phrase until the shape of his ideas emerged. Our conversation went on for hours, but Lue never looked at the clock. Furiously busy as he was, he wanted to be sure all my questions were answered.

A year or two after adoption, he was taken to visit his former family. "I believe that we visit my biology parent one time. See, I remember we went there, but I didn't even remember whether we get there and actually do something." But he remembers dry fields of rice, so different from the wet paddy fields of his new parents. What he wouldn't have known was that the difference showed that he had taken a step up in the world. Paddy rice brought a more abundant living than dryland rice.

Lue figured out for himself that he was adopted. "People around me didn't really directly say to me, but make some noise that I know that I'm not their biological son. And I can see, if I look in my mirror ..." Lue's mobile, non–Hmong face blossomed into its familiar, all-engulfing grin.

"But you know, my adoptive parent really protective. They just don't want anyone say anything. And I respect that it's OK. I'm in the family, and my life is like any Hmong son." It helped that his adoptive father was the headman of the village, which contained ten or fifteen families, all relatives. "He protected me, and people don't dare to say much." Lue laughed.

His new mother saw schooling in her son's future. It didn't matter that she herself had none. Her second husband, Lue's new father, would soon die in the war. But since managing finances is a common task for a wife, it was she who saw to it that Lue went to school. It was she who pushed and shoved to keep him on track. Later I attended a sit-down dinner for four hundred in California, with live music and balloons, a gathering to celebrate Lue's doctorate in education. After several hours of speeches, Lue appeared from behind the scenes and stepped to the microphone amid booming applause. He held up a photograph of his late mother and said that she had died in Laos "without a chance to say good-bye to

For Chamy Thor's twelve-year-old nephew in Laos, school means leaving home to live in the city. Laos, December 1994.

me." She was the individual, he said, whose dream of education he had just fulfilled. Both men and women in the audience sniffled. The only reminders of her that he had brought with him to America were the photograph, a silver bar sewn into clothing made of parachute nylon, and her tooth.

Lue had come a long way from his childhood in wartime Laos. Having lived in the war zone, his family had fled now here, now there. Lue's father had previously served the French as an officer during the "Japanese War"—World War II—and later during the battle at Dien Bien Phu. When Vang Pao, not yet a general, came to where Lue and his family were staying, Lue's dad once again signed on for military duty. They moved to the military base at Long Cheng, just as Ly Vong and so many others would do.

But war did not deflect his mother's plan for Lue's schooling. Lue was eight or ten years old when he started at a village school in 1962. It would have been one of the earliest such schools. Only twenty existed in Hmong villages in 1959, and there were no more than a hundred in 1968.

"I still remember my first day in the school. Oh, man! I get reaction to the smell of pencil and the smell of the paper. Headache, nauseas, whatever, because when you freshly sharpen your pencil? Phew! It make me throw up, or whatever. And the smell of paper when you open the fresh page, it is torture. I think if you have that kind of thing, you probably won't go very far.

"So I remember I come back to my mom and say, Mom, I *hated* school, I get nausea, I get headache. And then I have an older cousin who used to go to school and I asked him, I said, What is your first day in the school? Because mine is kind of terrible. And he said, Same thing, but you will get used to it.

"OK. So I hang in there. I knew [it was] something that my parents want me to have, because they see that they didn't have it. Means that a son who first can read and write Lao—I know that they really want me to be someone."

His eyes were fixed on me, and he laughed often. "At the time that I went to school, we do reciting, and I still remember those book that I have in the '62, '63, we still have some in here." He gestured toward the shelf of books beside me in the small library. "I still remember a chapter—not very long chapter—about five, seven sentence. I [can] almost say as by heart, and I can say as fast. And this is how my mom and dad want to hear. They don't know [how to read] it, but they want to hear it.

"So what I'm doing at night time, I'm built a fire or a lamp that use oil, and then that part of village about ten or fifteen houses all together, they will hear me to read Lao, to read in my book out loud." The houses were close and the walls thin.

"And so sometime I get so fed up that I have to read, OK, because they want to listen, right? And so sometime ..." Laughter interrupted the narrative. "... I actually say thing that is not really in the book.

"But later I really say [what's] in the book, because if someone come to tell my mom and dad, He just make it up, then I will be in big trouble."

Besides, boys who couldn't recite the lesson in front of the teacher had their hands or bare feet swatted. For protection, ten-year-old Lue cooked up a plan. If he didn't understand the reading, he would hire another student to explain it, paying in clean sheets of paper torn out of his notebook.

But being a good student got him in trouble, too.

"The second grade teacher [was] mean. Those days we used to have mean teacher. Even we change mountain to the city, we still have mean teacher." He laughed. "And later I think, mean teacher, is it really work?

"Second grade, we already read some French. You know, like *a*, *b*, *c* and then later *je ne parle pas l'anglais*. It's very, very simple, OK. And I remember one day we read a short chapter, but it [was] assigned long enough for us to prepare. I have five classmate which is my cousin. One is my stepfather's son." By this time, Lue's father had been killed in battle and his mother had married for a third time.

"And then when we come to time to read. And each one of us have to go in front of the class and read it. And the teacher really watch every word you read. And so, if you read and you pass, you come back to the bench. And I believe is forty-three of us. And fifteen or seventeen of us pass. If you make mistake five time, you go in that corner and wait for spank by your classmate. One person [would] spank five people.

"And that chapter I remember is like, *not difficult*, but they don't prepare themselves. I used to go ahead a little bit. And then the teacher *challenge* people, Who can read the next page? And I say, can I try? Three of us raise hand. And teacher say, After you try and you get through, you have bonus. You think that probably a pencil, book, or something, right? So we just want to get a bonus.

"Then we three try, and two of us pass. That's why, when the bonus come, is what? He give me a ruler and he say, Here is your bonus, and what I'm going to tell you to do is give each one three spanks.

"And I [went] red and I say, Gee, this group is all my relative. But I had to do it. That's why I say teacher mean, mean, mean, mean." A student's plight counted for nothing.

"So my step brother come home, cry. They say, Who beat you? We don't have the word spank, but we have the word beat. And he say, My step older brother. Then they come right on me without asking what caused me to do it, OK? So they jump all over me. And I say to them straightforward, This is my bonus." Lue was looking at me when I glanced up from my notebook.

"I remember that incident is vivid."

Like Lue's father, the village headman, Lue's mother also came from a prominent family, of the Her clan. Her eldest brother later became a district chief, governing a number of villages. But the greater influence came through a younger brother who went to Bible school.

About the time Lue's family fled from their first village because of fighting, Lue remembers, they went to church. "I didn't even know why we went there. I just kind of go with the old folk and they just sing a song, whatever. But I grow up, I don't really see the altar in my house that the traditional Hmong have.

"So I don't know much about those rituals *until* when my adoptive father was killed in the battle and then my mother remarried. And she remarried with a stepfather who have lot of traditional faith experience, and so I mingle with those children and those cousin, and that's why I learned why people do a different thing."

His mother's younger brother — the one who went to Bible school — became a pastor. (Later, he joined the military and was killed.) This brother gave Lue's mother her vision of an educated son.

"And so early on, in 1962, when I had a short time at school, she really push me, force me, convince me to go to school. And many time I kind of rebel. I say XYZ son didn't go, uncle, whatever. She said, Nope, you go to school and we go to the farm and we work very hard, carry rice, come back home, and you go to school.

Lue finished sixth grade at the military-run school in Long Cheng. He was fourteen, an adult. In the absence of his father, he took responsibility for the family. At this age a Hmong male began to give serious thought to earning respect. He took care to stay out of trouble, to stay close to his "roots and branches" — his kin — and to protect the family's reputation. He schooled himself in cooperation and the friendliness that Lue practices to a fault.

Lue describes the informal curriculum of the young male. A man must ask: "Do I care for and help my parents and relatives when I am needed? Do I deliver on my promises — by acting rather than by talking? Do I know the ways, roles, customs, and manners of my lineage, clan, and regional group? Am I willing to learn from the elder persons? Have I learned a special skill: courtship chants, wedding songs, funeral chants, blowing the *qeej* [kheng], understanding and using Hmong proverbs?"[1] I was astounded by the maturity of these questions and recalled that there is no Hmong adolescence. Adulthood indeed comes early.

At fourteen, Lue joined the military. He was based in Thailand and employed by the United States, a step that had a profound effect on his life. He flew into Laos as a radio operator, transmitting enemy locations to fighter planes. His next assignment, as a second lieutenant, was not quite so risky: managing a military rice warehouse and distributing food to battalions.

But Lue saw that being part of what looked like a losing effort held little promise. He left the war zone and became a security guard for the U.S. Agency for International Development. This took him to the lowlands around Vientiane. By then he had married his wife, a beautiful, serious Hmong woman with skin as delicate as a baby's. When the Lao government fell to communism, he fled with his wife by boat to Thailand. He studied English there for more than a year before being accepted for resettlement in the U.S.

His story in America begins as so many other Hmong stories did: factory work, ESL classes, a job as a community health worker and another as a bilingual aide in school. But the school job, and perhaps the spirit of his mother whispering in his head, ignited him. He gathered courage and began to teach American teachers at the state university in Sacramento. "There were not very many Hmong who were willing to teach American teachers the Hmong language [and] aspects of Hmong culture," he wrote in his doctoral dissertation, which looked at Hmong students in Thailand. "[N]one of us had any experience at that sort of thing." At the same time, he was earning a high school diploma by correspondence, emceeing at Hmong New Year celebrations, and helping organize a mutual assistance association that still serves Sacramento's immigrants.

This was no average individual. Eventually he was hired by a suburban Sacramento school district to work with immigrant students and quickly saw that he needed a college degree. He earned that, and a master's, from a private university in Sacramento. He was on a roll then, located an amenable doctoral program several hours' drive away in San Francisco, and set to work on the final step. In his dissertation he names each of the twenty-six cousins who lent him money for school. "I believe I have done, if not exactly then very close what my mother told me to do." Once over the phone he told me, "I think I haven't done good enough, but I look back and see that I worked like hell."

Twenty years after Lue Vang fled from Laos, he was awarded his doctorate in education. He was forty-three. He had achieved one of the three or four professional goals to which all Hmong parents aspire for their sons. At the time, he was one of seven Hmong with a doctorate in education.[2]

When I went thousands of miles away to college, I found myself thoroughly alone. I knew none of the other students, and my brother was three hundred miles away at his college. I was cut off from family and friends.

I chose my courses alone, planned my future with only myself in mind, and gratefully accepted tuition checks from my parents without believing I had to pay them back except by doing my very best.

When a Hmong leaves home to go to school, as is necessary beyond the lower grades, he or she, figuratively speaking, takes along ancestors, family, everybody in the village, and centuries of voices urging diligence. It's a psychic mob scene. Like every other Hmong endeavor, community suffuses education. Extended family may have contributed money, and in return the student's efforts are understood to be for the material and social benefit of family and kin, now and down the generations. On top of that, the entire village listens keenly for news of shirking. "To send children away to school is still a new idea," Lue writes in his dissertation, "and it means to live with the talk of others."

Lue calls this Hmong "groupness." It is pervasive and functions almost instinctively. Its pull is felt most strongly between parents and children and between siblings who "come from the same womb." "The parent can be ninety and the children can be seventy, and we still have a bond." And the parent continues to be responsible.

But that groupness suffers a head-on collision in encounters with Western-style education. Lue might have been writing about U.S. schooling when he described post-grade school education in Thailand. "It takes the child from the family and village and sends him back a different person." Basic structures of thought are changed. Mere chatting becomes a minefield. Hmong conversational style emphasizes narrative. School learning demands abstraction and summary. Educators teach logic. Hmong thought grows out of concrete reality and observable successes and failures. When an educated child challenges the old belief in spirits and ancestors as the cause of events, a parent can believe his world is in danger. It is. This alien, scary kind of education is key to success in the new land.

"Without continued Hmong identity, life is not worth much," as Lue expresses a widely held belief. "How much change can occur without interrupting thousands of years of linguistic and cultural identity as Hmong?"

If education both fractures Hmong families and enhances their status, conversion to Christianity brings both obvious and subtle changes to the Hmong. Clearly it competes with traditional religion, yet it also supplies a new Hmong village to replace the old. In addition, the "new" religion, embued as it is with Western culture, unwittingly teaches secular skills that ease Hmong entry into mainstream life.

I had already studied the Hmong language for some months under the easy-going, playful Lue when a language helper I had found through Lutheran Social Services suggested I accompany her to church. (I was to drive her, an unmarried woman, and later her unmarried male cousin to church on a number of Sundays. I was surprised to find two never-marrieds in their middle years.) The idea was that I would be helped by listening to a lot of spoken Hmong.

The sanctuary was broad and had room for maybe five hundred people. The pews were full, and a hubbub of men and older children clustered against the back wall. Women in the pews fed their babies from bottles. Church rules, a friendly elder who appointed himself my guide told me. No breast-feeding.

The service included a familiar alternation of speakers, singing, and praying. To my dismay I understood almost no words, although I did recognize hymn tunes — "Amazing Grace," "Blest Be the Tie That Binds." Later I learned from Lue, an elder and co-founder of that congregation, that I was hearing the Green Hmong dialect — which some call Blue Hmong — not the White Hmong I had been learning.

A visit to a third and fourth graders' Sunday School class taught me something about my view of time and children. Seven girls and fourteen boys sat for half an hour, more or less quietly, while their teacher wandered around preparing himself for class. I was alternately impressed with the kids and exasperated at the man for being so indifferent to the clock. ("Time is money," Lue had quoted to me from my own culture.) Finally the teacher spoke to the class, and all turned their attention to him. After teaching written Hmong to the kids for ten or fifteen minutes, he told some wonderful biblical story that had him grabbing one kid repeatedly by the shirt and then, his dignity remarkably intact, falling backward onto the floor.

Back in the sanctuary, elections for church officers were under way. I could tell by the newsprint pad, on which several people — including Lue — took turns writing names, that four or five individuals were nominated from the floor for each office. Nearly every nominee — men, except for candidates for the women's board — spoke a few words into a portable mike by way of electioneering. One toothless grandmother drew laughs with her statement.

Something was going on with these women. Seventy percent of Hmong women in the denomination — and perhaps in others — can read and write Hmong, compared with ten percent of non–Christian Hmong women, I was told by a Hmong leader. And not just the women were learning: Both men and women copied into notebooks the words of songs projected onto the front wall of the sanctuary.

After I had been attending Sunday afternoons off and on for a year, my self-appointed guide—an interpreter at the university hospital in Sacramento—invited me to the church's New Year party. The party was in an enormous elementary school auditorium. Arriving about nine a.m., I was of course late. Maybe six hundred people were already seated or bustling around long tables on which disposable pans full of food were being deposited.

I sat and made friends with a young woman next to me whose arms were draped about her husband in a most American fashion. She gave me a rough translation of the sermon. Its theme was the sojourner. The preacher told about Abraham starting out for a new land, Joseph in exile, and the Hebrews wandering in the desert. These stories are popular with refugees. He also talked about America, commenting that the old people think only about going back. "But we're going on to another country," his message was translated for me. "What country is it?" My seat-mate's young husband called out the answer: "Heaven." "That's right. We don't belong here per se. This is just a training ground." It seemed to me a way to help refugees manage their sorrow.

Between choirs and hymn singing, a man who looked young—he turned out to have thirteen kids—took the microphone to tell how he overcame being an orphan. (You are an orphan even if your mother is still alive, because the father is so crucial to one's training and status.) The orphan theme carries much emotional weight with Hmong. He had half the audience weeping. In this room there were probably few over the age of thirty who still had both parents.

These church-going Hmong are swapping old for new. They do not visit a shaman anymore nor venerate ancestors at household altars. Wedding customs are different. Adults write in Hmong. Children write in Hmong. Women are elected leaders of women's groups. One woman was alternately astounded and a bit horrified to find herself president of such a group, even though she was anything but meek within her family.

"I was so scared to speak [before the group]. I ready to cry I so nervous." She traveled to a women's conference without her husband, an astonishing step. She looked forward to the end of her term but was glad for the experience. "I have grown up."

Sometimes the old has been transformed instead of replaced. A Hmong sermon probably has roots in the ancient sung poems that urge virtue and hard work. The old village leadership segues into the new elected church leadership. Traditional Hmong hospitality gradually learns how to include non–Hmong.

But Lue Vang had more to reveal about the effects of church.

During my lengthy interview with Lue several years after the New Year's church party with all its food, I learned behind-the-scenes detail about his congregation, including the fact that it has a membership of fifteen hundred. As Lue spoke he watched me intently, and whenever I spoke he kept up a chorus of "Umhm" and "Right!" and "OK, OK, OK."

He touched only briefly on matters of belief before becoming practical.

He was eager to tell me about the way groups in his denomination had funded each other, helping his congregation buy an eight hundred thousand dollar church complex.

"If a group in Spokane [Washington], let's say, would like to buy a church, they send an announce through the channel. And we in Sacramento say, OK. And then suppose that each church send a hundred dollars." There are "seventy-three or seventy-one" congregations around the country, twenty-six of which own property. "You already get seventy-three hundred dollars. And this is something that I see that the non-tradition [Christian] Hmong do a lot."

But as always, Lue was careful not to boast. With classic Hmong hedging, he assured me, "I don't say that tradition didn't have anything [like that]. They do have something, but probably I haven't known yet of it. A number of tradition Hmong have done a wonderful thing, but more or less like a business." Clans of any religion pool resources, he reminded me. His congregation, however, includes not one or two clans but eight or ten.

Besides organizing to reach goals, these church Hmong were developing other skills. For example, they had agreed to shift from a headman-style government to a governing board, with elections such as I witnessed. Voices that hadn't carried weight before — the young and female — began to count. "We run it for one or two year," Lue said, "and kind of smooth to some extent that we learn the new way."

Then there was the matter of the unstructured meeting. "Sometime we meeting, it took seven or eight hours. I remember back in '90, '89, we take like a whole day to meet — means that almost like ten to twelve hours and still didn't finish our business. But now we try to make sure that if we say four hours, four hours.

"And we have a rule committee just chop you down and say," Lue was laughing, "'That is nonsense, excuse me, that's not in agenda.' Sometime make people really pissed off." Everybody wanted his say, even if only to repeat what was already said. "If I don't let you say [it], I won't see you next time." So in a village meeting, people could talk as long as they wanted? Yes, he assured me. "And then if they don't finish today, they can finish tomorrow. We don't do that here, because tomorrow we have something else!

"I think that the non-tradition Hmong have a sense of fitting into the mainstream easier, because they learn some of how organizations go."

I had moved four hundred miles south of Sacramento and again needed to find a Hmong language helper. What I found was a tiny congregation of the same denomination as Lue's, Christian and Missionary Alliance. It was the first Hmong congregation of that denomination in the United States.

I found it easily on a business corner in Santa Ana. As Lue's church had, this congregation rented space, from a Chinese congregation, and worshiped on Sunday afternoons. Instead of hundreds, I found dozens gathered for worship. There I met a plain-spoken, generous woman, and I spent many hours at her home absorbed into the life of her extended family.

I also met Pang Foua Yang Rhodes and through her, her brother, a seminary student who preached once a month at the church, Stuvy Yang. From him I learned which Hmong are likely to be attracted to Christianity.

Like Lue, Stuvy had been raised in a Christian family.

"My father became a Christian when he was still single, still a man in his teenage years. When he became Christian, it was early in the history of Christianity among the Hmong people. All his brothers forsook him, and so he was not able to live with them." Because he no longer appeased the ancestors, the others feared spiritual retaliation. "[His brothers] didn't allow him to farm the land with them, so he had to go farm by himself."

But the trouble his brothers anticipated — sickness, poor crop yields, even death — didn't happen. "Gradually his brothers began to see a change and a difference in him, and so that caused them also to convert to Christianity."

Stuvy enumerated factors that discouraged Hmong from becoming Christians. First was the lead role of the father. "We're a patrilineal [patriarchal] society, so if the grandfather or the father is still alive, the son wouldn't disobey the parent, especially their father." This is especially true when the father or grandfather is active in shamanism.

More telling, the demographics of conversion were clear: "The higher up you are, the harder it is for you to convert to Christianity." Stuvy explained. "Being the head, you have to perform all those ceremonies, you have to go to all those functions. And many time those functions involve invoking or appeasing or worshiping the spirit. Being Christian, we can't do that. And so they say, Oh, he's no longer one of us.

"If you're a leader, you can't be seen as an outcast. So that's the major reason why we don't see them coming to Christianity as readily as the peasant who has nothing to lose."

It is also true that some factors in Hmong culture support conversion to Christianity. First, the Hmong emphasis on right living is a natural entry point to Christianity. Then, too, the patriarchal structure can work to the benefit of conversion as readily as not. The religion of the family head is the religion of the wife and children.

About one-tenth of Hmong in the U.S. are Christian. Stuvy's denomination counts about twenty-five thousand Hmong members, he told me. He estimated that another ten thousand Hmong Americans are Baptist, Brethren, Lutheran, Mennonite, Methodist, Roman Catholic, Seventh-day Adventist, and Church of Christ members, among others.

Stuvy's was the first Protestant denomination to send missionaries to Laos, but it took more than twenty years for them to reach the Hmong mountains. That was in 1953. At that point a Protestant-Catholic team put together a written alphabet for the language.

After visiting with Stuvy I went to visit his sister, Pang Foua Yang Rhodes. I was eager to get better acquainted with her. She had ventured further than any Hmong woman I knew, including Chamy. Not only had she completed college. Partly as a result of her Christian beliefs, she had married a European-American.

In her apartment I saw but one clue that she is Hmong: A framed portrait on the wall showed her with her tall, brown-haired husband, both in Hmong fancy dress. On another wall I saw three portraits of their wedding, including his parents— sophisticated Westerners— and her parents— former subsistence farmers.

In some ways, Pang Foua was non–Hmong from birth. A Christian family, a father who encouraged his daughters. And yet she sees herself as Hmong. Her story challenges the sense of what constitutes "Hmong."

She was maybe four years old when they came to America. They arrived at the airport at night and were picked up by sponsors. "My first recollection of America was the lights."

They had been sponsored by the Christian Reformed Church in a Dutch town of eight thousand in Iowa. Different congregations in town had sponsored about ten families, the size of a Hmong village. Those families formed the Hmong congregation that met in the afternoon in a Christian Reformed Church building.

She knew her dad — Stuvy's dad — was unlike most Hmong fathers. Not only was he Christian from his early years and a faithful Bible reader. "He's physically affectionate. Traditionally Hmong men did not even touch their daughters or had anything to do with the kids while they were little. But my dad would braid our hair for church. He would play with us. And we were a very affectionate family — verbally affectionate, too.

"My dad did such a great job with his two daughters, teaching us that we were as valuable as his four sons. He wanted me to be college educated, to get a good job, to give as much to the family as any of the boys would."

In high school, she began to see that, though she once played football with the non–Hmong boys, there were still barriers. "I realized that I could probably never have a romantic relationship with someone who was Caucasian because, as open-minded as the Dutch are, there could never be the crossing of cultures in that." Yet she saw that her goal of college made her a daunting figure for Hmong boys.

At home, Pang Foua was the perfect Hmong daughter. Because her parents saw her as so faithfully Hmong, her father sent her off to college in Rhode Island, with the words, "Honey, I want you to know that you can marry anyone as long as he loves God and he loves you." Pang Foua continued with feeling, "And let me tell you, he lived to regret saying that!"

She chose to go to Brown University because a relative spoke well of it. There, a certain white student had decided not to attend the all-white Christian student group but another that was predominantly Asian. "He wanted to challenge himself and get to be in a position where he was less comfortable." Because Pang Foua was her friendly and talkative Hmong self, she provided a good gateway to the rest of the group.

"So we went out, and pretty much after our first date we were dating. And I was shocked, more than anyone else." In her mind at the time, God was challenging her to break out of her "old conservative scared kind of mode."

When the attraction didn't pass, her parents became alarmed. Her mother wrote and said, No more. You have to break up. But Pang Foua refused, and felt excruciating guilt. "I had to really struggle with the honor-and-obey thing — that in disobedience I could still honor them."

With her boyfriend, there were other cultural issues to hash through. "I was very up-front about the Hmong culture and about how there would be the head price or bride price [to be paid to her parents]. So he knew all that going into it."

But she would not have married without her parents' blessing. That meant continued conversation. "I said to them, 'OK, what is it that you don't like about this guy?' It came down to the fact they had to say it's their own prejudice."

But it also stemmed from a sense of insecurity as a people, Pang Foua believes. "The Hmong are very proud of being Hmong, but they're also very aware of our state of political and economic servitude to others. My mom's biggest thing was, 'He comes from a wealthier family, and we're so poor, and he comes from a culture that is dominant and we're, you know, just little people.'" They also raised reasonable questions about how she would fit into his world and how it would be for their children. But "I challenged them that God has called us into relationship with people, not just our own cultural people but people of the world."

Pang Foua sees Hmong culture as "a tight blanket we keep around us." "I feel like we restrict ourselves in how we can grow, because we don't want to become *white* or *American*, you know."

Time and lots of talk apparently worked. "They finally realized that I was still the same person, that I still loved them, and that I would always be there for them"—including taking them into her home, if they wished to live there. At the time of our visit, she had been married five years.

Pang Foua told me it would be simpler just to be American. Church and education have given her that much distance from the Hmong nest. "I would survive fine, you know. I am first a Christian. Second, I am female. And then third I am Hmong American. So culture is important, but it's not the main thing for me.

"But it's my conscious decision to say, I want to be true to what has shaped me as far as culture and family upbringing. And so who I am becoming must take parts of it with me." Those include humility, willingness to serve another, disinterest in winning for one's own sake, and hospitality. Of the latter she said, "If you come through the door, it's an invitation to sit at the table."

And she loves the Hmong sense of family. "The kinship network, I really cherish that—being part of my family." She knows that means that if you won the lottery "you would have to give money to them." She laughed. "You know, that kind of network. I hope that we Hmong never lose that."

12

Choosing a Path:
Mai Xia Cha

Siab ntxhov: turbulent heart, unsettled in mind.
—Heimbach, *White Hmong-English Dictionary*

I met seventeen-year-old Mai Xia Cha one winter when I needed an interpreter. I was researching how Sacramento Hmong deal with illness in the U.S. Mai Xia, pronounced "my see-a," had just begun her first semester at Sacramento's city college, taking classes in English, speech, and math. She was paying her own way. We chatted in the car as we drove between interviews. Clearly she was bright.

After she had helped me for about a month, she quit school to marry Zhen Fang, who had finished technical school and was doing computer work. They had fallen in love, American-style. Since she would be moving to San Diego to live with Zhen and his mother, Mai Xia found a substitute interpreter for me. He proved to be as gentle and intelligent as Mai Xia.

Hers was the first Hmong wedding I attended. She seemed quite apologetic about it. Since it would span two days and a night, consistent with the Hmong habit of not rushing important events, Mai Xia advised me to come toward the end. Even so, she said, I might get bored. Her comment signaled a dual awareness of her culture.

I parked well up the street and walked to her parents' house. I was greeted by a hand-printed sign beside the front door advising me that I couldn't enter there. The front room was set aside for negotiations, such as took place in Ly Vong and Pao Chao's stormy wedding. I went around the corner of the house to the small, steamy kitchen, where women chatted, chopped vegetables, and stirred huge savory pots on the stove. Their contented talk as they observed the ritual of food preparation only confirmed my sense that I was stepping into a centuries-old tradition.

Mai Xia appeared in jeans and invited me to her bedroom in back. A beautiful woman with perfect skin and elegant features, she showed none of the radiance — or fluster — that we associate with a bride on her wedding day. In the bedroom I joined an assortment of her female relatives sitting on quilt-covered twin beds while Mai Xia shoved belongings into suitcases. After a while her father appeared in the doorway and handed her a heavy silver neck ring. A wedding, it seemed, was a time to pass along family heirlooms. This gift was a smooth collar of silver with etched pendants on silver chains that hung down the back. Her father had bought it for himself some years before. Although Mai Xia had had her eye on one that had belonged to her grandfather — that one was being saved for her younger brother — she was content. When she passed this one along to a son of her own, she later explained to me, she could tell him that it had been worn by *his* grandfather. Her father gave her other valuable gifts, too, a nice touch since she admitted to having been a difficult daughter. "I always gave him a guilt trip. I would say that he doesn't pay attention to his daughters."

I went to the living room to have a look at the negotiations. Men sat on folding chairs around a Formica-topped table dotted with bottles and glasses. They were just finalizing the wedding contract, like government officials negotiating a treaty. A relative pointed out to me the main parties: relatives of the groom, relatives of the bride, and a professional negotiator for each side, with their apprentices. The groom was there, but he spoke little.

The two paid negotiators, or debaters, knew the rules of engagement and could chant the appropriate songs. One would chant, "They're asking …," and the other would sing the reply, "We need to hold and talk to the parents," who were elsewhere in the house. Mai Xia had missed these discussions. She had been asleep. Three-day weddings can sap one's energy.

Any problems between the families must be settled, to clear the air for the new clan relationships being formed. These might include "you insulted our cousin" or "you never paid off that debt." In Mai Xia's case, the groom had erred in the course of discharging a seemingly minor custom. When he had come to Mai Xia's house to take her away — the first step in this particular kind of wedding — Mai Xia's mother had followed them out the door. This is common and expresses the parent's concern.

Mai Xia later explained. "If a parent follows, [the groom] is supposed to give a gift. 'Here's a little something for you to go buy a drink.' Or, 'Here, go buy ice cream.' And he says 'Don't worry about us. We're just going to the movies.' He makes up an excuse." Everyone knows they're not going to the movies but are eloping.[1] "But he did it wrong. He didn't offer it. He just said, 'Don't worry about us, don't worry about us.' He gave the gift to my little brother instead." It was an insult to Mai Xia's parents, a lack of respect. The standard fine was two hundred dollars to each parent. But since Zhen had given five dollars to the younger brother, they went easy on him. "As my cousin said to him, 'You did something right, but you also did something wrong.'"

More important was negotiating the bride money. Though I didn't feel I could ask Zhen what amount he had paid to Mai Xia's family, half a dozen years later he told me that the asking price in his circle was now six or seven thousand dollars.

This giving of money for the bride is a tough issue for Americans, who, it should be remembered, still toy with the romantic image of a fragile, lace-bedecked bride carried away to happiness by a rescuing knight. We think of "bride price" as signifying the buying and selling of women.

But to traditional Hmong, the transfer of money from the groom to the bride's family makes sense. It is social cement. First, it honors the bride's parents. It's a reward to them for raising their daughter; it's called *nqe mis* meaning milk price, referring to the milk of the mother who nursed her. It is recompense for the bride's "home schooling," which produced skills from which they will no longer benefit. It marks her value to the household. Hmong bride money also honors the emotional cost of losing their daughter. In the traditional family, the bride's parents don't gain a son. They only lose a daughter.

It also honors the daughter. The higher the amount, the higher the esteem she can command from her husband's family.

I asked a Hmong couple in their forties about the custom of paying bride money — traditionally silver bars not spent but kept for the purpose. They replied with an account of a *man* marrying a *woman*, making sure I understood the distinction. Old-style Hmong couples don't "marry each other," nor does a woman do the marrying. It is the one who pays — the man — who chooses and marries the woman. (Most often he sensibly chooses a woman who has shown an interest in him, which Ly Vong evidently did not think to do.) As the following story, told with considerable feeling, begins, the wife has just explained that she didn't believe her future husband when he said he would come to claim her that night. Her reason was simple:

> SHE: He doesn't have money!
>
> HE: No, I got a part-time job! But ... (She exploded with laughter.) She only [costs] one thousand [dollars].
>
> SHE: I don't know how to call that money. It's not to sell but it's for ... promise?
>
> HE: Yeah, like any promise.
>
> SHE: ... to tell that you like to marry and you going to keep [her] forever.
>
> It's not a bride price.
>
> HE: Just like a promise. You pay more money and you know that it's worth [more]. But something you buy like at Pic-N-Save, ahhh (he made a deprecating gesture), too cheap!
>
> SHE: If he don't pay nothing for me, and later on he said, You're nothing to me, because I don't pay nothing for you.
>
> HE: Because I get you free!
>
> SHE: But when I got married to him, you know how much he have? Two hundred dollars! I cried! (She began to do so now.) Because he just bought a car, a ooold, stupid car [instead of saving the money to marry me]!
>
> HE: An ooold seventy-five Chevy Nova. Blue. But I worked! (Five hours a day at $3.35 an hour.)
>
> HE: I told her, don't worry about it. I get the money. I have an uncle. He say don't worry, we get it. No problem, you know? That's our custom. We say, we can help you. Five hundred for the food, for the drink, for the party. And a thousand is for ... for my wife.

At Mai Xia's house, the discussions about bride money were over, and the two negotiators had joined others at a larger table. There the agreement was rehashed, approved, and acknowledged with beer. Elders and ancestors were toasted. Fines of alcohol were levied on anyone who had mis-spoken: For minor infractions, beer must be given; for more serious mistakes, hard liquor. Each time, two glasses traveled around the table on a tray and everyone drank. The helpful relative who was explaining everything to me grinned and called my attention to the groom, who had become inebriated. The elders had mercy, however, and allowed him to moderate his intake.

The matters of money and honor settled, Mai Xia eventually made an appearance in her finery. This included much embroidery on apron, collar, and cuffs, and silver coins on double purses, set off by a black velvet jacket and the white pleated skirt for which the White Hmong are named. Around her neck she wore the neck ring given by her father. Her father had also given the groom a gold finger ring. "He knew him and knew he was good husband material," Mai Xia said.

Guests brought gifts, too. Quilts and bright-colored, fuzzy, Chinese-style blankets were stacked in Mai Xia's room. Money was given, too, in the amounts of five, ten, twenty dollars. A Hmong neighbor who would not normally give anything came to the house with twenty dollars, a generous gift. Mai Xia believes that it was a thank-you to her for giving a ride to the man and his son when she saw them walking in the rain. Had they not later moved away from Sacramento, she and her husband would be duty-bound to reciprocate with a gift when one of the man's children married.

The gifts are technically for the bride, although practically speaking they help furnish the new home. "They are recorded as value, how much you bring with you," Mai Xia said. "If it's a lot, you're up there." Her gifts were written down on a white lined pad, a document that she keeps in a drawer. The list also includes fines, donations, and any money borrowed — a financial record of the negotiated contract.

Everything spent on the couple seems to increase the marriage bond. This extends to the pig or cow bought for the wedding feast. Mai Xia translated a send-off song: "You better be serious about the wedding. You better be able to raise a cow or a pig from the dead if you have a divorce." That is, You had better be able to reimburse everything and throw a feast for everybody.

The final act of the marriage drama was lengthy and, for the groom, grueling. The bride's negotiator had written down every name in Mai Xia's family as far back as anyone could recall, from the oldest ancestor to the youngest baby. The groom was called and, with friends encouraging him, he bowed to the floor at the reading of each name. "He's on his knees and cracks his head," she said. "If you have a big family tree, it's going to take forever. Hours! It's when you prove yourself a man or a boy. My husband had red, red, red knees after. He was sweating!"

She continued. "When he bows it means, 'I will respect you. I will respect your daughter.'" Mai Xia admitted that people love this part. "Everybody looks forward to it, at least the girls. It's just my opinion, but we like to see a guy make a fool of himself for a girl."

Behind the surface differences between this and mainstream weddings I had noted something else. Vivid to my Western eyes was the fact that a Hmong wedding focuses not on bride and groom but on the new relationship between their families. The groom has pressed his forehead to the floor in respect for even the youngest among his new in-laws. The two families also now have rights and responsibilities with respect to each other. It is so well understood that it is not even mentioned. But perhaps most looming was the sense that dozens of people were watchers of this marriage. For reasons of honor or money, they had a stake in its outcome.

I asked Mai Xia what brings people to a wedding, mentioning to her some of the reasons why people go to weddings in my experience — to witness an important event, to enjoy a party, to see the wedding dress. She said, "They come to pay respect to the bride and groom or to the parents of the bride and groom. It's not like a happy moment they want to capture in their minds and hold forever or like a party where you go for fun. It's an event where one goes to create new bonds, re-establish and strengthen past family bonds, and to stake a claim in ensuring the continuation of the Hmong community and people."

A Hmong wedding simultaneously establishes a new family and, with its assembly of important men around a table and its Greek chorus of women in the kitchen, re-affirms the old Hmong way. Marriage is crucial to them. It is the frame around which Hmong culture is built. So tinkering with marriage — as is occurring in this country — touches Hmong society at its heart.

Within this context Mai Xia, more strong-willed than I first guessed, was about to negotiate space for herself, somewhere between the solid old ways of marriage and her brave vision of accomplishment in the wider world. It seemed that her brief taste of college was fresh in her mouth.

Mai Xia needed no reminders of a wife's role. She well knew the wife was meant to stay home and bear children, leaving education to males. In short order Mai Xia had a daughter and then a son. I was heavy-hearted about her leaving college in the first place, this bright young woman, and now she seemed to be falling into motherhood by default.

Within a few years I too moved to Southern California and one day headed to Mai Xia's for a visit. I hoped to understand the forces at work in her, and she had agreed to my taping our conversation. By then, she had three children, ages three and a half years to four months. The college student was filling her house with children, and irresistible ones at that. My visit included peanut butter and banana sandwiches, big glasses of apple juice, and a series of moves from indoors to back porch to front lawn to accommodate the energetic second child, Max. His mother and three-year-old big sister took turns retrieving him from the edge of the street and from the vicinity of a neighbor's dog, both fascinating attractions. Once Max contentedly sat down on my tape recorder.

In between rescue missions, Mai Xia told a few of her stories. By her own account, she had been a disobedient child. "You better be good," her parents told her as a four year old. "Don't pound on the walls or the ghost will get you!" The ghost seemed a live possibility to Mai Xia. She had heard the funeral drums for a neighbor who had died in an accident. She had run in fright from a miniature figure representing the deceased's spirit, set up inside the house for ceremonial purposes. "I had to pass every time we were going to farm. I was terrified." Now, as a mother herself, she could see her parents' side of it. "When you don't want to go to sleep, when you're naughty and make a lot of noise and bang on things, well, that's how I was. My parents had an exhausting day, and they wanted to go to sleep."

With the disruption of the war, her family came to the United States. She was still a small child. In preschool in Oregon, Mai Xia was enchanted by the curly hair, big blue eyes, and "these dimpled smiles" of her first American friend. To this girl she gave the eagle pin she had received on the flight from Asia.

Mai Xia skipped second grade, and in sixth grade she was offered admission to a class for gifted students, but she refused the opportunity. She preferred to stay with a beloved teacher.

"In eighth grade I had history and I started getting interested in school. I was like, 'Oh, wow!'" She researched English and French kings. "It was very fascinating. I wanted to be in that time and that place and see the person." Her intellectual energies had been engaged. She earned A's in English.

Meanwhile, the subtle influence of America continued to expand in her life. She acquired Chinese-American and European-American "best friends." An American boy "followed [her] like a dog," gave her presents, and asked her out. Dreams of joining the drill team or student government never came to pass. "I just couldn't do it because my parents didn't believe in it. Dad expected me to come right home after school. It contributed to my being outrageous, and that took a toll on my grades." She sounded like Sai Sue, vibrant and gifted. "I was pretty messed up. I didn't want to pay attention to school. I was absent a lot."

Just then Max headed yet again toward the street. "Ma-ax, come back, please? Come back, Sweetheart." To me she said, "You just have to ask him nicely. If you demand something, he won't do it." I stopped myself from saying, "I wonder where he got that?" Mai Xia decided we should move indoors. Without scolding she said to Max, *"Peb mus sawvdaws"*—loosely, "Let's all go."

I might have suspected that her meltingly gentle tone — it's the voice in which I always hear her speak — was for my benefit except for one thing: Her children show all the signs of being accustomed to it. They are at ease in their world, as beloved children are. Their mother is a safe haven.

The family's affection is captivating, producing a home that has spun a web around Mai Xia's heart. Once when Zhen had returned from work and joined us for conversation, Max sat down on his lap while Mai Xia nursed the new baby Billy. Marcy, the three year old, stuck out her lower lip, then went around behind Mai Xia and threw her arms around her mother. "All she gets is my back," Mai Xia said with sympathy. On invitation Marcy went to sit on her father's other knee. As she approached, Max held out both his arms to his big sister and then patted her when she was safely aboard.

I had often observed the tranquility of young Hmong children, such as at the Easter egg hunt and many other gatherings. No squabbling about toys, little crying. Similarly, I rarely hear parents yelling at their children. Mai Xia is not the only patient parent I have seen. In Thailand, during a village church service, I watched a small Hmong boy clamber all over his unperturbed father, the child obviously relishing the close body contact. The father seemed quite comfortable with the "disturbance," while the adults around him didn't even glance at the wiggly boy. Was this child-friendly atmosphere common or only a special case, perhaps triggered by the presence of an outsider? I was suspicious.

I continued my observations, and I continued to encounter peaceable children. I hear crying in Mai Xia's house, see red marks on cheeks where some sibling mischief occurred, but Mai Xia simply coaches the offending child to apologize to the injured one. Still, I couldn't fully believe what I was seeing.

Then I ran across research done by some academics and a pediatrician who came up with provocative information about Hmong parenting. I don't know that there's a clear connection, but I believe that the Hmong parenting style they uncovered contributes to the happy kids I see. The children in the study were Caucasian and Hmong, about Max's age. The researchers found a marked difference between the behavior of the mothers in the two groups.[2] Hmong mothers were more attentive to their young children, responded faster to their fussing, were more mindful of their child's whereabouts, were more patient, and expressed more delight. They also corrected them more rapidly. They were physically warmer and more respectful of their child's point of view.

Certainly it takes more than warm parenting to produce contented children. A culture built on community rather than individuals' rights will

Children are much favored in Hmong society. Laos, December 1994.

logically produce fewer cries of "Mine!" I also recalled that a Hmong mother has a network of supporting adults, aunts, grandmothers, even grandfathers, who will take a fussy baby or cook the dinner or wash the clothes. Caucasian mothers are more likely to do their job unaided.

I feel blessed when I am around these children. When I go to Mai Xia's house, Marcy sheds her reported shyness to sit close and look at a picture book. Max leans against me and talks in his personal language. Baby Billy, devoted passionately to his grandmother, holds my finger. Even when they squabble — Max often seems to precipitate the trouble — the waters quickly calm. Even as preschoolers they are good company, and I could see that Mai Xia, with a strong affection for humanity, derives deep pleasure from them.

Still, she was torn.

Every January I make a trip to San Diego and invariably spend Saturday evenings at Mai Xia's. On my latest visit I arrived with bags of fruit, tortilla chips, and salsa. Before a dinner of chicken, spareribs, and a buttery-flavored fish grilled by Mai Xia's mother-in-law on the side patio, Max had been eager to show me his new shoes — tough-boy boots. One of these contained a prosthesis that fit over his right foot. "He doesn't like to wear it," Mai Xia said as if in apology.

From birth Max's right foot has been like a leaf that never fully opened. He lacks a few toes, and his lower leg is not straight. Although that leg is significantly shorter than the other, Max has adapted to it and gets around at a good clip, as I had seen the day Mai Xia tried to keep him from dashing into the street. On that day she had told me that their doctor suggested removing the front of the foot, leaving the heel for support, and attaching a prosthetic foot. Besides wishing for him to have legs that matched, she was concerned about social consequences. "One worry I have is when they're teens and kids pick on him — how to deal with that."

On the other hand, surgery to remove a part of the body is abhorrent to the Hmong, Mai Xia reminded me. "You know the Hmong. We are skeptical about surgery," believing it will cause trouble in the next life.

They were planning to drive the five hundred miles to Sacramento to ask her father, an excellent arbiter by virtue of his being a shaman, if it would cause any harm to Max's spirit to do the repair. Later she phoned to say that her father had given his approval "if the doctor can guarantee that he will walk." Of course such a guarantee, often required by Hmong, could not be given. Would Mai Xia come down on the side of the old way or the new?

Mai Xia and Zhen chose not to do the surgery: "If God ordained him to be like that, it must be for a reason." The pull of her father's world, the old ways, was strong on Mai Xia's heart no matter how urgently the new ways called.

During the visit when Max showed me the prosthetic boot he wouldn't wear, Max and Marcy and I sat down at their father's computer. Max, scrambling between my lap and the computer table, brought his dimpled face close to mine to repeat everything Marcy said. He draped himself over my shoulder, a warm, little-boy-scented garment. This child, I believed, though his parents had chosen not to do the surgery, would arrive at adulthood emotionally whole.

I certainly found him irresistible, and I saw that Mai Xia did, too. Once she had said to me, "I have three beautiful babies. I just"— there was a second's pause —"adore them."

One day Mai Xia had called to say that she was starting a part-time job in a physical therapist's office. They needed the money. "Besides, I'm going stir crazy." During this phone conversation, Max was pounding on the breakfast table, she explained, and Marcy was folding clothes. And she was pregnant again.

"You know what's a tragedy?" she said. Girls such as her being raised without family support, she answered herself. They only want to protect her to *prevent* her from damaging the family reputation. Her voice was soft but her meaning was sharp. Nobody offered her money for college, she said. Nobody gave her guidance on how to survive once she got there. She worked to pay for college but ended up exhausted and sleeping in class. "I felt hopeless and just quit. Now I wish I hadn't." She had earned an A in history.

She and Zhen moved into a house, and they were expecting the fourth baby. A month passed and again we talked. She asked about a letter of reference for a job, but she was ambivalent. "Maybe I should go to school. I've spoken to a few community colleges." Her employer, Olivia, was encouraging her, but she had been daunted by her own uncertainty and the long line she found at the college registration counter. I drove down and together we got her registered. She told me again how glad she was for our talks.

Another month passed and she called again. She was about half way through her pregnancy and had been sleeping as much as fifteen hours a day. She and Zhen had talked. He offered to go back to school if she could find a full-time job. That meant no college for her. "In our culture the women take care of the kids and the husband doesn't," she pointed out. But "he never liked school, only working with his hands." Mai Xia admitted that she was disappointed. "I'm the kind of person that wants to change the world." Given her brains and drive I had no doubt that she still would, if she could achieve her dream of college. "It's going to be one of my goals, as soon as I have this kid."

The following January I made my usual trip. Marcy was now speaking good clear English and practicing jumping jacks in front of the TV. Max had learned how to remove his own diaper and use the toilet, and Billy, attached to Grandma, had a little smile for me.

Mai Xia and I chatted. "If I weren't Hmong, I'd be finishing college now," she told me. "I'm Hmong and I'm a mother."

By February Mai Xia had quit her job. Low iron. In April, six weeks before Georgina was born, Mai Xia called again. She had been watching the calendar, counting, but not the days to delivery. Her old girlfriends, she figured, must have finished college by now.

She was twenty-three years old.

13

A Different Path:
The Children of Long

As arrows are in the hand of a warrior,
   so are children of one's early life.
Happy is the man whose quiver is full of them.
      — Psalm 127:4–5

Long Yang and his wife, Cho Lee, the thirty-something couple I met in my search for language help in Southern California, live in Santa Ana, where Gen. Vang Pao had his headquarters. Their turquoise bungalow stands in a neighborhood where kids play in the street. The house is surrounded by a chain-link fence with a gate. The fence seems less an instrument to keep people out than a symbol of Long's arms, extended with intense care around his family. He is deeply centered on people.

Long had a special relationship with a neighbor across the street. John was a retired U.S. Marine officer who fought in World War II. John was in his garage every morning by five or six o'clock, smoking, Long told me. He talked to everybody and gave candy to the neighborhood kids. He kept watch, too, discouraging mischief by his presence near the street. When I came for language lessons on Wednesday afternoons I often saw him there, working on projects, and he always greeted me. John said he admired Long and Cho for what they had come through and also as hardworking neighbors. In fact Long learned from John, matching his care of home and yard to John's. I could picture the two men taking note of each other's activities across the street.

So when John dropped dead of a heart attack in his living room one day — "I just talk to him a few hour before!" Long lamented — it hit Long hard. Worse, John had not wanted a funeral, just cremation, but that left Long and Cho with no opportunity to pay their respects, real deprivation for Hmong. Instead, Long himself had "a little service" at home and remembered the good things about John. He went across the street to talk to John's widow, but in telling how much he missed John, he started to cry and soon the widow was crying, too. He apologized and retreated. Then Long went through a period of neglecting his lawn.

After several years of weekly and then occasional visits to the turquoise house, I asked Long and Cho for their stories. I was looking for a window into the evolution of this family of Hmong parents and American kids. On a May afternoon, a Saturday, I went to see them. One of the boys let me in. The four children — ages twelve down to seven — all neatly dressed, sat in a row with their mother watching a Rodney Dangerfield movie, about a kids' ball team. I sat with them and watched for a while. Zong, the only daughter and eldest child, sat cuddled next to Cho, peering at some papers I had brought for Cho. Zong has a pixie face, and that day her hair, captured in an elasticized cloth scrunchy, sat atop her head. Finally, Cho went and woke Long, who had been sleeping after his night's work. We went to the family room in the back of the house, empty but for a sofa, a coffee table, and a computer that Cho's brother had given them. As always, there was no clutter. "Long, he like to clean a lot, you know. He don't like the messy like this." She gestured to maps of Laos I had brought and laid on the floor next to me. Cho told me that Long also doesn't like the kids to play in the backyard because they "mess it up." On a stone fireplace mantle stood photos of the four kids who now were captives of the TV in the front room.

Long brought a metal folding chair and sat down. It put him a little higher than Cho and me, who occupied the sofa. Unlike the rounded Cho, Long is small and lean. Physically, he reminds me of a bantam rooster. He could be ferocious, I am sure, but more in the mold of a mother bear. A photo shows him with his arms spread protectively above the four children.

Long was born north of Xieng Khouang City in 1962 or 1961, or maybe 1965. The familiar discussion of birth dates ensued. In fact, Long's story promised to be a repetition of so many others I had heard, until I noticed how much it revealed about Long, that he was deeply tender-hearted.

Long was the eighth child of nine. His mother died in 1975, during rice planting. Long was perhaps thirteen or fourteen. "I'm *old* already!" His father remarried but would only live three years more.

The mother died just as Gen. Vang Pao was fleeing from Long Cheng and the communists started arriving. "People start moving out. Just like 'The Killing Fields,'" Long said. "People start moving closer to Vientiane, moving, like whole family, whole village. But some people they stay. They don't feel like they want to move. So that time my mom pass away." He cleared his throat. "So probably my dad, me, three brother, and one sister, plus my older brother family is still there.

"And when communism come over, you couldn't stay in the village, right? So we had to move place to place." ("play to play," he pronounced it, reflecting the lack of final consonants in Hmong.) They visited their homes only at night and lived in the jungle during the day when the soldiers came: "They shooting people.

"We try to come to the village during the night or the day, to get things or take water. People try to come [back] to live, but we can't because a couple day later the soldier come back again and they burn all the house. So the whole village, it just gone." Out in the living room a brief wail arose.

"Even the rice," Cho added.

And so the family lived in the jungle, still farming their rice fields. But after two crops, the soldiers realized villagers remained in the area and harried them out. Long's family moved to a mountain region called Phou Bia, where holdouts remain to this day.

"Lot of hunger, lot of hunger, because we couldn't plant any more rice. Then my dad pass away there." By now, just one brother, one sister, and Long remained from the parents' household, along with his oldest brother's family.

"Then my older brother, they decided to stay with the communism, because they know they cannot move no more. Because they have kids, and monsoon rain, like rain day and night. You have to *carry* the kids and *carry* lot of things, stuff, you know. So my brother say, 'We decide to stay, no matter what. When they come over, they kill us, it's OK, we die.' And I told my brother, 'OK, then we have to leave.'" His young brother stayed behind, too, and his sister married and left. Long retreated to the cold heights of Phou Bia to escape detection along with three friends—"Relatives. Same last name, so we're very helpful each other, so we trust each other." All his other family members had exited from his world.

Long and his three friends moved constantly through the jungle to avoid detection. "I remember [for] my whole life, one night I was sleep in the rain, all night, just with the rain."

"Nothing cover," Cho explained. Jungle homelessness.

"Everything open [above me], nothing there. I remember my whole life — it's still on mind. I still feel water dripping my face. Cold." He had

had no blanket, no shoes. "I have a knife." He laughed at the extremity of it. I asked what he had thought at the time.

"That night? You just think you die or you live, which is better? You want to die or you want life, and it doesn't matter." Desperation brought revelation. "I say, It's OK, doesn't matter if it rains. I still alive." He was sixteen years old.

Just then Cho and Long's three sons— Lao, Feng, and Dou — moved quietly through the family room to the sliding back door that led into the back yard. Evidently the movie was over.

Teen-aged Long, stripped of his family, also lost his three traveling friends. "They couldn't stay because they miss so much their parents. I don't miss my parents because my parents they all pass away." Of the three friends, two are still in Laos. The third lives in Minnesota, the only one Long has seen since the day they separated.

Long pressed on to find his sister, Ywg, whom I met at Cho and Long's house. ("Ywg" is pronounced with the sound "oo" as in "took," with no final g.) But when he arrived, Ywg and her husband were gone, in what turned out to be a failed attempt to cross the monsoon-swollen Mekong to Thailand. Long despaired. But still in the village was the older brother of Ywg's husband, "Older Brother-in-law." This man had "eight or seven wife" and was a village leader. "A pretty nice guy," Long said.

Once the rains stopped, the jungle dried, and the river dropped, this older brother-in-law announced that it was time to run for it. "So I told the older brother-in-law that, Ohhh, I don't know that I can go to Thailand, because I have family back there, my brother and my sister, and I don't like to left them behind. And he say, 'No, no way. You cannot stay no more. Just go with me. Treat me just like your own older brother or your dad or your mom, and I'll treat you just like my younger brother.'" But Long had no money to buy food or clothes in Thailand. His older brother-in-law said, "Don't worry about it. [If] I have something to eat, I let you eat. If I don't eat today, you don't eat." So Long said, "OK, now I got the main thing: You won't leave me." It was a wedding contract in action, two men bound by the marriage of Ywg. This older brother-in-law was filling the vacuum left in Long's life by the loss of father and older brothers.

For twelve days they walked in the jungle, thirty people, toward the Mekong. Long carried about fifty pounds, mostly rice. The load diminished each day as they ate. One day's distance from the river, they stopped to chop down bamboo trees and cut the culms into lengths. This bamboo would buoy them across the river. Belongings were dumped in order to carry the bamboo. "Forget all your stuff. Whatever you have, forget it."

At the river they pulled vines from trees and tied sections of bamboo into triangles. Long took pen and paper from me to sketch it. "OK, three bamboo, only three. You tie it up together here. And then we go inside there, [and get] in the water. One person at a time." Personal flotation devices. "And you hook one to another [with vines], so the whole family go together.

"Then take all your clothes, hook up to your head, hook up your neck, whatever" — he demonstrated tying clothes around his head. "OK, make sure they don't get wet, except your underwear."

Cho laughed. "Not even underwear!"

"Oh, it's just better if you have nothing! It's more faster," Long went on, grinning. "If I [make it across] alive, I don't die, I can wear the underwear any day in Thailand." Besides shirt and pants, Long carried a knife and a rifle with a few bullets in it, reserved for the direst encounters.

"No shoes." Long and a friend, also barefoot, had pulled sharp bamboo thorns from the soles of each other's feet after walking through a newly cleared field. "Osh, my goodness! We step in there, Oh! No choice! Have to go. You helped each other pick it out like monkey!

"Soon we just start going down to the river" in the dark of night. As dawn broke, the crowing of roosters and clanging of temple gongs told Long and his companions that they were near a town. "Along the river, the soldier pretty close there. They make a real good trail, so they can run fast or they can see you, because they know that people cross that area all the time. So just look for place to hide.

"And then, how about our children? Very small, like couple of months, one year, two year. And they don't know what's going on, right? So maybe they might cry. And so I say, OK, just give a little mix, you know, the opium? Mix with water and just couple drops in the mouth. Make them sleep, but not too much.

"But whoever gave too many drops, the children almost pass out. And the parents are crying like, Oh, if I know that my child is going to be dead, I'm not going to come here." Long's voice had fallen almost to a whisper. "I know [one] couple left one little girl behind. They thought she [was] dead. Because you can see only the mouth just barely open, just like that." He demonstrated. "They give too much! But don't worry. Because water — every time you give opium, jump in the water, then [the effect is] gone fast.

"So as soon as we get to the river, everybody plunked down in there. So the baby start get wet. So baby cry.

"That time, I already dead. Fifty-fifty [chance]."

Slipping into the water, half of the group pushed out into the river, each person in a bamboo life preserver. Kicking and paddling, they made it to the middle of the river, the border with Thailand, where they were legally safe.

"The communism soldier, they heard the baby cry. Oh! People crossing the river! And they run. They run and they start shooting. Start shooting everywhere, start shooting people. I can hear the bullet. Pewp! pewp! pewp! pewp! I can hear that.

"But I just, what we call it, call for help for …the Heaven. I did. We don't know Jesu. We call it only Heavens. 'You got to help me here. I do nothing wrong here. You got to help me get outta here!'" He laughed as he spoke. "OK. My parents. You always call your parents [to] help. 'Oh, my Dad or Mother, help me get out from here.'

"So they [the Thais] know when someone pass the middle of the water, [but that the Lao] still shooting. And then I heard couple shoot from the Thai people. Couple shots like"—he switched to a high pitch—"duh-duh-duh-duh-duh-duh. Machine gun. So [the Lao soldiers] know, Uh, those people pass to there, so forget about it. So they stop shooting. They stop shooting."

But only half their party had made it into the water before the baby cried and the soldiers started shooting. "Soon as the baby cry, they just move back, hiding.

"Then the sun came, then we know that we alive. We can see right there!" He pointed as if the river were just yards from him now. "Right there where we cross from. My brother-in-law older brother, he was crying." Long cleared his throat. "For everything he still left behind. Still have couple wifes left all way to Phou Bia, and still have son there, too." He coughed.

"But the group, they split back? They crossed the night after that. They cross like a little more close right there, and they got shot. They got killed."

"All of them?"

"Just a few." Again I heard kids laughing and chattering—they had come back into the house at their father's direction.

"The brother was carrying the mother-in-law. And his brother-in-law carry his wife. Pulling, pulling to cross the river." Two brothers-in-law pulling two women with vines attaching their rafts, the wife and the mother of one man. "And the wife got shot and her brother also got shot. The little daughter still on her mom's back."

"The baby still on the mother's back, but the mother died," Cho said.

"And she say, Oh, I got shot. But he keep pulling. And then the brother of his wife, he also got shot and he say, Oh, I got shot. And soon as he say it he just …" Long gestured down.

"So as soon as they got to Thailand, all [the husband] had to do, he just give to the Thai people to bury her. He just take only the little baby out. Her mom dead. Nothing he can do. So they don't know [if] they bury her or just throw her in the river."

Cho said, "When we go somewhere he talks about that a lot." I wondered if others had such stories to tell.

"Yeah, some people," Long said. "You stay here, or in the mail ..." And he cries.

Themes emerge as people tell their stories, songs, as it were, expressing something insistent. Long's stories conveyed the emotional cost of losing family and his astonishment at being alive. His experiences had made his heart tender and nurtured a passionate resolve to keep family and kin together, safely behind his chain-link fence.

Cho, too, experienced a peeling away of family like Long, but she responded differently, with resignation. Beneath her attention to responsibility lies immense sadness.

"My father, I don't know anything about my father. I'm only six or seven months when my father died. My aunt and my other [relatives], they always say that my father died while I was only crawling. They laid my father on the floor, and I still crawling to him."

A decade later, her mother fell ill the day after her bed broke beneath her. A broken bed is a sign that a dead parent has paid a visit, that something significant will happen. "About six o'clock I wake up and Mom look at me but she can't talk no more." Her mother was taken to a hospital, and eight days later she died. Cho was ten or eleven, the seventh child.

Only young Cho and two brothers remained at home, and, after an initial carefree time with their middle sister, Cho was shunted around like a foster child, a common plight of Hmong children of older parents.

They fled to Thailand just weeks before the end came in Laos, and Cho was asked by a brother to live with him and other relatives there in the refugee camp. "He want someone like sister to help him to cook." Cho found herself ejected from childhood. "When I got to Ban Vinai, I'm the one that's responsible. Only first week, my sister-in-law show me to get the water, how to cook, that's it. I'm the one responsible the breakfast, the dinner. The water finish, I'm the one that have to go get it."

At this moment in her narrative, two of Cho's children appeared and attached themselves to us. The twelve-year-old daughter, Zong, attached herself to her mother's knees while Dou, the youngest, made small motions toward my tape recorder. They giggled, and Cho shushed them. Cho in the refugee camp was the age of the daughter whose chin now rested on her knee — twelve.

"I miss my sister." She stopped to clear her throat. "I had nobody."

Then an aunt needed her services. "I go with her to take care of her little girl." This aunt harvested corn for the Thais, and Cho went along to babysit. "And their baby was crying, and I have to follow and carry the baby on my back, carry the baby with them everywhere they go! Ai-yi-yi!

"A lot of their cousins, they tease me, they say they going to make me marry their son. When I look at the [road] to go home, I cry every day!" She spoke in a wavering voice. "I feel so bad that time. That's the baaad time I ever have." I began to see, in that twelve year old, grief mutating into depression.

In the United States, Cho again found herself responsible for a household, going to high school, cooking for six males— including Long, a close friend of her brother's. "I go to school, I have no friend, I come back home, I have nobody to talk. I always in my room to study, or I do the cooking.

"Long and my brother helping me sometimes. And I feel so bad I cry every time I talk to them. I say, Oh, yi-yi! And then of course at that time I start to talk to Long." I pictured a houseful of teenage roommates, taking uncertain care of each other.

Then, as Long told me later, he decided to marry her. This is how he put it: "Finally I said, Oh, maybe she could be my *wife*! Maybe she's the right person for me. Because their parents pass away long time, OK, and actually my parents are pass away, so oh! we probably match each other. We know how suffer we are before, and how poor we are." But rather than asking her to marry him, Long had tricked her into getting into his car.

Cho said: "I get inside the car and he drove off. And I say, You crazy! He drove off to his cousin's house. I got there, I cry, I hit him, I scratched him, I ..." She dissolved into laughter. This was the modern American version of the way Ly Vong captured his bride. "So his cousin told me that, you a lady? You have to go [with a husband] one day no matter what." Cho was a senior in high school.

"You know why I say it's so terrible? [The cousin], they living only one-bedroom apartment. We have to sleep in the sofa [in the front room]. Imagine!"

Zong, still leaning close to her mother's legs, spoke up for the first time. "In the sofa?"

"No fun at all," her mother said. "No life at all." Cho conceived no child for two years. "Long say that, 'Oh, you don't have a kid; I don't know what I gonna do.'"

She went to a shaman, and before long she became pregnant, giving birth to Zong.

"But [Zong] is sick very much. And I [called] a future teller. And the future teller say that she's not my girl." Cho was told that in a former life she had many children and had told God that she didn't want any more. "So that's why I cannot have a kid. So Zong going to be dead [when] she's four months. At that time she's three months. Only one more month she going to be dead!"

The fortune teller consulted cards and Cho's hand and doubled her client's dismay. "She say that I'm not going to have any more kids. Long going to get married again. Another wife! I was crying and then Long said, You're stupid. I told you not to go looking [for a fortune teller]."

Relatives became involved. "My cousin told me, 'You know, the only way you can forget about that, you have to believe in God only.'" Long's uncle had already extracted a promise that they would attend church, but they had reneged. "And then my cousin, they pray for us very much." The uncle prayed, the church prayed.

Cho was in crisis. "Long and me, we have a lot of argue. We have a lot of bad time. And I be like crazy. Like I go to work, I say, What I doing? I not even remember the way I get there.

"So one of the [church] elders, they call me, they say, Do you like us to come to tell you about God? And the day that they coming I'm so happy. I'm so happy that they coming! I say, Yeah, I would like to go to church. So the next day I go to church."

Long went, too, but it did not go well at first. "Every time he pray God before he go to sleep, his parents come to chase him. He not even asleep. We just lay down!" Long stopped praying for several years. But the church's pastor visited and told Long he had to pray. "Couple days [of praying], his parents didn't chase anymore."

Long works nights and Cho works days for a company that makes intravenous solution. In the absence of other adults in the household, babysitting has been a problem. For years Cho has gotten the kids out of bed in the dark, piled them into blankets in the back of the van and driven them to work. There Long comes off his shift and drives the children home, getting them ready for school and, according to one of the children's teachers, attending every parents' function religiously.

"When we come over here, we think that we gonna have money, have things. But [when] we got here, it's not what we think in Thailand. We know that it might be different." She laughed. "But we don't know!"

Throughout Cho's story, Zong listened at her knee, tracing her hand on paper, drawing a ring on it, and adding a pen. Today was Zong's twelfth birthday, Cho said, giving her daughter a loving swat. In the view of Cho and Long, she was now too adult for such things as toys. At her father's insistence, she gave away her Barbie doll.

I knew that Cho sometimes got cross with Zong. Now, with Zong listening, she said: "I told her every day, Of course sometimes I yell at you, mad at you. Not that I don't love you, just because you don't do the way I like. And she says, 'Mom, I heard that already.'

"Long always wants me to get along with her. When she young, we always fight. Now she grow up, she act better. She says, 'Mom, I'm trying.' 'I don't want you to try. I want you to do it.'" Cho didn't consider Zong to be a very good student.

I asked what hopes she had for her daughter. She said: "To grow up to be a good girl — even if she doesn't have good education, as long as she have good personality." What makes a good girl, I asked. "Respect mother, father, respect old people, listen to us." An ancient Hmong wish.

I had listened to many adults, the refugee generation, and absorbed the heaviness of their lives. Now it was time to listen to the children outside their parents' circle — at school. This institution lies at the core of immigrant parents' dreams but subtly changes everything.

I took a few days to visit Long and Cho's four children at their schools. With each child I observed a different blending of cultures. Cho had yearned to go to school while still in Laos but was denied the chance because she was female. What she didn't fully grasp was that her children were not merely becoming educated. They were also being wooed away from the old life to one of individual autonomy and independent thought. American education bears the fingerprints of American culture.

The May morning was fresh. Students assembled in the outdoor lunch area, where they were greeted by the principal.

"Good morning, students," she intoned into a microphone.

"Good mor-ning, Mis-sus Mac-Cor-mack!" all chanted back to her. The dialogue moved to Spanish and then Lao. "Sabadee, students," she said, eliciting a matched response from the crowd. This was a diverse student body, and she was proclaiming that to be a good thing. Latinos and "Lao" — in fact mostly Hmong — predominated, with a quarter as many Vietnamese, and a few Cambodians and Chinese. There were half a dozen African Americans and even fewer European Americans, besides the teachers. The students, now squirming at the lunch tables, wore neat white tops

The sons of Long and Cho Lee Yang. *From top:* Feng (third grade), Dou (first grade), and Lao (fourth grade), horse around with a cousin, April 1998.

and navy blue skirts or pants, not so different from the French uniform Chamy wore to school. But in everything else, this school was vastly different. It was kid-friendly. No teachers required a student to beat his cousins with a ruler.

Feng, the Yangs' eight-year-old third grader, had spotted me during the morning assembly and shyly gestured for me to follow him. He turned out to be the most nearly classic Hmong of the children, a boy with a hospitable heart. Beside him as we walked was David, a Hmong boy who reminded me that I had met him at a recent picnic. In the third-grade room, Feng draped his backpack over the plastic chair at his desk.

The children dove into private word search, giving the teacher an opportunity to tell me that, of the twenty-nine students in the room, Feng's family was among the best off. "The parents both speak English," she explained. For my benefit, she asked the students how many spoke Hmong at home. Eight raised their hands, although a number of children of Hmong refugees nationwide have already lost the ability to understand Hmong. Six clans were represented at the school — Chang, Kue, Lo, Vang, Xiong, and Yang.

Feng's room reflected the students' activities. Along the window, wheat grew lanky in green plastic strawberry baskets. Storage shelves standing next to students' boxes sported spelling words printed on big cards. Although it was an ordinary room by American standards, the carpeted, well-lit and amply supplied room might easily seem opulent — even indulgent — to a refugee parent. I thought of the fresh-air classroom beneath the raised home of Nom Npis Lis's relative in Kilometer 52.

The students bent quietly over their desks, writing. Feng rested his head on one arm while he wrote. Beside a big name card on which he had printed "Feng" in huge, self-celebrating capitals stood plastic cups containing a bounty of pencils, pens, scissors, crayons, and a big Elmer's glue. On his feet, tucked under his chair, Feng wore white running shoes with laces that kept coming untied. No one fussed about them.

Next to him sat Pang, a diminutive Hmong girl, her hair fastened into a ponytail with a scarf. Their two heads often leaned together. It turned out that half the belongings in the plastic cups were hers. Absently now, Feng fiddled with her ponytail with a pencil, to no response from Pang or the teacher. Later Feng told me, "See that small girl? I like her."

It was time for Feng's book club discussion at a table in the back. The group consisted of four children, two of them Hmong. A bag of cheese popcorn lay open on the table, part of the effort to make reading fun. (School should be happy!) In a soft voice, Feng read his book report to the others, tracing the words smoothly with his index finger. "Dear Book Club,

The title is … It is about …" The book was about a farm, with red-painted barn, tidy house with curtained windows, and aproned white farm wife.

At recess the kids made a run for an expansive grass playground. Feng, making sure that I was following, streaked off with a Latino boy to the monkey bars. "Michael is my best friend," Feng announced when I caught up. Then he continued, "You stay the night? You play with us at recess?" He had taken my hand. "You can stay the night." Feng and Michael and I were joined by William, who chattered uncontrollably about a coin collection. William grabbed Feng from behind and hoisted him playfully from the ground. Feng protested loudly.

I asked the growing cluster of boys how many were Hmong. Only Feng was, I was pretty sure, but exuberant William assured me he was, too. Feng challenged this assertion by speaking to William in Hmong. William answered in a pretty good imitation.

Back in the classroom Feng counted out arithmetic problems by tapping fingers against his head. When the arithmetic test was scored, Feng got 70 out of 90. A Hmong girl got them all right. Feng stuck a hole-punch in his mouth and twiddled it. (Hole punch? I imagined a teacher in old Laos exclaiming.)

Outside after a lunch of tacos and carrot coins, I was transferred into the care of Lao, the fourth grader and oldest son. Cho had told me that Lao put off doing his homework and had a hard time making friends. I'd heard the wiry Long fuss at his chubby nine-year-old, first-born son, telling him to skip breakfast to lose weight. It seemed that Lao might not feel so comfortable at school as his brother Feng.

I found Lao playing soccer with eight other boys, including one of the school's African Americans. Lao was the only Hmong, the remainder being Latino. Sweating and red of face, he tore around the field and laughed boisterously. Somebody on Lao's side made a goal and the four of them cheered and hugged. Some of them took fake falls, out of high spirits. I have seen boys like Lao turn into athletic powerhouses in high school.

Boys kept making passes by my station. "Are you Lao's … her … aunt?" one struggled to ask in English. "Friend," I said. The soccer game wound down, and Lao and some of his soccer mates hovered near, purposely within my hearing, I think, laughing. They were teaching each other "bad" words in their native languages—the universal back-lot subject. With a buddy wrapped on either side, Lao showed off a wound on his elbow. The bell rang and Luis, Lao's best buddy, pinched him on the cheek as they headed to class. I wondered why Cho thought her eldest son had trouble making friends. Did she mean cousin-friends? Hmong-only friends?

Inside Lao's fourth grade classroom, the nineteen students settled into their places. The teacher said, "Shut your eyes and think of what you want to be or do when you grow up." After a minute, she called on students.

Luis, Lao's friend, said, "I want to be a good soccer player for a Mexican team so I can help my family, my cousins, all my uncles and aunts, and my grandmother."

Carlos: "I want to be a basketball player to help poor people, like giving them food."

Lisa, the only girl who spoke, said, "A model."

A boy named Jason said he wanted to be a scientist. "What do you want to do as a scientist?" he was asked. "Discover a different kind of species."

Lao did not raise his hand, but his homework drawing on the subject showed a car. On pale blue lines below the car he had written, "I want to be a racing car so I can meet the famous guy and because to help [my family]."

Such a familiar exercise. So innocent. Yet so American, to ask a child, without an adult relative in the conversation or even in the room, to contemplate what they wanted to be. Interestingly, because so many of these children were from newcomer families, their vision included taking care of others.

I found my way to the third son and youngest child of Long and Cho, first-grader Dou. Cho considered him a good student, but even he might disappoint them, she said. "Sometime when they grow up they change," she had told me ominously. Dou wore a huge purple and yellow T-shirt with "Aloha" on it. His teacher wore Dockers, a T-shirt, and running shoes. She had a loud, firm voice and gave shoulder hugs—an affectionate person. She had taught some of Dou's siblings and was now close to retirement. She was Japanese-American. She told me that she often saw Long at school but didn't know Cho. I described the couple's work schedule.

The children gathered before the teacher's easel to practice reading. Dou, seated in the middle, was on the verge of giggles. The teacher chanted out familiar songs and poems, and then all read in unison. Dou's voice sounded a split second ahead of the others. The teacher pointed to "pig" and asked what words could be made by changing the first letter. Dou's hand shot up like fireworks. "Fig!" His voice was loud and the final consonant, tough for Hmong, was clear. Dou continued listening raptly, rolling up both arms in the front of his shirt. Somebody had clipped chunks of hair off the side of his head. Between poems he flashed a smile that squeezed his eyes nearly shut and showed big, new front teeth. A happy child.

Dou and five others moved to a back table to read. There they came under the direction of a seasoned teacher's aide, a Chinese American woman of managerial character. Perhaps she was aiming for old-country student decorum here, bucking the free-wheeling, child-centered atmosphere of this school. The reading posed little challenge for Dou, who first sat on his right foot, then kneeled in his chair, and finally, seal-like, swam up onto the table and extended his feet over the back of his chair. "Dou, sit down," the teacher pronounced sternly. He rotated his reading book in a complete circle, regarding it briefly upside down, in rebellion, and then sat.

Recess took the kids out into the sun, where Dou and a half dozen others ran and ran, finally settling like elves in an outlying swath of tall, unmowed grass.

The day's events included a musical program presented by older students in the library-auditorium, where students sat crowded on the polished hardwood floor. I wondered how the wiggly Dou would fare. The choir, dressed in bright red shirts, sang, and most of Dou's class watched avidly. The number ended, but Dou didn't clap, only gazed at the singers. A tall, crew-cut teacher played his trumpet, and many of the students laughed. Dou sat still. The choir sang again, a Spanish song that required the audience to clap along. Dou stirred only slightly.

Forty minutes into the program Dou's classmates were wiggling, looking around, whispering. Dou remained transfixed. He blinked and looked aside when a teacher took a flash picture. Fifty minutes and he still hadn't moved. What was it about music that captured him? Had some ancestor gifted this child with a gene that brought him close to a trance?

At lunch Dou showed me how his milk, in a small plastic bag, acted like a balloon. With a straw poked through the side of the pillow-like container, Dou squeezed, inadvertently siphoning milk onto my lap. He looked at my skirt and then at me. We both laughed, and he took off for the playground.

It was hard to picture this child going wrong. At least not in the American world.

My last visit was to the middle school, where Zong was in sixth grade. At twelve years old she was approaching the age of matrimony in the old country. Here, she was on the threshold of teenage independence and, possibly, defiance. Cho had called her a poor student.

I caught up with her in math class, where she smiled sweetly and wiggled her fingers at me from the back row. I smiled back, then stood near the door and observed. A couple of students were lectured for not doing their homework. Zong and a friend, sitting with elbows touching, com-

Zong Yang, right, daughter of Long and Cho Lee Yang, watches an Easter egg hunt with her friends at Santa Ana, California, April 1998.

municated with eyes and a whispered word or two. Zong was not one to draw a teacher's attention unnecessarily.

Outside during a break, Zong and I were joined by three of her friends, one Hmong, one European American, and one Latina. The inner courtyard of the campus swarmed with young people dressed in variations on the school uniform. For most this meant blue jeans, a white shirt, and — not required — expensive running shoes. Not Zong. She was dressed like an apprentice businesswoman with an appointment to keep. She wore a navy blue shorts-skirt and white blouse with a stylish checkered windbreaker. White tights were tucked into perfect patent leather shoes, and her hair was gathered neatly on top of her head. It was as if she was taking herself as far as possible from her parents' past.

"Does she always dress up like this?" I asked her Hmong friend, Jenny. Jenny was outfitted in loose jeans, sloppy jacket, and a water bottle that she used as a weapon. "Yes," Jenny said. "Every day."

The four girls bought spicy Cheetos, and we headed toward a guard at a chain-link gate, which cut off access to several banks of classrooms. The girls told the guard they were going to see Segal. I didn't know who or what "Segal" was.

Down the row of classrooms we stopped at a locked door. Zong surprised me by banging on the door, and all four of them yelled, "Segal, let us in! We know you're in there!" "His car is there." Jenny squirted the door with her water bottle. I couldn't imagine what was going on or what kind of person Segal was. Finally, with the arrival of some older students, the locked door was opened and we went in. Segal turned out to be the music teacher, a hefty, plaid-shirted fellow with an unruly red beard. He presided benignly over the high-ceilinged band room, which had cupboards with instruments along the back wall and a supposedly soundproof practice room where a drummer drummed. This was a different kind of adult for Hmong kids, and Zong responded enthusiastically to his easy, egalitarian style. On a VCR a video of an electric guitar competition played, watched by half a dozen young people including a mother and child. I introduced myself to Segal, who explained that the video-watchers were former students of his who were on break from high school. "Their parents aren't home, so they come over here."

The bell rang, and Segal finally drove out his returnees in a booming voice. Zong and about a dozen other girls brought folding chairs and violin cases into a semi-circle. Segal explained to me that it was hard to teach them on the every-other-month schedule he shared with physical education. "They could do well if I had them all the time," he said, "especially these sixth graders." His hand swept an arc to include Zong and her buddies. "They're very bright."

It became obvious to me that Zong was entirely at home in this American school, at ease with these informal teachers as no student would have dared to be in the Hmong mountains. So were her brothers. I don't think either Cho or Long, their hearts heavy with memories of bullets and death and homelessness and early responsibility, guessed just how at-home their children feel in America.

One December morning I drove with Cho and Long to the Los Angeles Convention Center where they and eight thousand others from more than one hundred countries would be sworn in as citizens. Long hummed the national anthem on the way.

Cho had considered taking a new name for the occasion, but decided to stick with Cho. The judge, a first-generation American of Armenian ancestry, administered the oath of allegiance, gave a brief speech, and, before showing a video about America, asked the new citizens to try something. "Shout the name of the country of your birth," he directed. At a signal, the assembled new citizens did so. "Did you notice?" he said. "Together, those cannot be heard!"

I know the judge meant, "You are American now." But I wondered how much of those old lives might indeed be dismembered under pressure from the new. "Forget the past; this is a new country." It seemed sad that the sturdiness and selflessness I had seen in the Hmong culture might be slipping away, that so many family stories would die with each generation. Perhaps it is unavoidable, given the radical difference between a society built on the individual and one requiring people to cluster for survival.

Because children such as Long and Cho's will never experience the kind of lives their parents lived, one wants to take their hands and say, "Come, listen to what your parents survived." But those stories are largely unhearable by children, Hmong or not. Kids by nature are non-historians. History is the business of maturity, available only after we accumulate a past of our own and begin to scan it for meaning. A child's task is to achieve adulthood in the here and now, in whatever location they find themselves.

14

Buried Treasure: Mai Xiong

Our parents are a sun getting ready to set.
— Hmong conference speaker
Mai Zong Vue

Mai Xiong wasn't getting any younger. She acquired eyeglasses, which she used for stitching. She no longer performed the rigorous shaman's ceremony. There seemed less urgency about her gardening, more enjoyment. She continued to reveal what it meant to be Hmong, but now a *retired* Hmong.

Visits to see Mai Xiong in Sacramento still meant delicious traditional cooking—and limited verbal communication. Despite her attendance at language classes, Mai's English remained skeletal. And despite hours under a trained Hmong teacher, stacks of books and tapes and vocabulary cards, plus conversation practice with two other women before Mai, I never managed to master more than the simplest visitor chat. This proved discouraging for both of us. What would we talk about? "Cannot talk is like a prison," an author wrote.[1] Driving to her apartment I'd review adverbs that always gave me trouble. "Soon," "after a while," "right away"—words that, misunderstood, could get a person into difficulty. Together, we sometimes simply fell into silence, diverting ourselves with stitching or TV. Once when a bilingual friend was present, Mai said that it was hard to be my friend since we couldn't talk.

Before my second visit with Mai, I had phoned to see if she was available for some language study. Telephoning with my limited language was a rash deed. No, I couldn't come, I thought I understood; she was going somewhere. I checked and double checked with her what she was saying, and after hanging up called a Hmong friend, asking her to call Mai to verify my impression. I was right, but it turned out she was only going to her garden, a mile away. I drove the dozen miles to Mai's apartment building, knowing that someone there would notice me and come out to point the way to the garden. Instead, a woman called out from her door that Mai hadn't set out yet. I headed up to her apartment.

After some explaining, little of which I got, and some chatting, Mai and I recreated the old mountain trek on foot to the fields. Crossing her quiet side street together, she said *"Tsheb los"*—"Car coming"—and I was thrilled to realize that I had gotten the message. Later I also understood when she said that she was afraid of dogs.

The community garden, equipped with spigots and hoses, spread over several acres. Mai sprinkled down her patches and picked some lemon grass, cilantro, and mustard greens for me. Nearby, women were picking dried peas. One woman walked by with a child and said to me in English, "You like Hmong people?" I said I did. I wondered what Mai meant to this woman. Had she learned any herb lore from Mai? Had Mai been a model she found herself emulating? Walking back home, Mai and I chattered and gestured.

On a visit a month later, I found Mai dressed up in a black skirt, blouse, and top. She wasn't wearing her usual scarf, and her hair was nicely done. She appeared to have had a perm. Some special occasion? We worked on stitching and stitching-related words for a while, in both Hmong and English, while individuals occasionally peered through her window. A man came to the door selling a video about Malaysia. Then a woman, tiny, possibly retarded, came first to the window and then inside with two little girls, a baby on her back, and a little boy who soon misbehaved and was sent out. He had tried to investigate Mai's back room. The baby started to cry, and the mother swung him off her back, pulled up her shirt and began to nurse him. Mai moved over and started good-naturedly spanking his legs. Over a meal of lemon-grass flavored chicken and sweetened cucumber "soup," I tried more vocabulary.

But every time she looked at me and with a school teacher's perfect enunciation tried to communicate on a subject other than children, food, or speaking Hmong, I was stumped. I wasn't any more comprehensible to her. I had asked to use the bathroom, and she had responded by clearing out the bathtub for me.

In July I went looking for her again at the garden, since I did not find her at home. I spotted Mai in her garden patch and hailed her across the field. She looked up and gave me a broad smile. We puttered for a while, and I said something in Hmong to two nearby women and their children. Mai gave me a large bag to hold and began to fill it to the brim with cucumbers. One of the mothers said it was for me. I protested that, since it was just my husband and me, I needed only one cucumber. So Mai took one cucumber out of the bag and left me with the rest.

Some visits were pure delight. A neighbor would see me and say "*Koj tuaj los*" ("You've come, eh?"), and I would answer, "*Kuv tuaj os*" ("I've come.") One day in August, kids from the building waved to me when I arrived, children whom I had seen squeezing close to Mai. At the top of the outside stairs Mai waited, a big grin on her face. She touched me on the arm, and then we went inside. There I found the sweet-faced relative of hers from across the street. Mai chattered about my coming and about what I left on her door on my last visit. (I no longer phoned before coming.) I gave her the pears and cantaloupe I had brought, and she motioned me to a folding chair. Immediately she announced she was going to feed me and told me to wash my hands. (It was not yet 11 a.m.) She placed on her little bamboo table rice, green beans, and cabbage and pork in broth. I forgot the word for "full" and decided it was an important word to learn.

Later, two women came in without knocking. One, with a short haircut unusual for a Hmong woman, said in English she was Mai's sister-in-law. It turned out that this woman had come for mosquito "medicine." Mai went for a plastic bag that had money in it and a dozen containers of a cream. The sister-in-law took seven of them.

After she left with her mosquito cream, Mai and the young woman remaining started telling mosquito stories. It became hilarious. The visual cues I depended on were ambiguous, but Mai's hilarity was infectious. She seemed to be saying that a mosquito bit her here and here and here (arm, other arm) and here (with her gathered fingers she dove mosquito-like for her lower torso) and here (her top lip, which she depicted as having grown very swollen from the bite). The whole show was repeated several times, to much laughter. Mai is a sight when she laughs—big, white, gold-trimmed teeth, big generous mouth, and triangles for eyes. I was grateful for the visuals, because I was a floundering immigrant in this Hmong village, struggling with a foreign language.

One day while placing my empty dishes on Mai's sink shelf, I noticed a woman's angry voice outside over the swish of traffic. I peered out the screened kitchen window and saw three tall African Americans and one small Hmong man standing in the street facing each other, in battle formation. Nobody appeared armed, so I went downstairs. The two African

American men were walking away, so I talked with the woman. She was a good twelve inches taller than the Hmong man, and she was high. Soon she drifted off, too, shouting.

I listened to the frightened Hmong man. He had been visiting in one of the apartments, he told me, then drove out of the parking lot and pulled to a stop at the corner of Martin Luther King. There the three adults, all apparently high, had closed around his sports car, talking loudly. I knew that was threatening behavior to Hmong. The woman opened his passenger door and climbed in. Hot words were exchanged. The frightened driver got out the other side. The two belligerent men told the Hmong driver to stay out of the neighborhood and then wandered off. The woman had gotten out of the car, ranting across its hood at the Hmong man, and then I had arrived.

Hmong from the apartments gathered around us. After hearing him out, I encouraged the driver to keep cool, not escalate a fight like that but to continue coming here as he wished. Then he, too, left, shaking visibly, his passenger door locked.

Soon after, a police black-and-white pulled up. Two policemen got out and ambled over to where a group of us still hashed over the incident. One policeman was tall, blond and slim, the other nearly as tall, and dark. Their size and easy demeanor contrasted markedly with the agitated Hmong.

The excitement is over, I told the policemen. Everybody's gone. The two policemen heard my story, the crowd of Hmong still gathered around us. The tall blond officer thanked me for bringing things to a smooth close.

"Can we call you next time?" he said.

Then the scene struck me. On one side were the policemen — like me at ease, tall and well-fed, in charge of ourselves and much of what goes on around us. On the other side were the Hmong, small, baffled, fearful of yet another unknown from this strange culture. Momentarily I saw through the policemen's eyes, where I had been not long before — the Hmong a nameless crowd, big kids holding little kids, moms and grandmoms and dads and granddads. "Can we call you next time?" the blond one had said. The Hmong were people with whom he could not communicate.

"You can talk to them yourself!" I said. "A lot of them here speak really good English." I gestured toward the bank of faces, people who had wandered in Mai Xiong's door or greeted me with small talk. "Look at 'em! They're glad to help."

I wondered if the policemen believed me.

After I moved to Southern California, my visits to Mai's apartment became rare. Now and then I sent her a picture postcard or note with a drawing of myself on it as a humorous identification. One December day, after visiting my father, I stopped in and, as often happened, showed her some new pictures of the family. She took from me the picture of our year-old granddaughter, a sweet child who had been born early but was now thriving. First Mai exclaimed about the baby's pink cheeks, chattering and pointing to them. Then I watched as Mai stroked the picture with her nose, a traditional sign of affection.

Visits to Sacramento became more infrequent. One such visit occurred not long after my trip to Laos with Chamy and Nom Npis. I had come north with slides of Laos and a slide projector, and I wanted to offer Mai the option of seeing pictures of her homeland. We hadn't seen each other in a long time. She opened the door and a big smile crinkled her face. "Ohhhh, come in," she said in English. She motioned me to the sofa and said, "*Zaum os*," sit. Her relative from across the street was there. Then Mai began to say in Hmong how I "didn't come and didn't come." She stopped talking to cry, then continued talking and crying at the same time, lengthening her words with a wavering tone as I had witnessed in Laos but had never seen from Mai. Then she couldn't talk at all and began shedding big tears. I hugged her and smoothed her hair and wished I knew exactly what the sadness was. I knew she had been sick.

I asked her if she had received the bracelet I bought her in Laos. She held her wrist up. She was wearing it. She showed me the padded envelope in which I had sent it, stashed carefully behind a cardboard mail holder she had made from a Tide box. Then she took a heavy silver ring off her finger and gave it to me. It was like a man's ring, sculptured, with a dark gray marble stone. It was still warm when I slipped it on my hand.

When I returned from my car with the slides and slide projector, Mai took to kissing me. Later, any slide in which I was seen triggered more kisses and, "Oh! Sue!" Then she would leap up to work a bit on the dinner she eventually laid out: rice noodles, chicken in broth with mint and lime, and some leafy vegetable with lavender flowers. She was very interested in the slides, and then we watched Brian Boitano and Nancy Kerrigan skating in competition on TV.

On a recent trip to Sacramento, I heard that Mai died. I was stunned. Many older people were suffering from flu at the time, and a few had indeed died. Chamy hadn't heard anything about Mai, but she tried Mai's phone number for me and then three other Mai Xiongs in the phone book. I called the three funeral homes the Hmong use, and I tried calling Sai Sue Lor's wife, who had told me that Mai was "Grandmother" to her. No luck. I decided to drive down to Mai's apartment.

I parked my car and went in through the open chain-link gate as I had done so often. Some children were playing there, and I asked a girl of about twelve what she knew about Mai. "She lives here," she said. Next I spoke to several men toward the back. One said Mai had been very sick two or three months ago and had spent a week in the hospital, but she was better. Upstairs a woman said, "She's gambling at Lake Tahoe." That was Mai, all right. Reassured, I wrote a message to her on a piece of paper and drew my picture on it. The woman said she would give it to her.

I went back to my car, started the engine, and burst into tears. Even though she was alive, I had experienced the certainty that one day Mai Xiong would not be there. And that on the day I learned of it, I would need to cry.

15

Peb Hmoob,
We Hmong: Chamy Thor

If you live like the old people, you will have a son.
If you live like the old people, you will have a daughter.
— Hmong funeral text[1]

I went to Northern California in February to visit Chamy for the weekend. She had called to say that there was a funeral and a healing we could attend and that she would explain the rituals to me.

Chamy had moved to a new location, still in the country — a new center for the Chamy enterprise. This house had just been finished, and the front yard featured broomstick-size trees in a sea of weeds. I knocked on the door and Patty, the first of Chamy's two daughters-in-law, answered.

"Hello, Sue!" Chamy called out from within the room. "You got lost! Too bad! Come in!" The entire family was gathered in the front room, sprawled or modestly seated on three matching blue sofas. On a fourth sofa Chamy sat, half buried beneath a sewing project. Sunshine, Chamy's first grandchild, was already asleep in her crib for the night, I was told. I had not met her yet but had a charming photo of her pinned to my bulletin board. In it she wore a flowered pink and blue dress, lacy socks, and bright red shoes. Nom Npis greeted me good-naturedly as always and went off on a chore. John, the eldest son, sat quietly, almost disappearing into himself — like his grandmother Kia Lis, I thought. I have always seen him like this. This was the father of baby Sunshine and husband of the cheerful Patty. On the VCR a bad movie was playing, and after having my bags

266

stashed at the end of one sofa I sat down with the rest to watch. It was "GI Jane." After it finished, Ken, the tall, gregarious second son whom Chamy once nearly dumped out of his basket-cradle, turned to me. "Why would women want to be in the military?" he wanted to know. I attempted to explain about opportunity, the varied abilities and interests of women, access to power. He said, "Why can't men invade women's territory but women can invade men's?" The two of us pursued this briefly, while Chamy continued bent over her work. *Sib tham* was not her preference.

With quick-flashing needle she was stitching a purple turban, the pre-wrapped kind I had seen for sale at her relative's store in Fresno. Chamy had just visited the store and learned how to make them. Instead of tediously wrapping yards and yards of the silk into the traditional head-dress each time it was needed, you just popped this onto your head. Chamy paused to lift scissors out of the big Danish butter-cookie tin that served as her sewing basket. "You only need half the silk," she said, "so it cost only twenty-five dollar instead of fifty." So! The keeper of cultural arts was tinkering with tradition in good Western fashion to save time and money. She was nothing if not realistic. But in the process, I thought, what was lost was the intimate touch of an older woman's warm hands as she wrapped a daughter's head.

Most of the family had scattered, and as Chamy worked I looked around the living room. The now-blank TV was centered in a wall of shelves where books leaned against one another. There was the two-volume one about word power, a binder about business writing, a guide to rocks and minerals, another on crossing cultures, help for those with allergies, and one that must surely be Chamy's, *How to Feel Younger Longer*. In the for-mer house I had also seen books on electrical work and general construc-tion and had wondered about them. On the wall hung a familiar framed *paj ntaub* of animals, and I wondered if Chamy had time for such work now.

Soon Chamy called out to the girls in Hmong, and I noticed again the emphatic, staccato quality of her speech, to which this language lends itself. Chamy's daughter May did not respond — she had morning sickness, I soon learned. But John's wife, Patty, and Ken's wife, Virginia, took them-selves to the kitchen without a murmur, as good Hmong daughters-in-law have always done.

In due time we were summoned to the dining room, where I sat again at the familiar table. Patty and Virginia carried in big bowls and platters filled with chicken, mushrooms in broth, rice, and buffalo fish — "It's like carp," John said, and I remembered his fish ponds. Hanging opposite me on the walls were a framed picture of Jesus shepherding sheep and another of a mill pond with a straw-hatted white American boy lolling beside shining water, a Tom Sawyer kind of picture. We ate, ladling servings onto our plates not with our personal spoons but with serving spoons. Chamy does not follow Hmong custom out of concern for germs.

While the two girls—they were both in their teens—cleaned up, Chamy gave directions to Ken and to May's husband, Ku, that I did not understand. However, they soon appeared in the living room carrying brand-new double box springs and then the mattress. These they installed in the middle of the living room. Behold the guest bed. The arrangement left about a yard of clearance between bed and sofas. Sheets, fuzzy blankets, and pillows appeared, and the girls made up the bed. It struck me that Hmong custom continues to place the guest bed in the main public room even when American houses aren't built with such in mind. But then, where else would they have put it?

Soon everyone disappeared and I crawled into bed, thoroughly awake. Within moments the house fell silent. Briefly, I heard two young people talking animatedly and laughing, and once I heard a door shut, the latch carefully pulled to. Otherwise, silence. No creaking beds, no baby noise (Sunshine was seven and a half months old), no snoring, no drawers or closet doors being shut, no voices. There were nine adults and one baby in the house. Around midnight, soft rain tinked in a drain pipe, and at 5:30 a.m. the wind came up and played falsetto notes with a house vent. Someone crept past me to the kitchen.

The sun came up and the family began appearing. Through sheer curtains I could see more clearly the dozens of trees and bamboo clumps that someone had planted in front. The bamboo was looking vigorous. May's husband, Ku, came through and I commented to him about the bamboo. "I am glad for that bamboo," he said in heavily accented English. He had only been in this country five years and missed the towering bamboo of his childhood.

I tidied up my bed and stowed my bags next to the bookshelves. Nom Npis appeared and sat down, looking fresh and ready to visit. I commented on his fine bunch of kids. In what turned out to be a reply, Nom Npis said:

"Hmong fortune teller said before the Vietnam war that the rock will come up from the bottom of the river and looks like the leaf, and the leaf will sink. And people said, 'What's that mean?' And he said, 'Listen carefully. In future, rich people will become poor, poor become rich.' When you're rich, your children spend whatever they want. When the rich left the country, they left everything behind, but the children continued to spend. Poor know they're poor. Their children keep going to school, become Ph.D."

Opposite: **Chamy Thor chats with a Hmong villager who has come to town. The woman represents the way of life Chamy wants Hmong Americans to remember. Laos, December 1994.**

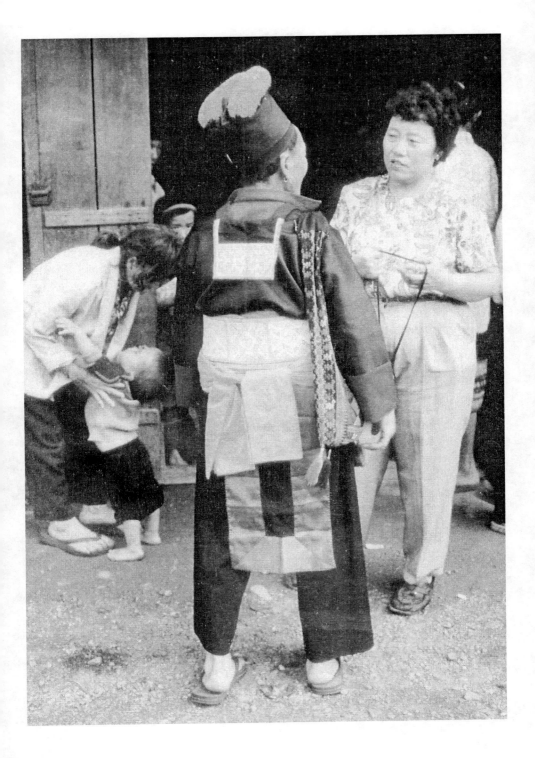

Chamy had arrived in time to hear this. Nom Npis continued. "People now see we were right not to have more children."

Indeed, the three children, now securely launched into responsible adulthood with their marriages and, soon, their degrees, are never far from Chamy's mind. Chamy had secured part-time jobs at her office for two of them as student assistants. Her boss later told me that he was glad to have them since they had inherited their mother's work ethic. That way, Chamy said, "I can keep my eye on them." (Ku had remarked, with a cheerful smile, that his mother-in-law kept all of them in line. I had no reason to doubt it.) The whole gang was also involved in the dance program, as I had seen for myself. Chamy leaned heavily on all six of the younger ones to stay in school — high school, as in the case of Virginia, and college for the rest of them. She directed them firmly toward graduate school. May and Ku had even broken with tradition to live with the bride's parents rather than the groom's, since they could better afford college by doing so.

"They going to stay with us until they finish college, so they don't have the expense of room and food," Chamy said. "Then they are free to leave."

I commented that when everyone left, the house would seem empty.

Chamy shot back with a twinkle in her eye, "Ken will stay here [according to tradition]. Or if he leave, we go, too!"

Nom Npis, grinning, had his own version. "Chamy will go with Ken, I go with Johnny!" They both laughed. It seemed that each parent had a favorite son. I was amused that Chamy preferred the sociable, cheerful child who was most like her husband, and Nom Npis favored the quiet, sober one who was most like his wife.

But then, reflecting on the business of living with one's children, Chamy veered away from her statement. "People like us might not want to babysit kids, like Americans [don't]. It's going to change. It is already." I knew that she had spent entire weekends babysitting Sunshine — a second job, she called it.

It was Saturday, and most of the family was going to the relative's healing, one of my reasons for coming.

Outside in the fresh February morning, I counted six vehicles parked in the gravel drive, symbols of the multiple directions the household members take in pursuit of classes and work. That morning, Nom Npis was first to leave, in the white pickup truck: He had the task of transporting the shaman and his bench to the healing. Three older sedans — more or less sporty — belonged to the three young couples, and a fourth, a venerable dark blue Toyota Corolla, got Chamy to work. The sixth vehicle, into which we piled, was a van that I knew was used to carry young dance students to practice and performances.

Ken climbed in behind the wheel, and Chamy and I sat two rows back.

"So, Ken gets to drive instead of Mom," I observed loud enough for him to hear.

Ken said, "It's too big for her to drive."

Chamy was right on his heels. "Oh, yeah? I can do anything!" The familiar refrain set us all laughing. I liked the warmth between Chamy, Nom Npis, and their kids. Later Chamy told me that when the three young ones don't want their parents to understand, they talk together in Spanish. Chamy and Nom Npis, in turn, hide information from the kids by speaking in Lao.

We spent the day at the relative's house off Mack Road, where I observed a family reunion of a unique sort and experienced the hours-long, brain-jangling rhythms of the shaman's iron ring. Nom Npis had joined Chamy in explaining the ritual to me, and he continued to talk on a variety of subjects after we got home. As always, I was intrigued by what interested him. Did I know about the Hmong philosopher from Vietnam who had developed a script for the Hmong language? "He foretell events. He could find water underground. In future, his writing will be in the nation." I had indeed heard of this man, now deceased.

Nom Npis also told me about a recent dream, fixing my attention with his eyes. A tiger came close to his house, it seems, but he shot and killed it. For the first time I noticed a blackened scar on the back of Nom Npis's right hand. "Cut by bamboo when we try to go from Laos."

That evening, left to myself for a few minutes, I spotted a video titled "Hmong and General Vang Pao: The Secret War in Laos 1960–75." It was produced by a Hmong company in St. Paul, Minnesota, in 1997. I commented on it to Chamy.

"You want to watch?"

Sure, I said, some of it. It turned out to be important in this family's solidarity. Nom Npis slipped one of the two tapes into the VCR, and settled down to watch and offer commentary. I learned an assortment of things: In 1967, Sam Thong, the second most important Hmong military location after Long Cheng, had a school with thirty-six teachers and more than a thousand students — school! The town was built to be the Hmong capital following the loss of Xieng Khouang. The Lao king came to Sam Thong and gave Vang Pao the insignia of major general. Nom Npis was translating the voice-over, or giving me his own comments, I wasn't sure which.

"In 1970 the king visited Long Cheng," Nom Npis interpreted. "Everybody turned out with flags to wave." There were some two hundred thousand Hmong in Long Cheng then, he said, and maybe fifty Lao families. "The war was very close," Nom Npis continued. "The queen gave awards for good housewives." Five hundred thousand dollars were spent to build a palace for the king at Long Cheng, Nom Npis said. "It had lawn, flowers, everything." The king stayed in it only three or four days.

But much of the video was devoted to soldiers, officers, military equipment, airplanes—war. The voice-over moved into a wavering chant. Chamy said, "Very sad. Because of the war, all the family relative had to leave their own land." Nom Npis took up the translation. "Everybody looking back to the homeland. Very sad."

This video was important to Chamy. She had tried to tell her children why they had come to the United States—all the stories Chamy told me about their lives, the fleeing, the captivity, the fighting, the deaths— keys to her psyche. "They weren't interested until they watched video," Chamy said. "Then they started asking questions."

Blessed children! How many parents who have suffered wish that their children understood. I had already sensed that Chamy, though professedly shy, found it overpoweringly important to tell her story. She would desire it most that her offspring would listen.

I asked Chamy how her Hmong arts organization was going.

"You want to see scrapbook? I have a scrapbook." I had my own collection of newspaper clippings from Sacramento papers, notes from my earliest days with Chamy, drafts of grant applications we had worked on, paragraphs describing Hmong arts for a booklet, even my diagrams of how to do Hmong cross-stitch. Mine was a modest folder. Chamy's padded scrapbook was huge, and a work of perfect order. On the cover it read "Hmong Cultural Arts Center."

Chamy had begun teaching *paj ntaub* when she first arrived in America, to save it from extinction, she told one reporter. She had already been teaching for years when I sat in a small desk in her after-school class in Sacramento. Now she — or rather the Hmong Cultural Arts, Crafts, Teaching and Museum Project — had won a forty thousand dollar, two-year grant from the National Endowment for the Arts and was getting requests for proposals from the Department of Corrections for a bigger grant. Her embroidery had been featured in newspaper articles, and her dancers, favorite subjects of news photographers, frequently appeared in large color photos.

Chamy told me that she had been interviewed by the local public television station "about the embroidery, to explain the tapestry and the war." She herself had been too busy to watch it. "A lot of my co-worker say, 'I saw you on TV.'" I could see that pleased Chamy.

The NEA grant would supplement funding from Sacramento's arts council and other sources to pay for some new teachers and for a woman who was already teaching. "Funders like it when someone already show commitment," Chamy said. The program includes classes in embroidery, Hmong reading and writing, folk dance, and kheng dance "to get the boys." There are two sites, three groups.

"The dance teacher is one of our students since seven years old," Chamy said. That group had won first place at the New Year's competition that year, in a field of twenty groups. Mothers make the traditional costumes, with help from the daughters.

From her bedroom Chamy brought out fat booklets. The covers read *Phau Xyaum Nyeem Ntawv Hmoob*, Hmong Practice Reading Book, used in her classes. I flipped through one. Letters of the alphabet were paired with pictures: tus *t*wm, lub *k*aus, lub *x*ov; water buffalo, umbrella, thread. The cover of each book featured the scanned photo of its young owner, along with the student's name. Chamy misses nothing.

"How much of this are you involved in yourself?" I asked, recalling an earlier comment about the few hours she sleeps a night.

"*Paj ntaub* at Taylor Elementary on Tuesday and dance on Thursday," she said. "We have a lot of helpers. I just check to make sure the program is running as planned." Then she added, "I come up with projects." At the second location she teaches embroidery and writing.

While Chamy was turning pages in the scrapbook—articles, programs, photographs—I noticed her hands. They were smooth and white now, with teal veins showing through the skin. The nails were neatly manicured. Were these just winter hands, soft and pale now but to be toughened again come spring, or had she indeed been forced to abandon her beloved gardening? She seemed to have chosen the tougher path of preserving their culture's values over growing lemon grass. She and Nom Npis wanted to do it for the kids. She said, "When I see kids drop out of school, and there is no one to help them out, help them know what's right and what's wrong, that's not good. I felt something needs to be done to help those kids understand and stay out of trouble."

At the same time that she was struggling against the tide of cultural evisceration, she was proving herself a thoroughly self-starting, strong-minded American woman. At the California Department of Transportation her boss, William Bell, described her over the phone for me. He had a businesslike manner, but he was nonetheless effusive. "She's very diligent, independent, and dedicated. Her ethnic background is one with the work ethic." Chamy had earned a commendation from the Cal Trans director for having developed a faster reporting system to handle storm damage. "It was used all the way up the line of management, and we're using it again this year," he said. I told him she had not mentioned it to me. "She's very unassuming," he said. "Very dependable, very resourceful. I'm pretty demanding as a manager. She's exemplary in that she works independently and well.

"Ken and May have the same work ethic," he continued. "Chips off the old block. She's generating a role model."

As to Chamy's work mates, Bell suspected that her strong work orientation was off-putting to some. "She comes to work to *work*. Some people maybe don't react to that well, but people go to her for information. There are people she socializes with at her desk."

For her part, Chamy appreciated Bell. "He's an exceptional supervisor. He never put you down. If somebody say something, he would find out the truth and support you. He's fair and he's really nice." Chamy didn't take this kind of fair treatment for granted. Customs regarding women, she was finding, were far different from Laos. Bell had promoted her, and she was given an "almost corner office," as she told me, an upgrade from the cubicle where I had visited her. The advancement didn't surprise me. Chamy was doing her job the same way she had done school and college and motherhood and farming and jungle and arts organization: with all the intelligence, ingenuity, and strength she could muster. It's not luck, she had once stormed at her brother in Laos when he complained about his wife. Forget luck. It's hard work!

Sunday morning. Today we would attend a portion of a funeral while the younger generation, Sunshine included, drove to the mountains to play in the snow. Chamy and I were chatting briefly in the front room when Nom Npis emerged with freshly ironed slacks for Chamy to wear. He had ironed Chamy's clothes during our trip in Laos and showed me how to do mine on the sagging bed in the guest house.

It was this funeral, held in a recreation-type hall at a mortuary in South Sacramento, that allowed me to visualize Ly Vong's ceremony, which had taken place in the same room.

After the morning portion of the funeral, Chamy, Nom Npis, and I went to have brunch at a buffet restaurant. We heaped our plates with French toast, poached eggs, ham, pilaf, and biscuits. Nom Npis went for a second plate, of fruit. When Chamy came back with her third plate — dessert this time — she said, "Too bad, they just brought out a roast beef. Why they don't bring it before now?" I could not explain why Americans eat bacon and ham before noon but not roast beef.

The three of us ate mightily for twenty-one dollars. "We eat here a lot when we worked on house." What house? "Oh, didn't I tell you? We have house here and we remodel it." In fact I had overheard Chamy say to

Nom Npis in perfect Hmonglish, "*Koj puas mus* fix roof *los?*" Now, with tummies crammed, we stopped by a rental house of theirs. I was continually amazed by this couple. I stood in the entryway with Chamy as Nom Npis talked to the renter about the recently leaking roof. Nom Npis had fixed it within hours, and the report now was that everything was fine. Chamy tallied for me the properties they held, with their bank, and how they took care of them.

"Nom Npis can do roofing, electricity, kitchen counter-top, restroom," Chamy enumerated. He has a heating and air-conditioning license and contractor's license. Ah, yes. The books. How had I missed it? He built three houses in the north area for a company before the two of them launched into their own real estate. Their renters have included Hmong, Mexican American, African American, and Caucasian. Mostly they rent to Hmong families who can't find a house because of their many children. "We want to help them out."

Chamy had learned about leveraging, fixer-uppers, and property exchange. I wondered where. "I always thought there must be a way to do it," Chamy said. "I learn from the rich. I go to the library." She and Nom Npis had read a book on how to make a fortune in real estate. Once Nom Npis completed a tuition-free regional occupational program class in home construction, they got to work. They bought a couple of "junky houses," and the entire family worked to bring them into shape. She and Nom Npis had bought whole-heartedly into the capitalist economy.

That evening just before saying goodnight, everybody gathered in the living room, the kind of impromptu event I particularly enjoy. We had been joined by Nom Npis's young niece, whom he teased as I had seen him do with youngsters so often before. Perhaps it was I who brought up the subject of scary dreams, the kind Mai Xia Cha had once told me about in which you knew you were awake but could not move. Yes, they all knew about it. It had recently been featured on "Oprah." And, yes, all but the niece had experienced it. Ken and May described their experiences. "You see a shadow and feel heavy pressure on your body," Ken said. He had awakened frozen and tried to call to Virginia to help. Shaking the person stops it, he said. But he had been unable even to call out. John, in contrast, had experienced a cool hand on his calf.

"I know how to cure it," said Chamy, commanding instant attention. "Remember the word relax. You just know it will pass in about three minutes, and you don't fight it."

John said, "That's what I did, and I've never had it again." I was not surprised that John, so like his mother, had arrived at the same conclusion. Others I've talked to believe it is an evil spirit.

"See!" said Chamy. "She know that, too." She had meant "he," referring to John. In response, May, Ken, and the others laughed and laughed,
while John fell silent and red-faced. Second generation embarrassment at
the immigrant parent's language.

Later, I asked a physician friend about the phenomenon. We searched
the scientific literature on the Internet and discovered that it is well known
to the medical community. In fact, my physician friend realized that his
own frequent childhood waking-nightmare of having a bear sitting on his
chest, ready to attack, was exactly this.

With that discussion over, we all headed for bed. At least I thought
so. Instead, Ken's wife, Virginia, and Nom Npis's twelve-year-old niece,
who hadn't a shy bone in her body, reappeared and plopped down on sofas
near my bed. They had things to say about being married. While the young
niece was full of theory and opinion, Virginia, still a high school student,
was feeling some first-hand regret at having married so young. People had
warned her that it would be tough. She was fifteen.

She had gone to a Catholic school in Wisconsin. "I loved sports like
basketball and volleyball." When they married, she asked Ken if she could
join teams here. He had said no, she needed to come home to cook for the
family. But, she told me, she is determined to delay motherhood until she
finishes school. "I saw what it was like for Patty." The niece, meanwhile,
proclaimed that she would put off marriage for the sake of independence
and would in the mean time lead a respectable life to maintain "face."
These two were seamlessly blending old ways and new, sentence by sentence.

About one a.m., far later than I ordinarily remain awake, they said
goodnight. The next day when I was leaving I told the two I had enjoyed
our talk. The niece replied, "Yeah, that was *good.*"

I have thought a lot about the Virginias, the Pattys, the Mai Xias, all
the young women I know who have married early and moved into their
husband's family. And I've thought about how Chamy fits into the old system, with two daughters-in-law under her own roof. The paradox is that
Chamy suffered as a daughter-in-law. She might have died during her first
pregnancy because of a mother-in-law's insistence that she work in the
field. And yet Chamy now makes use of the labor of her daughters-in-law
for cooking and cleaning.

Chamy is aware of the contradiction. She values female independence
but also couldn't run this productive household without the girls' help.
More than once she has told me that she takes extra care to instruct and
encourage the girls politely as they learn to cook instead of complaining
behind their backs when they do something wrong. Certainly I have never

heard her speak harshly to them. And the truth is that Chamy and Nom Npis are supporting the girls financially. Work might seem a reasonable trade for the benefit. Chamy is also strongly encouraging them to continue their education, a source of future security for a female in America that she herself has struggled to achieve.

The Hmong community is in the throes of change as regards women. While men in the refugee camps were refusing to emigrate to America for fear of losing control over their wives, many women must have yearned for such liberation. Some must have had bitter memories of being overworked and overlooked. They wanted out.

Once here, the men's worry and women's hope came true. Women went to school, began to speak their own mind, and chafed against boundaries they no longer saw as immutable. Grandmothers refused to babysit. Young women entered the professions—claiming the respect once granted only to female shamans like Mai Xiong. They became activists. Ly Vong's daughter Nouzong Lynaolu picked up her father's mantle of leadership. And the momentum increases.

The Hmong are searching for their footing. A few men quickly saw the economic necessity of female autonomy, but others cannot relinquish old ways. Chamy has surely encountered such resistance, even if she held back telling me the details. At conferences, in living rooms, in chance meetings, I've learned that retaliation against a strong-willed, educated woman can be harsh. One self-motivated woman might be disdained by relatives, who make use of her special talents while scorning her for having them. A man with a strong wife must listen to taunts about wearing a dress. And there are those death threats Chamy received for being in a role of power at the welfare office, telling men what they had to do. It wasn't likely to happen, but it gives one pause.

Sunday night, twelve of us settled down to sleep in the house, plus baby Sunshine, who cried briefly during the night. Several extra teenage relatives had materialized. Invited to look in, I saw that John and Patty's small room was three-quarters filled by a four-poster bed and Sunshine's crib. One of the teenage visitors had slept on the remaining floor space there, and the others apparently moved in with the two other young couples. Still, I thought as I had rolled into bed in the living room, it didn't seem crowded.

As I drifted off I thought: This house, so full of these people — it feels safe.

Monday morning. I would be going home this afternoon. About eight-thirty, Chamy sat down on the sofa that had served as my night stand

and answered more questions about Hmong funerals. The morning before, we had driven again to South Sacramento, where Chamy and Nom Npis conducted me into the funeral crowd and I observed the playing of the drum and khengs, the ritual bowing, and the clusters of people who poured in through the door, bearing food and money. I recalled Lue Vang telling me how important it was to show up at a funeral.

In the evening segment of the funeral we had listened to lengthy chants sung over boiled chickens as hundreds of mourners stood listening. One of the chanters had a beautiful tenor voice and carried himself like a cantor or priest. I wondered what the chants said, and now Chamy was ready to tell me.

Nom Npis suddenly appeared in the living room with glasses of hot, sweet tea and bite-size Snickers. Chamy said to him in English, "Do you have plate?" As he went agreeably to get plates, it struck me: Nom Npis likes Chamy. I had watched him ironing her slacks and now he was going, unruffled, to bring plates. I don't know how I had missed it. This man, powerfully muscled, adept at jungle survival, equally fearless in the face of tigers or house-building, married to his brilliant, driven, powerhouse of a woman — Nom Npis likes and respects her.

Once we were settled with plates for our snacks, Chamy picked up the first of two thick paperback books she had brought, French publications — in Hmong — that she had acquired in Minneapolis. She opened the first volume and held it for me to see. It described the traditional funeral procedure, with photographs. The second gave the ritual text, including the words to be "spoken" by the kheng. Nom Npis settled down next to us.

Soon after someone dies, Chamy explained, a kheng player comes to guide the person's spirits back to Heaven. Nom Npis said, "They say thank you to one village-land-water-tree [where the deceased lived most recently], then to the next village-land-water-tree, back, back to the place where they were born. And the last stop is to get placenta. Then they can go to Heaven to be reincarnated." We carry ties to each of our homes, and each link must be acknowledged before we can complete our life.

Chamy described for me the flow of the old tradition, including preparation of the body and the rituals associated with burial. But I still wanted to know what the chants said. "Can you translate something for me?" I asked Chamy.

"OK," Chamy said. She suggested we go to my car.

"My car?"

"We can sit in your car. Because there is a superstition about not doing it in the house." It's bad luck. So we went out into the cold morning and climbed into my small rental car. "You can start the heater," Chamy suggested. There she translated bits of the chants.

When the person first dies, the kheng plays *tu siav*, "just died." The tune says, "The devil has an evil heart, has no good heart. And the devil dropped the sickness, and it spread all over the world. Whomever the sickness—" Chamy fished for the word, doing a hugging motion with her arms. "Embraces," I offered. "Whomever the sickness embraces, they must die." This part is performed next to the body laid just inside the home's back door. "This has very good rhyming," Chamy said. "*Naj* and *nrag, coj* and *ploj, puag* and *tuag.*"

Chamy read the Hmong aloud and continued translating: "First the person create water to wash face. He speak to the body. 'This is what I'm going to give you, three drinks. After that I'm going to give you water to wash your face. Right now I'm washing three layers of bad, dark things. I'm washing the face so you can go to the dark place.'"

Chamy continued, "Then they sing why people exist on earth, the origin of people." I had heard other versions, but it had special significance here — especially to Chamy. "In the beginning," Chamy translated, "the Bride and the Groom live together in the world for seven years without any children. They both go together to ask the Wisdom why they don't have children. The Bride and Groom don't have any children, so they don't qualify to stay on the Earth. The Wisdom says, 'Bride and Groom, let's go back to the Earth and you follow the old people knowledge and experience of living,' so that they will have son."

Chamy interrupted herself. "This one is very powerful poetry, very good saying." Then she returned to Wisdom's words. "'If you live like the old people, you will have a son. If you live like the old people, you will have a girl.' Then the Bride and Groom have children. They named the first Shine Sky — like a bright star — and named the second one Sky Shine. And then they mature. They keep growing, growing [in number]. If people don't die, the world can't hold everybody, so that's why we have to die.'"

The chant continues, touching the well of grief. "Now, deceased's family, your parent all pass away. Right now your parent fell and never got up, and it's compared [to] your house collapse.

"Because they die," Chamy translated, her voice hesitating "they don't have chance to teach you anything." Losing an elder is like losing an arm. "Because he pass away, he leave his children behind crying around the bed. Right now your parent die, nobody warms leftovers for the children. Parent die and leave children orphaned." Chamy added, "When they say this, some cry and cry."

She turned back to the page. Though the parent had died, that parent's voice continued, now heard teaching through the funeral ritual. The chant went: "We meet your father and he told us to come back and teach you this. Your parent said, 'Other people weaving, all you children must go weaving with them, not telling lies. If you don't listen to your parent and other people weaving and you don't go and you go telling lies around, you won't have any clothes to cover yourself.'"

She continued. "[You] children and grandchildren left behind, stay behind and keep on working hard so your children won't get jealous when other people get to eat meat."

I asked Chamy what she thought was good about the traditional funeral, now so often truncated and altered. Chamy thought a bit, catching her lower lip between her teeth, and finally said, "The way they teach the descendant, not to be bad person. 'Grandfather say that, say this, and you should do what he told you.'" She who had consistently broken rules while breaking new ground still believed that the Hmong elders were worth heeding.

Chamy stopped. It was enough. The February wind rocked the car a bit. Out in the front yard stood the bamboo clumps that, I had been told, caused old Hmong to cry when they saw them.

I asked Chamy about her goals. She had talked about losing weight and building a bigger house with a separate building for a kitchen. Now she told me about the museum she wanted to build, a place to put her collection of stitchery, books like these about the funeral, videos like the one about the war. And outside the museum she would plant bamboo for the elders to love. That was her Hmong side. The American Chamy talked about financial security, studying to earn her way up to the highest level at work. She talked about seeing that her children and grandchildren earned doctorates "so have a better life than I do." And she wanted to clean the yard.

I asked about her life so far, what made her happiest, saddest, most angry, most disappointed.

"I'm too late in this country, don't have chance to learn English from beginning. If I started here, I have Ph.D. That's the disappointment." It seemed that disappointment was never far from her thoughts.

"OK, sadness. I leave all my family behind. All the people that die from the war, all the bad things I've gone through still haunting me. Changed my life forever. You can't forget." She paused briefly, took a breath, and continued, ticking off the list of feelings I had given her.

"I'm angry about, even [when] you try do good things for people, some just badmouth about you. I'm powerful, so they don't like that. But I have to be successful. That's why I have to break out of the crowd." I thought how much easier it would be if these ground-breakers didn't also crave acceptance.

"Right now, because my family [in Laos] so poor, I have to help them out. That's why I work so hard. Everybody looks to me for help.

"Sometimes I will panic: How come I come this far and didn't enjoy my life? I work seven days a week. On the weekday, after working on my full-time job I head up to teach Hmong arts. On the weekend I help Nom Npis remodeling the house, cleaning windows, kitchen, bathroom and even climb with him on top of the roof to put on new shingles. Some days I work sixteen or fourteen hours per day and sleep only five hours."

"What makes you happy?" I had to remind her. She had forgotten that one.

"Ohhh, what makes me happy." There was a long pause while she looked out the car window. "OK, what makes me happy, when you have very, very small chance to go to school — over here your children have very good opportunity. I'm glad they almost graduate [from] four-year college. I'm glad they might have a better life.

"I'm a person that always struggle and try to find better life. I don't just sit there. I have to think what I have to do tomorrow. I'm never satisfied. I haven't reached my goal yet, that's why not happy yet."

Everyone had gathered in the living room around my bed — Nom Npis, Chamy, and all the kids. John held Sunshine. Chamy was perched on the edge of her chair, frowning as if scrolling through a list of things to do. Then Patty took Sunshine from John and put her in the middle of the guest bed, the center of attention. Slowly Sunshine rolled this way and that, raising herself on her tiny hands to look at the members of her court. Each of us was alert to danger should she roll too near the edge, but mostly we gazed in some primal devotion at this child.

I marveled that she was so firmly surrounded by family in this room. I contemplated the paths open to her and wondered most whether she would in time develop that odd hunger to stay connected to her large circle of kin, living and dead, or would let them drift from memory. Immigrants' children are unwitting forgetters, at the same time as they are inventors, bringing into being an approach to life like no other. As to Sunshine, I think that some day she will listen to Grandmother Chamy's stories, told in crisp sentences, and perhaps even notice the compassion that dwells in her Grandmother's persistence. I think she will adore her grandfather and gradually become aware of the beauty of his practical knowledge. From both she may discover the textures of life.

But she might just as easily allow consciousness of her people to fade. If so, she'll lose an anchor, the certainty of connection. She'll know less about herself. It will be easier to get lost, easier to be eaten by tigers.

Sunshine's eyes shone. Her small ears stood out just a bit from her head, and her smile curled up at the corners—all charming attributes to enthrall us. She rotated to where she could see Grandmother Chamy and broke into a grin. Chamy leaned over and gathered Sunshine into her arms, something I had not seen her do before. Chamy stroked Sunshine's cheek with her nose, as Mai Xiong had nuzzled the photo of my granddaughter.

"Ohhh, big girl!" Chamy said. The grandmother's face relaxed, and I saw the similarity in the smiles of grandmother and granddaughter, the upward curve at the corners, the shape.

Too soon, someone stepped up and lifted the baby away from Chamy. There was work, it seemed, for the matriarch to do.

Appendix A

Hmong Language and Names

Language

Dialects

The Hmong language is divided into two main dialects, White Hmong and Green — sometimes called Blue — Hmong.[1]

Because White Hmong is spoken by more people, and because it is more likely to be the dialect of those with education, some assume that it is superior.

The differences between the two dialects can be compared with those between British and American English. At times a single word may cause confusion, and at other times one might think, "He was speaking Hmong, but I couldn't understand a word he said."

The following joke turns on this same-but-different factor. A White Hmong and a Green Hmong went hunting together. One says, "If we catch something today, we eat. If not, I'll eat you tomorrow." They separate. Later the White Hmong calls out, "A deer is coming your direction." The Green Hmong thinks he said, "A tiger [the White Hmong hunter] is coming back," and the Green Hmong hunter runs.

Long-term geographic separation in China created the dialects. In the flight from China and then from their homes in Laos, the two groups have resumed contact and have learned to speak or at least understand each others' dialect.

Geographic separation also created some fairly superficial cultural differences. The most obvious is the difference in women's clothing styles,

from which the subgroups take their names. White Hmong women traditionally wore white skirts on special occasions and Green Hmong wore
blue batiked skirts dyed with indigo. (White skirts now are frequently
made from cloth printed with patterns, and the batik of Green Hmong
skirts is barely visible beneath appliqué and embroidery.) Striped Hmong
clothes feature horizontal stripes on the sleeves. Other categories that surface occasionally are Flowery Hmong and Chocolate Hmong. Men of all
groups traditionally wear black pants, shirt, and Chinese-style cap. Sai Sue
Lor, whose story is told in Chapter 10, describes himself as Striped Hmong,
and his wife, Ge Vang, as Black Hmong.

The groups readily intermarry.

Origin

The Hmong language belongs to the Hmong-Mien family. Hmong-
Mien has variously been included in the Chinese-Tibetan and Austro-Tai
families, but scholars increasingly believe that it developed independently.
Other languages in the Hmong-Mien family include Mien, Mhu, Qo
Hsiong, and some twenty others spoken by groups of various sizes in China
and Southeast Asia.

Orthography

In order to produce Christian materials, Protestant missionary Dr.
William A. Smalley and researcher G. Linwood Barney teamed with
Roman Catholic missionary the Rev. Yves Bertrais to devise a written form
for Hmong. The Romanized Practical Alphabet, RPA, was completed in
1953. According to a language-development paper by Jonas Vang-na Vangay, the roman alphabet was chosen so as to mesh with Western type-
writers and presses. The Laotian government disapproved of a Hmong
orthography, Vangay writes, so in the 1960s the three linguists went directly
to the Hmong. Three general meetings in Long Cheng, which included the
key leader Gen. Vang Pao, and five meetings of Hmong intellectuals in
Vientiane—students, teachers, administrators, and religious representa-
tives—were required before the issue was resolved and the orthography
accepted.

Characteristics

Hmong is largely monosyllabic, like Chinese and Vietnamese. The
infrequent multisyllabic word is usually a composite. Examples are
pojniam, "female + mother or wife of," meaning woman, and *menyuam*,
"little + little," child.

Hmong is tonal. That is, the meaning of a word changes when spoken with a different tone, always indicated by the last letter, or absence of one. Bliatout et al. in *Handbook for Teaching Hmong-Speaking Students* illustrate the principle.[2]

Tone	RPA symbol	Example	
high	-b	*pob*	ball, lump
high falling	-j	*poj*	female
mid rising	-v	*pov*	throw
mid	–	*po*	spleen
breathy mid low	-g	*pog*	paternal grandmother
low	-s	*pos*	thorn
low falling (creaky)	-m	*pom*	see

(Low rising -d may occur in place of -m at the end of a phrase.)

Hmong is not inflected to show plural or possession (boy, boys; boy's, boys'), gender or case (he, his, him; she, hers, her), or forms of verbs such as tense (take, took, taking, taken). Rather, these distinctions are indicated by the order or combinations of words, as in "will be going" in English or as in the case of *kuv*, "I" or "my," which changes meaning depending on what follows. Thus in *kuv noj*, "I eat," *kuv* means "I," but in *kuv tsev*, "my house," it means "my."

Hmong does, however, have classifiers, placed before the noun. Examples include words indicating bulky or round objects, long or slender objects, a length of time or road, a slap with the hand or a sheaf of rice, and pairs. The classifier can change the meaning of a noun, as with *ntawv*, "paper": *daim ntawv* means sheet — or "flat thing" — of paper but *phau ntawv* means "book."

Names

Clans

Traditionally, a Hmong person's name was simply a given name. So a Hmong person might introduce herself to another Hmong by using the pattern, "My name is Sue, and my clan is Murphy." With the increasing adoption of the clan name as last name, the issue of word order arises. In traditional Asian usage, the clan name comes first, as in *Vang* Pao. Most American Hmong now use Western order, with clan name last. The wife may also adopt the Western style of using her husband's clan name instead of her own. Some Hmong go beyond the use of a simple clan name, choosing instead a composite of an honored forebear's name. An example is Ly Vong Lynaolu, in which Lynaolu is the last name.

The number of clans is commonly given as about eighteen. A folk tale explains the origin of some clan names. The story tells of a great flood, during which only a brother and sister survived, perched on top of a hill. After lengthy protestations by the sister, they finally married and produced a child that looked like a pumpkin or a stone, round with no arms or legs. Disgusted, they cut it up and threw the pieces to the ground below them. Some pieces fell in a garden, others in weeds, others on a goat house, and still others on a pig house. Vang, the story continues, sounds like the Hmong word for "garden," Thao rhymes with "weeds," Lee rhymes with "goat house," and Moua sounds like "pig house."

Certain clan names closely resemble Chinese names, such as Lee. Nicholas Tapp suggests in *Sovereignty and Rebellion* that historically, in the rich ethnic mix in Southwestern China, clan names could easily have been adopted across ethnic lines. Marriages and feudal relationships might well have encouraged the adoption of clan names.

Clans are subdivided into descent groups, each comprising kin who can trace their lineage to a common male ancestor. In such groups, distinctions of ritual are carefully observed.

Members of a single clan might speak either White Hmong or Green Hmong.

Given Names

A child is named at the age of three days, not by the parents but by an important man in the village who is invited to call the child's soul into its body. Should a shaman later determine that someone's illness or misfortune is caused by the "wrong name," the shaman may change it. The practice offers a telling example of how the individual is not an independent figure with ownership of his or her name but is embedded in the community.

Married men who have become fathers commonly receive an adult name from the wife's father. But legal complexities in this country, including the difficulty of getting a name changed, mean that some babies now receive their adult names at birth.

Appendix B

Child-Rearing Study

Twelve Caucasian and twelve Hmong mother-child pairs in Minneapolis–St. Paul were studied by pediatrician Charles N. Oberg and Sharon Muret-Wagstaff, Shirley G. Moore, and Brenda Cumming.[1]

All twenty-four families came from low-income backgrounds. The children ranged in age from eighteen to twenty-one months. Most of these families had participated in earlier research beginning in the children's infancy. Since then, a quarter of the Caucasian families had experienced separation or divorce. None of the Hmong families had. During the same time interval, eight of the Hmong families had had another baby, but only two of the Caucasian families had. The ratio of adults to children in the household was the same in both groups, but the raw numbers were larger in the Hmong households. Hmong grandmothers were significantly involved in child rearing; Hmong fathers were only slightly more involved than their Caucasian counterparts.

The researchers used three scales to measure mother-child interaction, as described in the article by the authors mentioned above. The first measured the mother's patience, responsiveness to fussiness, attentiveness, and expressiveness toward the child. Another measured the mother's emotional and verbal responsiveness, avoidance of restriction and punishment, and involvement with her child.

The most elaborately described of the three instruments, by M. Ainsworth, uses four scales, worth describing in detail.

1. Sensitivity to the baby's signals and cues. A mother rating 9, or highly sensitive, responds quickly and appropriately to her baby's signals.

"She is empathic and respects the child's point of view," according to the article. "Her interactions with the child seem complete and well-rounded, and she monitors the child and the environment closely, anticipating problems." The sensitivity levels dwindle to "highly insensitive," in which the mother is motivated almost entirely by her own needs.

2. Cooperativeness rather than interference. The high-scoring mother "sees her baby as a separate person whose activities have a validity of their own" and avoids interrupting him or her arbitrarily.

3. Acceptance of the positives and negatives of parenthood in relation to the child. The accepting mother respects the child's will, does not resent responsibility for the child, and experiences frustration and irritation only briefly. The other end of the scale is marked by "pervasive irritation and scolding, rough handling and ill-concealed anger, and maternal escalation of conflict in power struggles."

4. Accessibility rather than neglecting or ignoring the child. An accessible mother "is aware of the baby consistently; she actively acknowledges and responds to him or her." The quality of her response is measured in number one above.

On Ainsworth's 1-to-9 scale, the Hmong mothers rated from 8.58 to a perfect 9.0 (Acceptance) compared to the Caucasian mothers' 5.17 (for Sensitivity) to 6.5 (for Acceptance). Comparable numbers appear on the other scales. There, the Hmong mothers' highest score came in "Frequency of expression of negative regard," namely, fussing at the child.

As to other aspects of the children's well-being, Caucasian children were significantly more likely to have accidents, hospitalizations and "ingestions." For these (and cultural) reasons, the Caucasian children made far more visits to emergency rooms. Caucasian children were more up-to-date on immunizations, but the Hmong children were fed more nutritional diets. Hmong children were somewhat slower in language development.

In discussing their findings, the authors of the study quote H. A. Bernatzik who wrote in 1963 that the Hmong child is regarded as "the most treasured possession a person can have." The baby's life is "rich in physical contact and social interaction" with mothers, grandmothers, and older siblings. Caucasian babies, on the other hand, while enjoying attentive, playful, and vocal interactions with their mothers, live in "object-filled rather than people-filled environments," according to another researcher quoted.

Oberg and his fellow researchers conclude that all twenty-four of the children in the study were healthy and normal. But they point to studies that connect early, secure attachments, based on consistent, sensitive caring, to a child's later cooperativeness, persistence, enthusiasm in problem-solving, and ego resilience.

Hmong mothers' success, the authors suggest, comes from "a cultural priority for attentive child-rearing and the availability and use of a strong extended family network."

Chapter Notes

Preface

1. Vang and Lewis, *Grandmother's Path*, 66.

Introduction

1. Throughout, the terms "Lao" and "Laotian" appear. I have chosen to distinguish them as follows: "Lao" indicates the ethnic group, their culture, and their language. They live primarily in the lowlands. "Laotian" refers to all citizens of Laos and may include the Lao, Hmong, Mien, Khmu, and other peoples. Exceptions are found in the name Royal Lao Army and Pathet Lao, which may include individuals of any ethnic group in Laos.

2. Geert Hofstede, "Foreword," in *Individualism and Collectivism*, ed. Kim et al., ix.

3. Michael Harris Bond, "Into the Heart of Collectivism: A Personal and Scientific Journey," in *Individualism and Collectivism*, ed. Kim et al., 69.

PART I. JOURNEYS

1. Word definitions (Parts I and III) are from Heimbach, *White Hmong-English Dictionary* and (Part IV) *English-Hmong Phrasebook with Useful Wordlist (for Hmong speakers)*, adapted and translated by Cheu Thao (Washington, D.C.: Center for Applied Linguistics, no date). The proverb beginning Part II is from Vang and Lewis, *Grandmother's Path*, 71.

Chapter 1

1. Chamy and her husband have chosen the Hmong spelling, Nom Npis Lis, for this book. It is pronounced "naw bee lee." Lis is the clan name. Other spellings are Lee and Ly. Nom Npis and Chamy's children spell the clan name Lee. Nom, meaning officer or king, is his adult name. For years he was called just Npis (Bee). Chamy's Hmong name is Tsab Mis Thoj. See Appendix A on Hmong Language and Names.

2. The count may reach twenty-eight, depending upon how subdivisions are grouped. Spellings also vary. Here are some common clan names: Cha or Chang or Tcha, Cheng, Chue, Fang, Hang, Her or Heu, Khang, Kong, Kue or Ku, Lee or Ly or Li, Lor or Lo, Moua, Pha or Phang, Thao or Thor, Vang, Vue or Vu, Xiong, and Yang.

3. Mee Her, *Gender*, 194.

4. Daniel and Knudsen, "Introduction," in *Mistrusting Refugees*, 6, 9.

5. Knudsen, "When Trust Is on Trial: Negotiating Refugee Narratives," in *Mistrusting Refugees*, ed. Daniel and Knudsen, 28.

Chapter 2

1. Vang and Lewis, *Grandmother's Path*, 84.
2. Ibid., 116, 120–123. In the poem, "Eating only a little" and "wearing only a few of the clothes" refers to the singer's total lifetime allotment. That is, he had to leave home while still young.

Chapter 3

1. Vang and Lewis, *Grandmother's Path*, 136–137.
2. Loc.cit. Some ambiguity exists as to the best translation of the Hmong word *ntsuab*. Generally it is translated as green, but the color distinction from blue is not exact. That is why a blue skirt can be referred to as "green." Therefore the term *hmoob ntsuab*, designating one major segment of the Hmong people and their dialect, is usually rendered Green Hmong but not always. The author of the book referred to in this note, Lue Vang, translates it as blue — Blue Hmong.

Chapter 4

1. Vang and Lewis, *Grandmother's Path*, 80.
2. Ibid.,163–183.
3. Hawke, *Everyday Life*, 33.
4. Vang and Lewis, op.cit., 157–8.

Chapter 5

1. Yang Dao, *Hmong at the Turning Point*, xiii.
2. This rendering is condensed from one told by Kao N. Vang, in *Hmong in the West*, 29–31.
3. This discussion draws upon the insights of Jared Diamond, *Guns, Germs, and Steel*. Other references used in writing this chapter, not all of them indicated in the text, include Sucheng Chan, *Hmong Means Free*; Wolfram Eberhard, *China's Minorities*; Jane Hamilton-Merritt, *Tragic Mountains*; HarperCollins, *Past Worlds*; Roger Lewin, *In the Age of Mankind*; Hy V. Luong, *Revolution in the Village*; E.C. Machle, M.D., "The Aboriginal Tribes of China"; Alfred W. McCoy, *The Politics of Heroin*; Gayle L. Morrison, *Sky Is Falling*; Leo J. Moser, *The Chinese Mosaic*; Keith Quincy,

Hmong; Christopher Robbins, *The Ravens*; J.A.G. Roberts, *A Concise History of China*; William A. Smalley, in *The Hmong in Transition*; Nicholas Tapp, *Sovereignty and Rebellion*; Vang and Lewis, *Grandmother's Path*; Eric R. Wolf, *Europe and the People Without History*; K.C. Wu, *The Chinese Heritage*; and Yang Dao, *Hmong at the Turning Point*. See Bibliography for complete publication details.
4. See Wu, *Chinese Heritage*, 56–58 for the Yellow Emperor's story.
5. Quincy, *Hmong*, 36–38.
6. Some also settled in western Shandong, southern Hebei, central and southern Shanxi, eastern Shaanxi and parts of Jiangsu and Anhui provinces.
7. Quincy, *Hmong*, 40.
8. Moser, *Chinese Mosaic*, 16.
9. Andrea Shen, "Ancient script rewrites history," in *Harvard College Gazette* (March 2001), 8.
10. Wu, *Chinese Heritage*, 12–13.
11. Moser, *Chinese Mosaic*, 23–24.
12. Quincy, *Hmong*, 42–44.
13. *Ibid.*, 44–47.
14. Eberhard, *China's Minorities*, 102.
15. Ching-Ching Ni, "China's *Other* Wall," *Los Angeles Times* (4 August 2000), 1.
16. McCoy, *The Politics of Heroin*, 80.
17. See Machle, "The Aboriginal Tribes," 2–3, for both quotes.
18. Yang See Koumarn, *Glimpses of Hmong History and Culture*, 4.
19. Robbins, *Ravens*, 115.
20. *Ibid.*, 118.
21. Morrison, *Sky Is Falling*, 87.
22. *Ibid.*, 4–5, 18.
23. Robbins, *Ravens*, 73.
24. Chan, *Hmong Means Free*, 30.
25. Vang and Lewis, *Grandmother's Path*, 7; Yang Dao, *Hmong at the Turning Point*, 13; Bliatout et al., *Handbook for Teaching Hmong-Speaking Students*, 4; and Hamilton-Merritt, *Tragic Mountains*, 334.
26. Yang Dao, *Hmong in the West*, 12–13.

Chapter 6

1. Vang and Lewis, *Grandmother's Path*, 81.
2. McCoy, *The Politics of Heroin*, 80. McCoy uses "kaitong," the Vietnamese word. For the name Lynhiavu, see Appendix A, Hmong Language and Names.
3. Gayle L. Morrison, personal communication, Dec. 2, 1996.
4. Rolland and Moua, *Trail Through the*

Mists, 186. This source supplied other insights as well.

5. Vang and Lewis, *Grandmother's Path*, 84.

6. Quincy, *Hmong*, 44.

7. Morrison, *Sky Is Falling*, 103.

8. For a close-up of the escape from Long Cheng, see Gayle L. Morrison, *Sky Is Falling: An Oral History of the CIA's Evacuation of the Hmong from Laos*. I am indebted to Morrison for much of the material that follows.

9. Morrison, op.cit., 162.

Chapter 7

1. In fact, they are trying, with outside assistance.

2. Hmong use two barrels. Storage barrels are quite large, like the ones we know. For carrying water on the back to fill these, grownups use a smaller wooden barrel about twenty inches wide and two and a half feet tall, bound together with horse hair twine. Children too young to manage this are given a length of stout bamboo about six inches across to use as a bucket.

3. Luke 11:5–8, a parable of Jesus. Translated by David Mote, with thanks to Kenneth E. Bailey, *Poet & Peasant: A literary-cultural approach to the parables in Luke* (Grand Rapids, Michigan: William B. Eerdmans Publishing Co., 1976):119–141.

4. Haing Ngor was murdered a few years later, in February 1996, outside his apartment in Los Angeles.

Chapter 8

1. Vang and Lewis, *Grandmother's Path*, 74.

Chapter 9

1. Statistics in this chapter come from the following: Roy Beck, "The Ordeal of Immigration in Wausau," *The Atlantic Monthly* (April 1994): 84–97; Amy Pyle, "Poverty, disease haunt Hmong's life in limbo," *The Sacramento Bee* (8 March 1987), A1; Dorothy Korber, "Counting America: Hmong make major strides," *The Sacramento Bee* (16 August 2001), A1; Hmong National Development, Inc., "Hmong Population by States—2000"; Public Broadcasting System, "Legacy of the Vietnam War," (KPCC, Pasadena, Calif., 4 May 2000, special broadcast); Cheu

Thao, former executive director of Lao Family Community, Inc., Sacramento, Calif., personal communication, 3 December 1987; U.S. Bureau of the Census, Population Division, *Profiles of Asians and Pacific Islanders, Selected Characteristics, 1990*; and Kou Yang, "The Hmong Community in Fresno," *Hmong Council Newsletter* (Fresno County, vol.1, issue 1, December 1990): 6–7.

2. Mymee Her, Ph.D., "Hmong Resiliency: Surviving a War and Living a Dream" (paper presented at Hmong National Development Conference, Denver, Colo. 17 April 1998, Denver, Colorado).

3. The federal poverty level for a family of four was roughly $16,000.

4. Frank Viviano backs up the veracity of this promise in *Dispatches from the Pacific Century*.

Chapter 10

1. The following story of Doc is taken from "Life and Death in a Lao Gang: A Local Refugee's Story," by Ya Po K., a Hmong, in *Sacramento News & Review* (13 January 1994): 16–17.

2. Thek Moua, "The Moua Family of Sanger," in *Hmong Means Free*, 223.

3. See Jack Katz, *Seductions of Crime* for a discussion of psychological motivations toward crime.

4. This and other observations in this section are thanks to Judy Lewis, unnamed author of "The 'code of the streets,'" *Context* 15, no.111 (1994): 1–7.

Chapter 11

1. Lue Vang, *A Cultural Interpretation of Thai Hmong*, 13–14.

2. At about the same time that Lue Vang received his Ed.D., roughly thirty percent of Hmong-American men and fifty percent of Hmong-American women over age eighteen had zero formal education. Two percent had a bachelor's degree. (Ryan Marblestone, presenter at Hmong National Development conference, Denver, Colo., April 1998.) Another way of looking at it: Five years earlier, in 1990, nearly a third of Hmong age nineteen to twenty-four were enrolled in college. That compared to thirty-nine percent for white Americans. (Case label, "Documenting the Southeast Asian Refugee Experience," UC Irvine Library exhibit, October 1998.)

Chapter 12

1. Mai Xia described three kinds of marriage, skipping some variations and a blizzard of options and etiquette detail. The "catch-hand" marriage, of which Ly Vong Lynaolu and Pao Chao Lor offer an example, is out of favor in the United States. It is, as Mai Xia put it, "primitive and barbaric," since the girl has no say. The second and perhaps ideal form begins when the man presents himself at the girl's home and announces to her parents his desire to marry their daughter. He comes bearing money, lots of it, to show he is serious— one or two thousand dollars in this country. The matter is discussed all around. The father asks the daughter if she accepts the offer. If she does, she goes with her groom the same day and stays with him. The pair returns in three or so days to arrange the actual wedding. In Mai Xia's case, her husband didn't have the necessary money to present to her parents, so the young pair chose to elope.

2. See Appendix B, Child-Rearing Study.

Chapter 14

1. Linda Crew, *Children of the River* (New York: Delacorte Press, 1989), 32.

Chapter 15

1. Translation of Hmong funeral text by Chamy Thor.

Appendix A

1. Sources for this appendix include Nom Pao Mouayaaj of Sacramento, Calif., personal communication; Quincy, *Hmong*; Tapp, *Sovereignty and Rebellion*; Jonas Vang-na Vangay, *Hmong Language Development* (Merced, Calif., unpublished paper); and innumerable individuals who were delighted to talk about their language and its use.

2. Bliatout et al., *Handbook*, 52.

Appendix B

1. Charles N. Oberg, Sharon Muret-Wagstaff, Shirley G. Moore, and Brenda Cumming, "A Cross-Cultural Assessment of Maternal-Child Interaction: Links to Health and Development." In *The Hmong in Transition*, ed. George Hendricks et al. (New York: Center for Migration Studies of New York, Inc. and The Southeast Asian Refugee Studies of the University of Minnesota, 1986), 399–416.

Bibliography

Beck, Roy. "The Ordeal of Immigration in Wausau." *The Atlantic Monthly*, April 1994: 84–97.

Bliatout, Bruce Thowpaou, Bruce T. Downing, Judy Lewis and Dao Yang. *Handbook for Teaching Hmong-Speaking Students*. Folsom, Calif.: Folsom Cordova Unified School District, 1988.

Bliatout, Bruce Thowpaou. *Hmong Sudden Unexpected Nocturnal Death Syndrome: A cultural study*. Portland, Ore.: Sparkle Publishing Enterprises, 1982.

Chan, Sucheng. *Asian Americans: An interpretive History*. Boston: Twayne, 1991.

_____, ed. *Hmong Means Free: Life in Laos and America*. Philadelphia: Temple University Press, 1994.

Conquergood, Dwight (ethnog.), Paja Thao (shaman) and Xa Thao (trans.). *I Am a Shaman: A Hmong life story with ethnographic commentary*. Southeast Asian Refugee Studies Occasional Papers No. 8. Minneapolis: University of Minnesota, 1989.

Cooper, Robert, Nicholas Tapp, Gary Yia Lee and Gretel Schwoer-Kohl. *The Hmong*. Bangkok: Artasia, 1991.

Daniel, E. Valentine, and John Chr. Knudsen. *Mistrusting Refugees*. Berkeley: University of California Press, 1995.

Diamond, Jared. *Guns, Germs, and Steel: The fates of human societies*. New York: W.W. Norton & Co., 1999.

Dinnerstein, Leonard, Roger L. Nichols and David Reimers. *Natives and Strangers: A multicultural history of Americans*. Oxford: Oxford University Press, 1996.

Downing, Bruce T., and Douglas P. Olney, eds. *The Hmong in the West: Observations and Reports*. Papers of the 1981 Hmong Research Conference, University of Minnesota. Minneapolis: Center for Urban and Regional Affairs, Southeast Asian Refugee Studies Project, 1982. See also individual authors.

Dunnigan, Timothy. "The Process of Identity Maintenance in Hmong Society." In *The Hmong in Transition*, edited by Glenn L. Hendricks et al., 41–53. New York: Center for Migration Studies of New York, Inc. and The Southeast Asian Refugee Studies of the University of Minnesota, 1986.

Eberhard, Wolfram. *China's Minorities: Yesterday and Today*. Belmont, Calif.: Wadsworth Publishing Co., 1982.

Fadiman, Anne. *The Spirit Catches You and You Fall Down: A Hmong child, her American doctors, and the collision of two cultures*. New York: Farrar, Straus and Giroux, 1997.

Goldfarb, Mace, M.D. *Fighters, Refugees, Immigrants: A story of the Hmong*. Minneapolis: Carolrhoda Books, Inc., 1982.

Hamilton-Merritt, Jane. *Tragic Mountains: The Hmong, the Americans, and the Secret Wars for Laos, 1942–1992*. Bloomington: Indiana University Press, 1993.

HarperCollins. *Past Worlds: HarperCollins Atlas of Archaeology*. London: HarperCollins, 1991.

Hawke, David Freeman. *Everyday Life in Early America*. New York: Harper & Row, 1989.

Heimbach, Ernest E. *White Hmong-English Dictionary*. Southeast Asia Program Data Paper No. 75. Ithaca, NY: Cornell University, 1979.

Hendricks, Glenn L., Bruce Downing and Amos Deinard, eds. *The Hmong in Transition*. New York: Center for Migration Studies of New York, Inc., and The Southeast Asian Refugee Studies of the University of Minnesota, 1986.

Her, Mee. "The Art of Giving." In *Gender: Multicultural Perspectives*, edited by Judith T. Gonzalez-Calvo, 192–195. Dubuque, Iowa: Kendall-Hunt Publishing Co., 1993.

Katz, Jack. *Seductions of Crime: Moral and sensual attractions in doing evil*. New York: Basic Books, HarperCollins, 1988.

Kim, Uichol, Harry C. Triandis, Çigdem Kagitçibasi, Sang-Chin Choi and Gene Yoon, eds. *Individualism and Collectivism: Theory, Method, and Application*. Thousand Oaks, Calif.: Sage Publications, 1994.

Kirton, Elizabeth Stewart. *The Locked Medicine Cabinet: Hmong Health Care in America*. Santa Barbara: Unpublished doctoral dissertation, University of California, 1985.

Lewin, Roger. *In the Age of Mankind: A Smithsonian Book of Human Evolution*. Washington, D.C.: Smithsonian Books, 1988.

Luong, Hy V. *Revolution in the Village: Tradition and Transformation in North Vietnam, 1925–1988*. Honolulu: University of Hawaii Press, 1992.

Machle, E.C., M.D. "The Aboriginal Tribes of China." Paper presented at the Canton Missionary Conference, Nov. 29, 1911.

McCoy, Alfred W., with Cathleen B. Read and Leonard P. Adams II. *The Politics of Heroin in Southeast Asia*. New York: Harper & Row, 1972.

Morrison, Gayle L. *Sky Is Falling: An Oral History of the CIA's Evacuation of the Hmong from Laos*. Jefferson, N.C.: McFarland & Co., Inc., 1999.

Moser, Leo J. *The Chinese Mosaic: The Peoples and Provinces of China*. Westview Special Studies on East Asia. Boulder: Westview Press, 1985.

Moua, Thek. "The Moua Family of Sanger." in *Hmong Means Free: Life in Laos and America*. Edited by Sucheng Chan, 223. Philadelphia: Temple University Press, 1994.

Oberg, Charles N., and Sharon Muret-Wagstaff, Shirley G. Moore, and Brenda Cumming. "A Cross-Cultural Assessment of Maternal-Child Interaction." *The Hmong in Transition*, edited by George Hendricks et al., 399–416. New York: Center for Migration Studies of New York, Inc., and The Southeast Asian Refugee Studies of the University of Minnesota.

Quincy, Keith. *Hmong: History of a People*. 2d ed. Cheney, Wash.: Eastern Washington University Press, 1995.

Reeder, Allan. "The Other Immigrants." *The Atlantic Monthly*, Aug.1997: 69.

Robbins, Christopher. *The Ravens*. New York: Simon & Schuster, 1987.

Roberts, J.A.G. *A Concise History of China*. Cambridge, Mass.: Harvard University Press, 1999.

Rolland, Barbara J., and Houa Vue Moua. *Trail Through the Mists*. Eau Claire, Wis.: Eagles Printing Co., 1994.

Sanday, Peggy Reeves. *Female Power and Male Dominance: On the origins of sexual inequality*. Cambridge, England: Cambridge University Press, 1981.

Smalley, William A. "Stages of Hmong Cultural Adaptation." In *The Hmong in Transition*, edited by George Hendricks et al., 7–22. New York: Center for Migration Studies of New York, Inc., and The Southeast Asian Refugee Studies of the University of Minnesota.

Tapp, Nicholas. *Sovereignty and Rebellion: The White Hmong of Northern Thailand*. Oxford: Oxford University Press, 1989.

Thao, Cheu. "Hmong Migration and Leadership in Laos and in the United States." In *The Hmong in the West: Observations and Reports*, edited by Bruce T. Downing et al., 99–121. Minneapolis: Center for Urban and Regional Affairs, Southeast Asian Refugee Studies Project, 1982.

Trueba, Henry, Lila Jacobs, Elizabeth Kirton. *Cultural Conflict and Adaptation: The case of Hmong children in American society*. New York: The Falmer Press, 1990.

Vang, Kao N. "Hmong marriage customs: A current assessment." In *The Hmong in the West: Observations and Reports*, edited by Bruce T. Downing et al., 29–47. Minneapolis: Center for Urban and Regional Affairs, Southeast Asian Refugee Studies Project, 1982.

Vang, Lue, and Judy Lewis. *Grandmother's Path, Grandfather's Way*. Rancho Cordova, Calif.: Folsom-Cordova Unified School District, Special Programs Office, 1984. Zellerbach Family Fund.

Vang, Lue. *A Cultural Interpretation of Thai Hmong: Beliefs, traditions and values about education and leadership*. San Francisco: Unpublished doctoral dissertation, University of San Francisco, 1995.

Viviano, Frank. *Dispatches from the Pacific Century*. Reading, Mass.: Addison-Wesley, 1993.

Warner, Roger. *Out of Laos: A story of war and exodus, told in photographs*. Ipswich, Mass.: self published, 1996.

Wolf, Eric R. *Europe and the People Without History*. Berkeley: University of California, 1982.

Wu, K.C. *The Chinese Heritage*. New York: Crown Publishers, 1982.

Yang Dao. "Why Did the Hmong Leave Laos?" In *The Hmong in the West: Observations and Reports*, edited by Bruce T. Downing et al., 3–18. Minneapolis: Center for Urban and Regional Affairs, Southeast Asian Refugee Studies Project, 1982.

Yang Dao. *Hmong at the Turning Point*, edited by Jeanne L. Blake. Minneapolis: Worldbridge Associates, 1993.

Yang, Kou. "The Hmong Community in Fresno." *Fresno County Hmong Newsletter*, vol.1, issue 1 (Dec.1990): 6–7. Fresno: The Hmong Council.

Yang See Koumarn. "The Hmongs of Laos: 1896–1978." In *Glimpses of Hmong History and Culture*, General Information Series No. 16, Indochinese Refugee Education Guides. Washington, D.C.: Center for Applied Linguistics, 1978.

Index

The alphabetization of Hmong names varies by individual preference between traditional usage (surname first) and Western order (surname last). In either case, the name is alphabetized here by clan or surname.